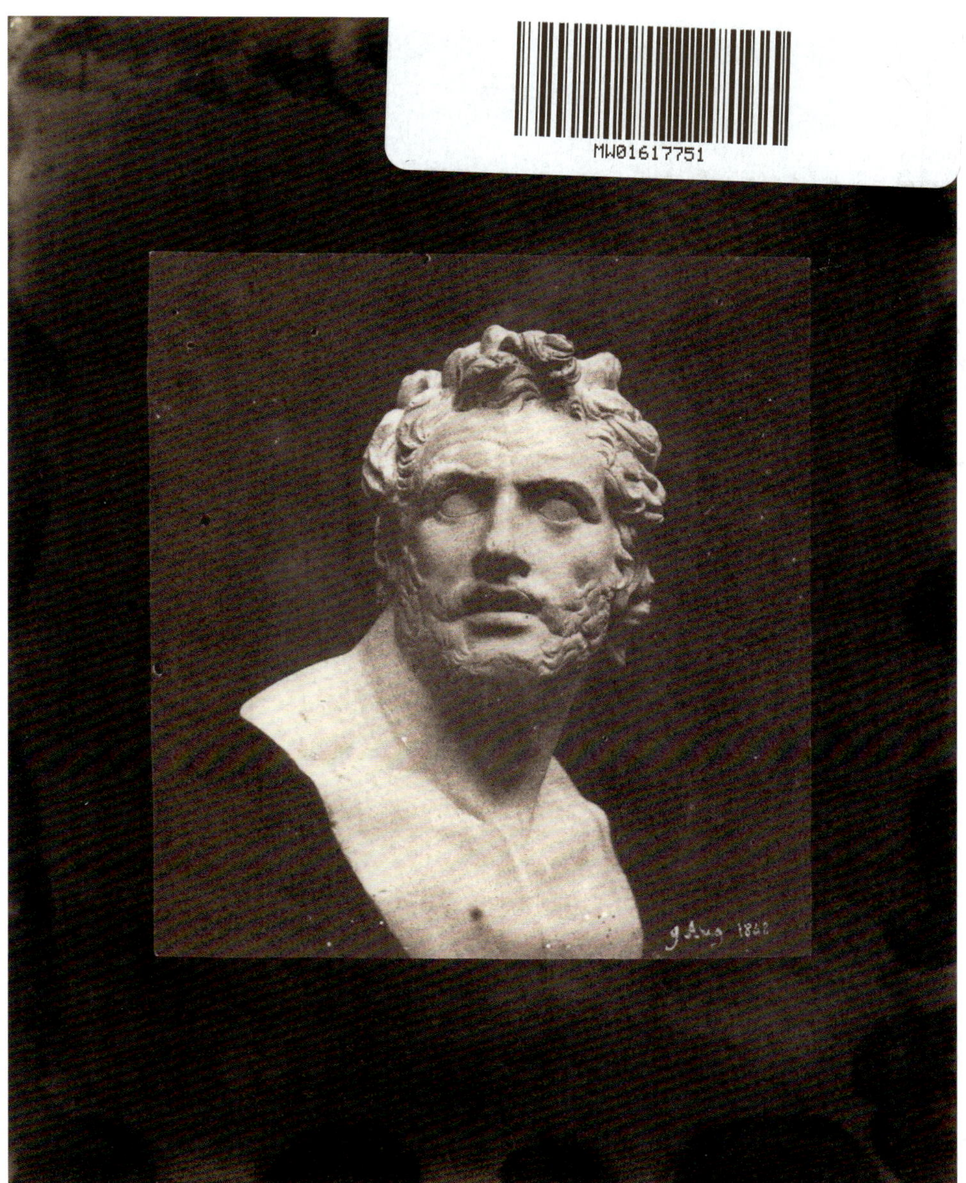

William Henry Fox Talbot (British, 1800–1877). *The Bust of Patroclus.* 1844. Salted paper print, 5 7/16 × 5 1/16 in. (13.8 × 12.9 cm)

Plaster casts gained in popularity during the nineteenth century as a way to bring renowned artworks before audiences who could not travel to view the originals. The cast in William Henry Fox Talbot's photograph—misidentified by the photographer as representing Patroclus, but believed today to depict a companion of the mythic adventurer Odysseus—duplicates a marble bust that itself is likely an ancient Roman copy of an earlier Greek sculpture.

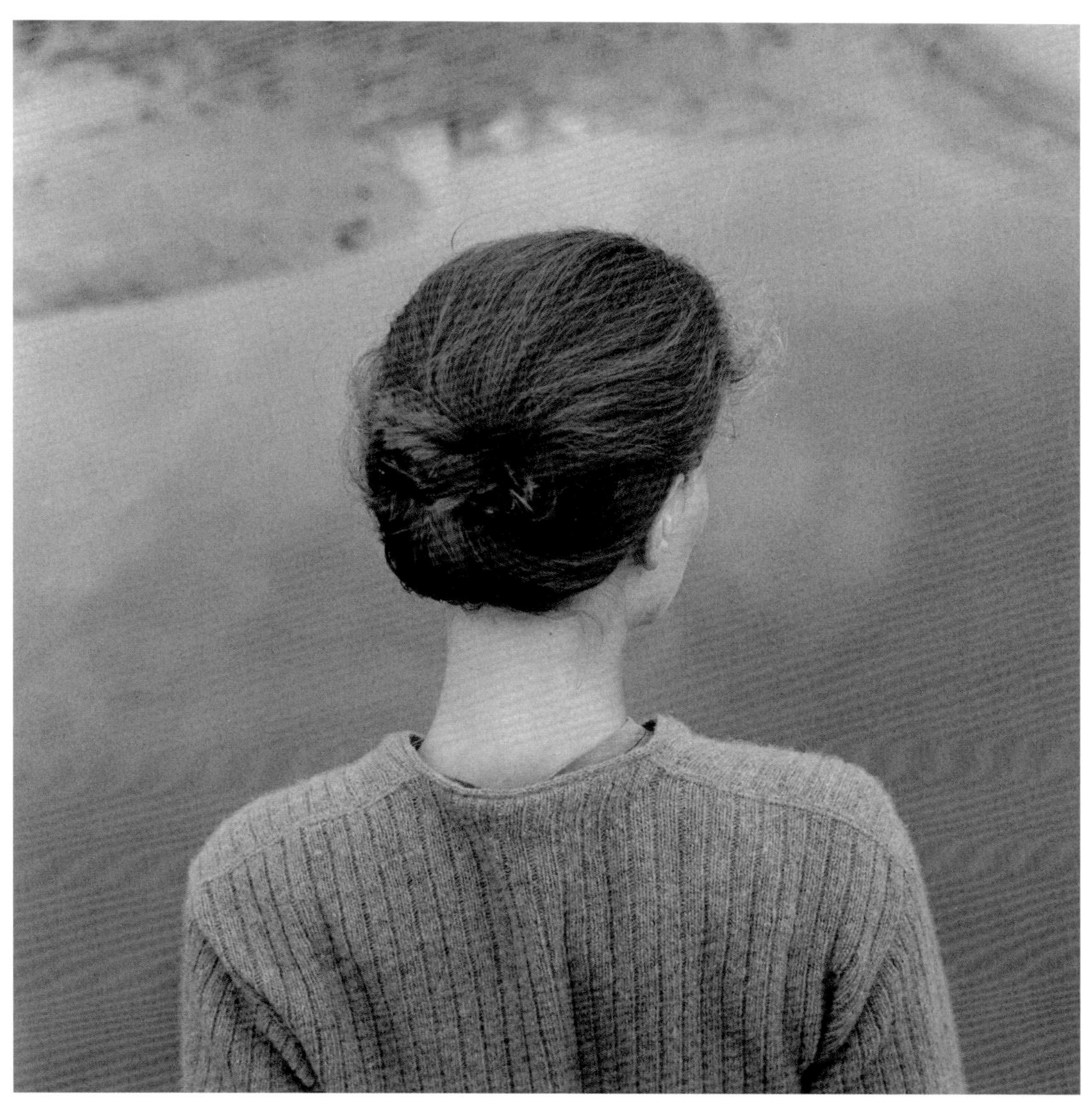

Emmet Gowin (American, born 1941). *Edith, Chincoteague, Virginia.* 1967. Gelatin silver print, 6 7/16 × 6 1/2 in. (16.4 × 16.5 cm)

Emmet Gowin's photograph depicts his wife, Edith, during a trip to Chincoteague Island, where he lived briefly as a teenager. The same year he made this image, the photographer wrote: "For me, pictures provide a means of holding, intensely, a moment of communication between one human and another."

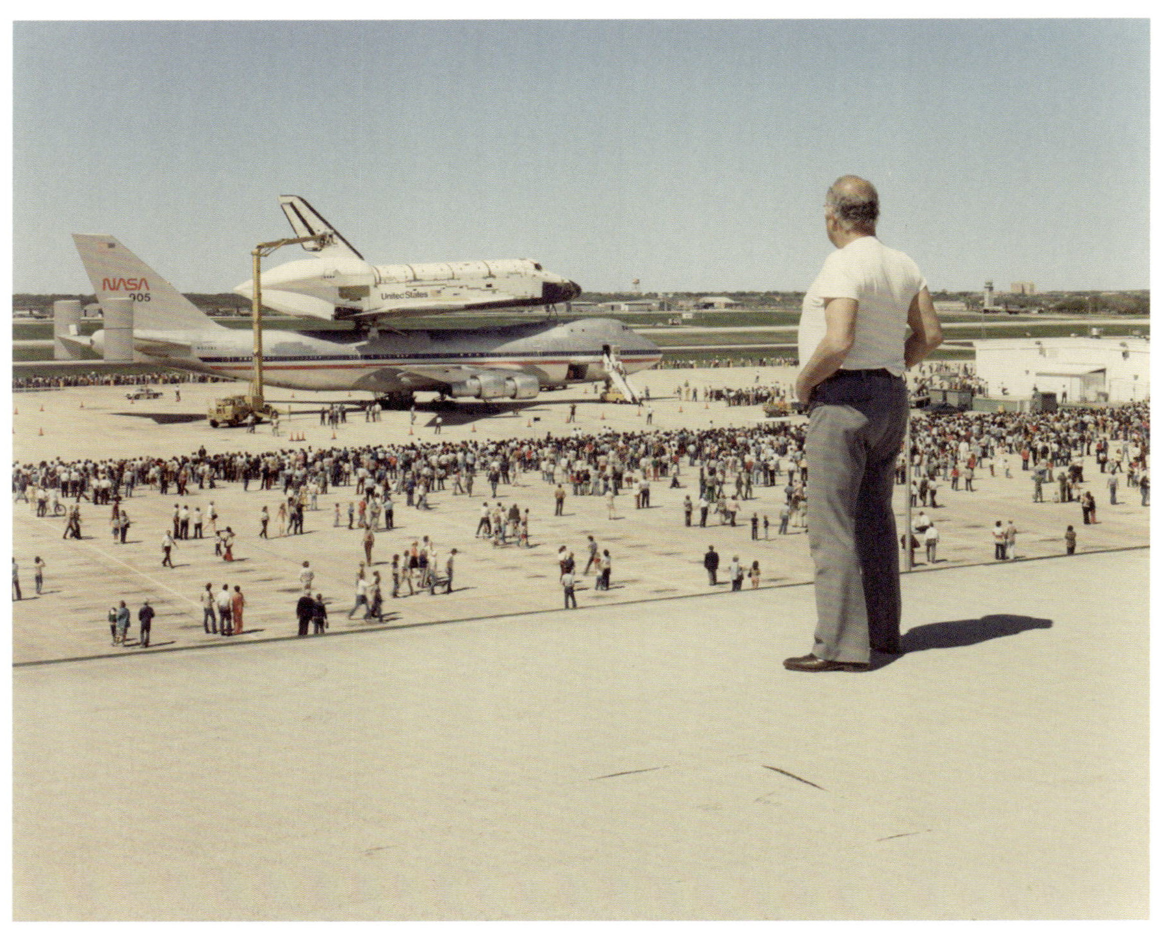

Joel Sternfeld (American, born 1944). *The Space Shuttle "Columbia" Lands at Kelly Lackland Air Force Base, San Antonio, Texas.* March 1979. Chromogenic print, 13½ × 17 in. (34.3 × 43.2 cm)

In March 1979, NASA's first space shuttle orbiter to reach space, the *Columbia*, traveled atop a modified Boeing 747 from Palmdale, California, where it was constructed, to Cape Canaveral, Florida, where it would launch two years later. Joel Sternfeld's photograph records the scene during an overnight stop to refuel at San Antonio's Kelly Air Force Base, where it drew a crowd of approximately two hundred thousand spectators.

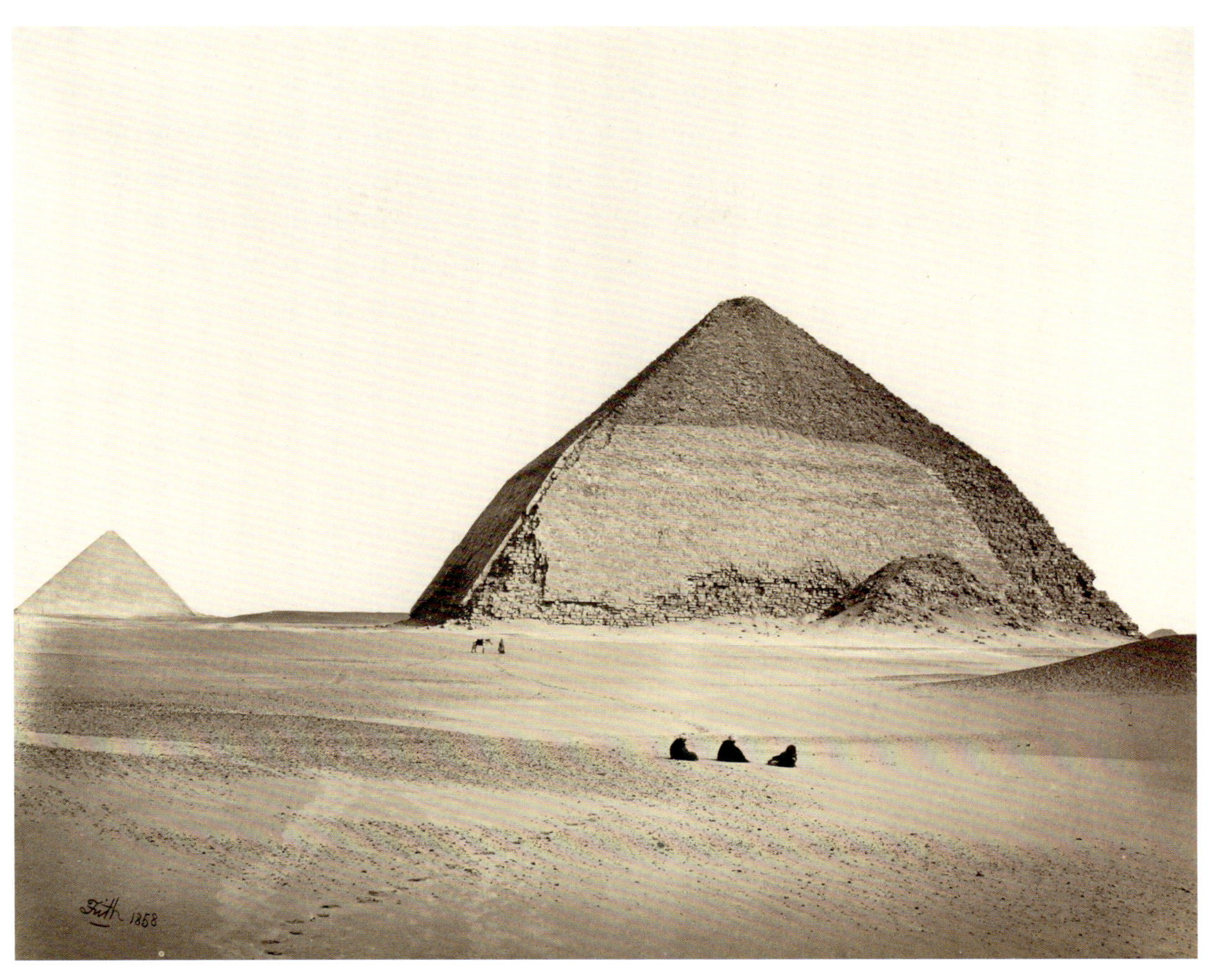

Francis Frith (British, 1822–1898). *The Pyramids of Dashoor [Dahshur], from the South West.* 1858. Albumen silver print, 14⅞ × 18⅞ in. (37.8 × 47.9 cm)

The Bent Pyramid, known for its unusual sloping angles, was built around 2600 BCE as a part of a complex of monuments south of Cairo. Francis Frith photographed it on his second trip to Egypt, during which he captured images of both ancient and modern architecture for a primarily British audience.

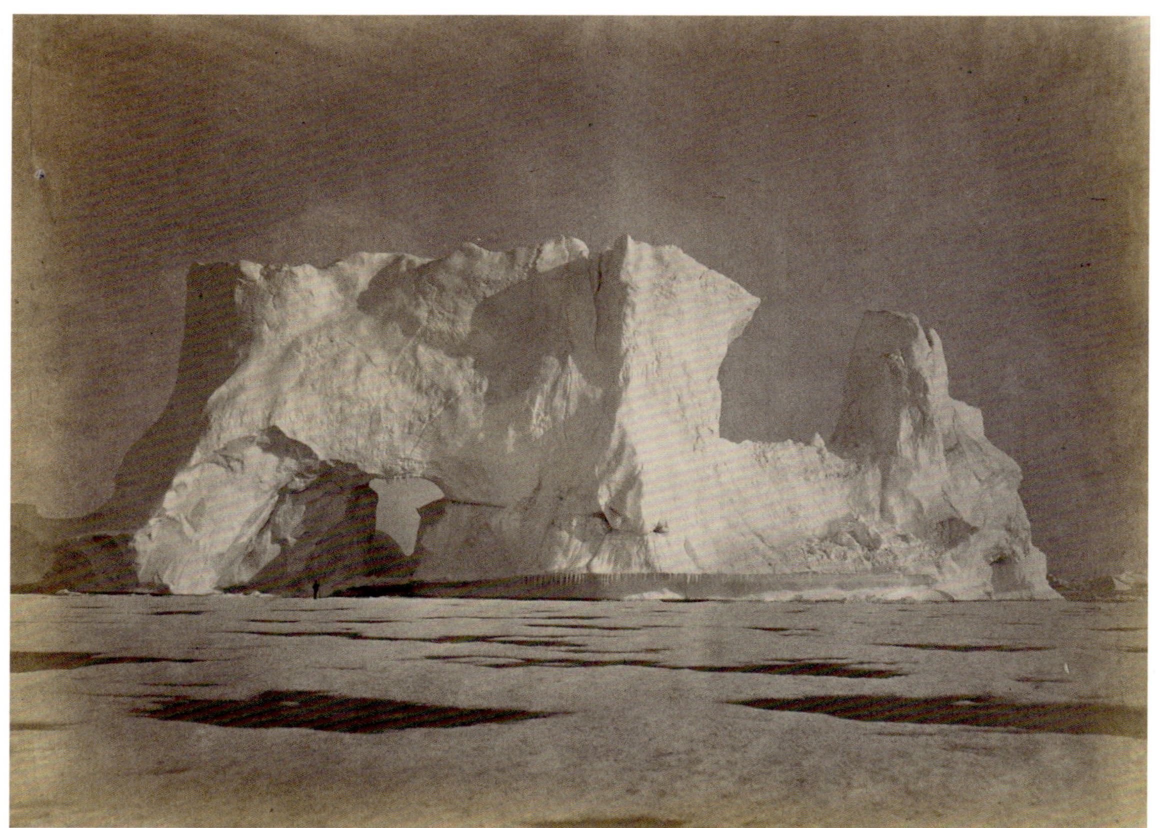

John L. Dunmore (American, 1833–1897) and George P. Critcherson (American, 1823–1892). *Castle Berg in Melville Bay over two hundred feet high. The Fig., which is some seventy-five feet from the Base, gives an object to compare with the Berg. The Ice in the foreground is about eighteen inches in thickness.* 1869. Albumen silver print, 10 15⁄16 × 15 1⁄4 in. (27.8 × 38.7 cm)

John Dunmore and George Critcherson created this and other photographs while accompanying the American painter William Bradford on one of his many voyages to Greenland "solely for the purposes of art," as Bradford recorded in his 1873 publication, *The Arctic Regions.*

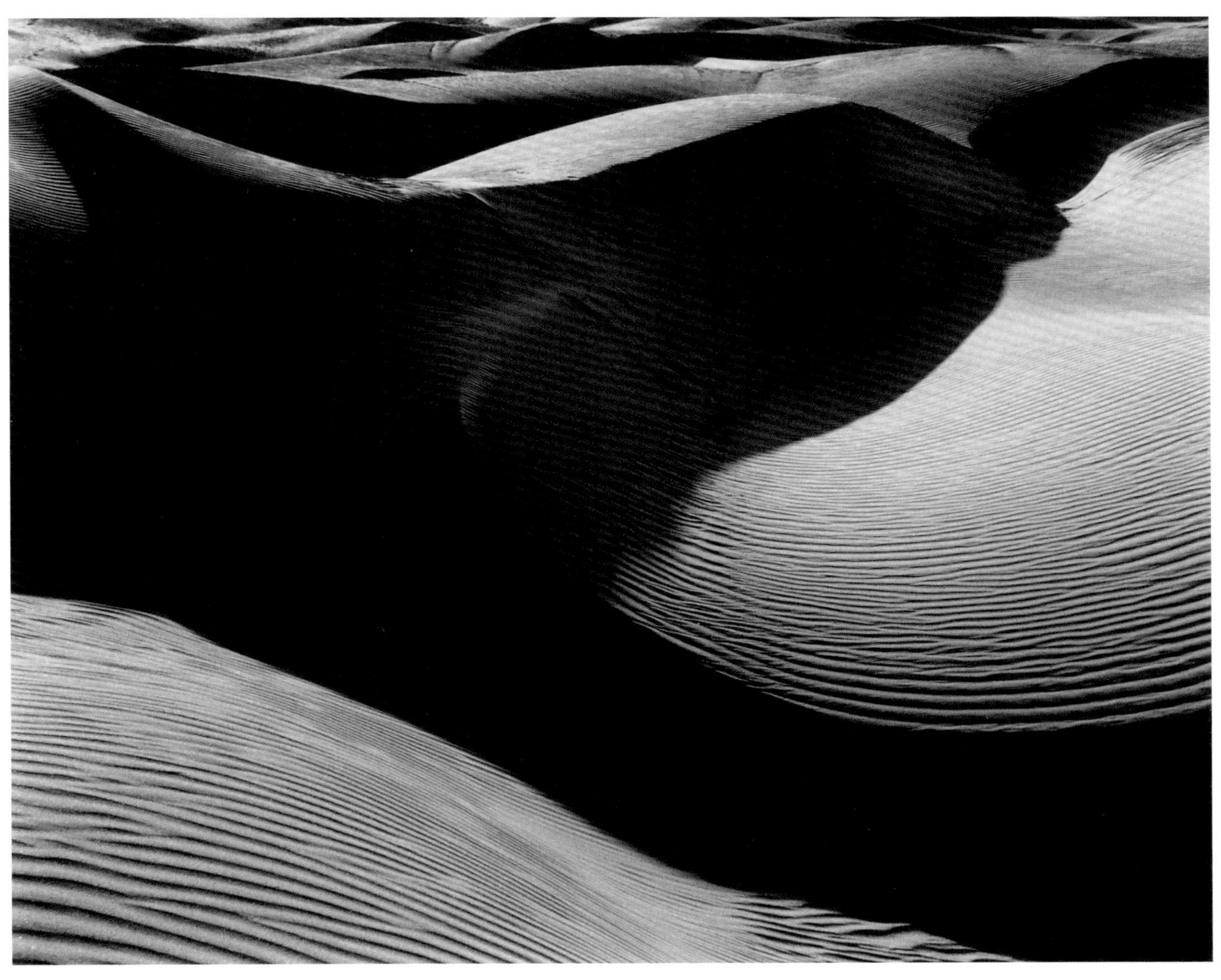

Edward Weston (American, 1886–1958). *Dunes, Oceano.* 1936. Gelatin silver print, 7 7/16 × 9 9/16 in. (19 × 24.3 cm)

The short-lived utopian commune of Moy Mell occupied the sand dunes outside Oceano, California, in the 1930s. A frequent photographer of the dunes, Edward Weston grew acquainted with this community of artists, poets, drifters, and the spiritually inclined, and one of his depictions of the landscape appeared on the cover of its magazine, *Dune Forum*, in 1934.

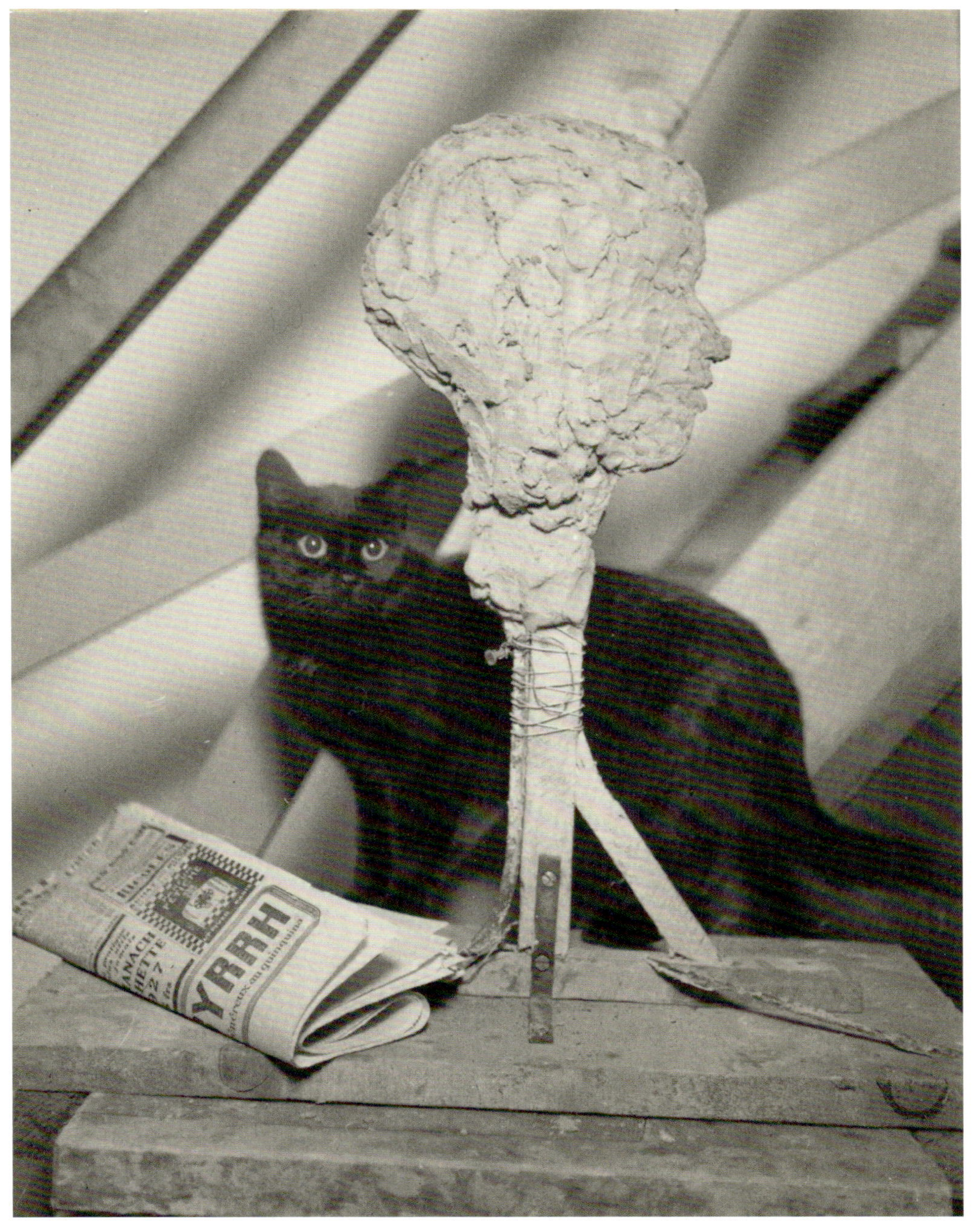

André Kertész (American, born Hungary. 1894–1985). *The Studio Cat*. 1926–27. Gelatin silver print, 3¾ × 3 in. (9.5 × 7.6 cm)

For a three-year period in Paris, André Kertész printed his images of interiors, artist studios, and portraits on commercially available postcard, or *carte postale*, paper, valuing its warm tones, sturdy support, and affordability. The choice of medium provided him a practical way to print and share his work.

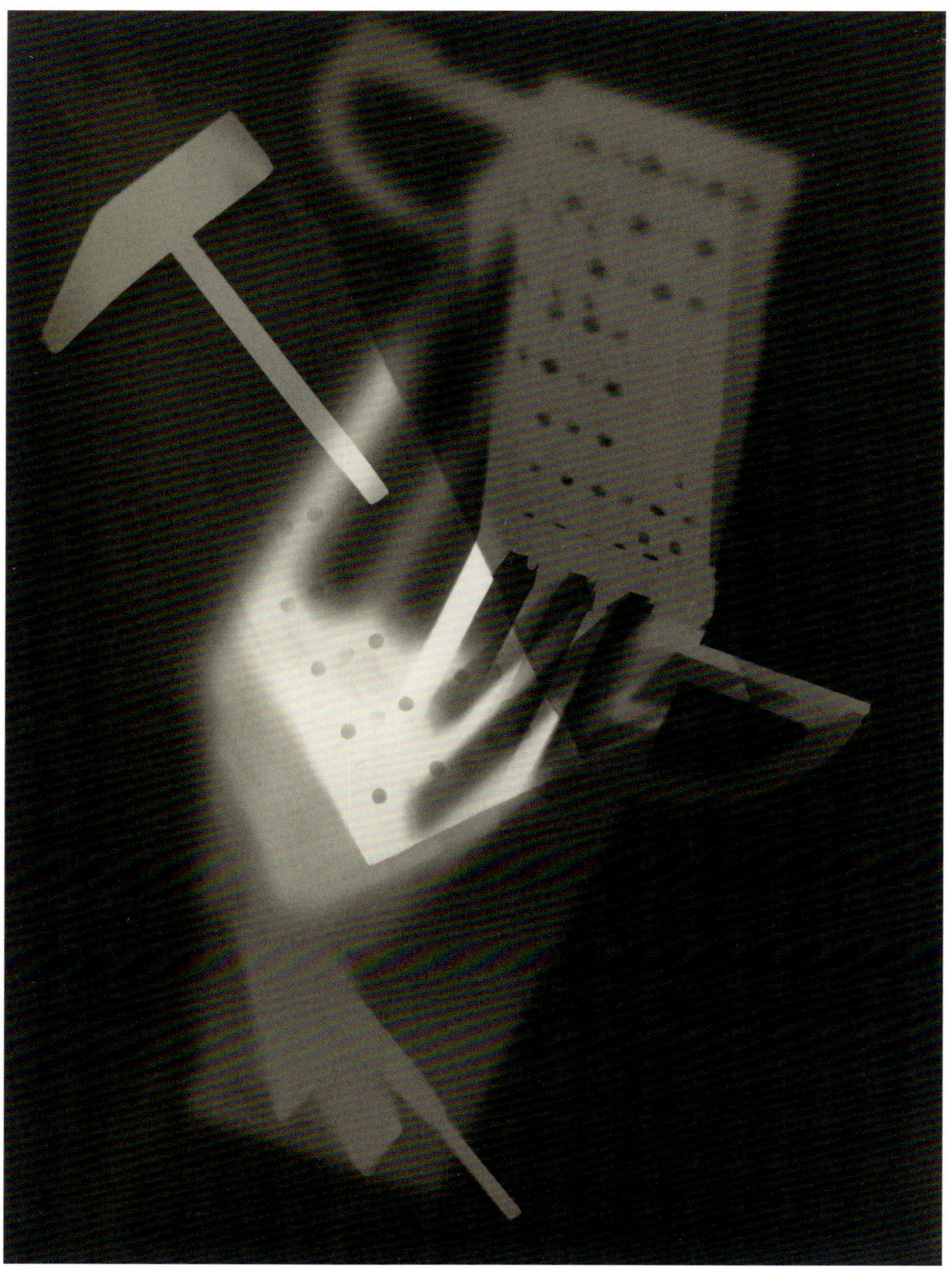

Man Ray (American, 1890–1976). *Rayograph*. 1922.
Gelatin silver print, 9⅜ × 7 in. (23.8 × 17.8 cm)

In 1922, while working in the darkroom without a camera, Man Ray began to arrange objects on photographic paper and expose the paper to light. He called the resulting photographs "rayographs" and compared the process to painting: "I have freed myself from the sticky medium of paint and am working directly with light itself."

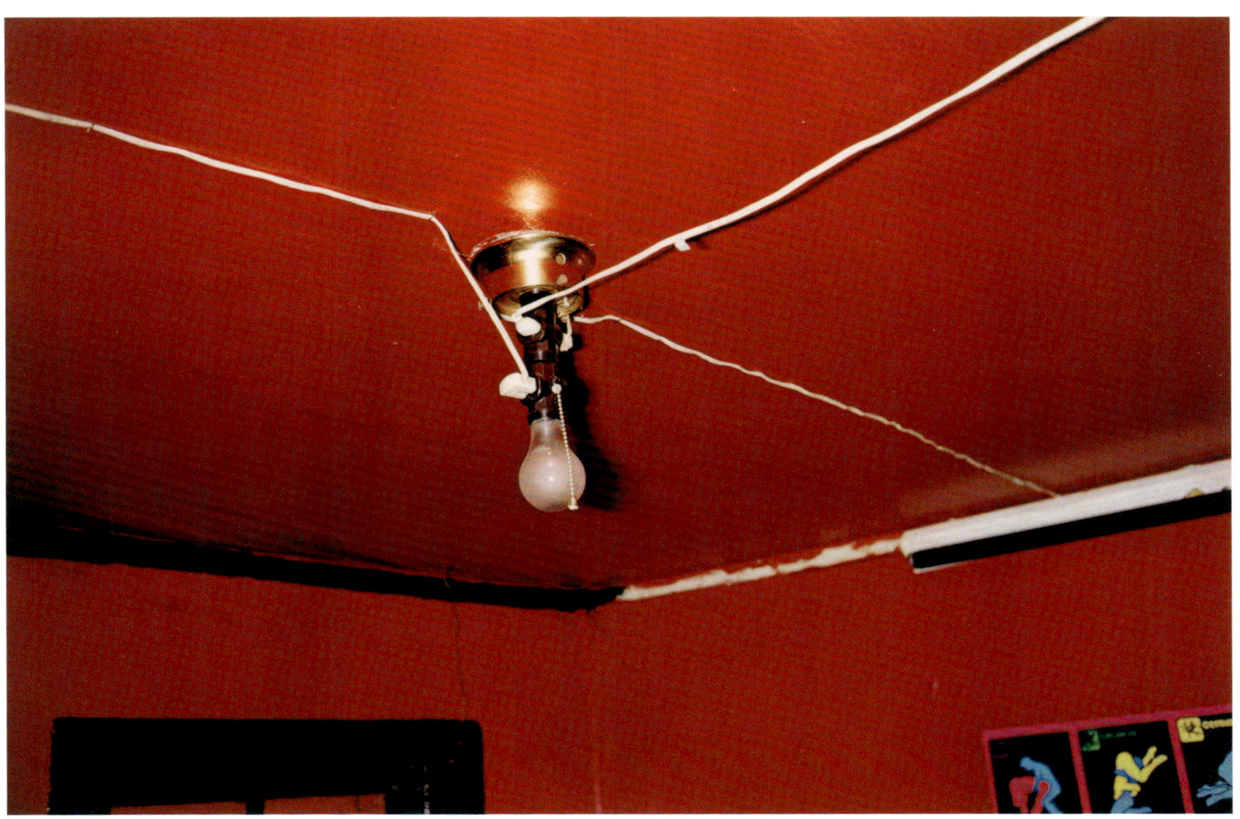

William Eggleston (American, born 1939). *Greenwood, Mississippi.* 1973. Dye transfer print, 11 9/16 × 17 3/4 in. (29.4 × 45.1 cm)

William Eggleston described this shot of his friend's home as an experiment in color photography and printing. "I knew that red was the most difficult color to work with," said Eggleston. "A little red is usually enough, but to work with an entire red surface was a challenge. It was hard to do. I don't know of any totally red pictures, except in advertising. The photograph is still powerful. It shocks you every time."

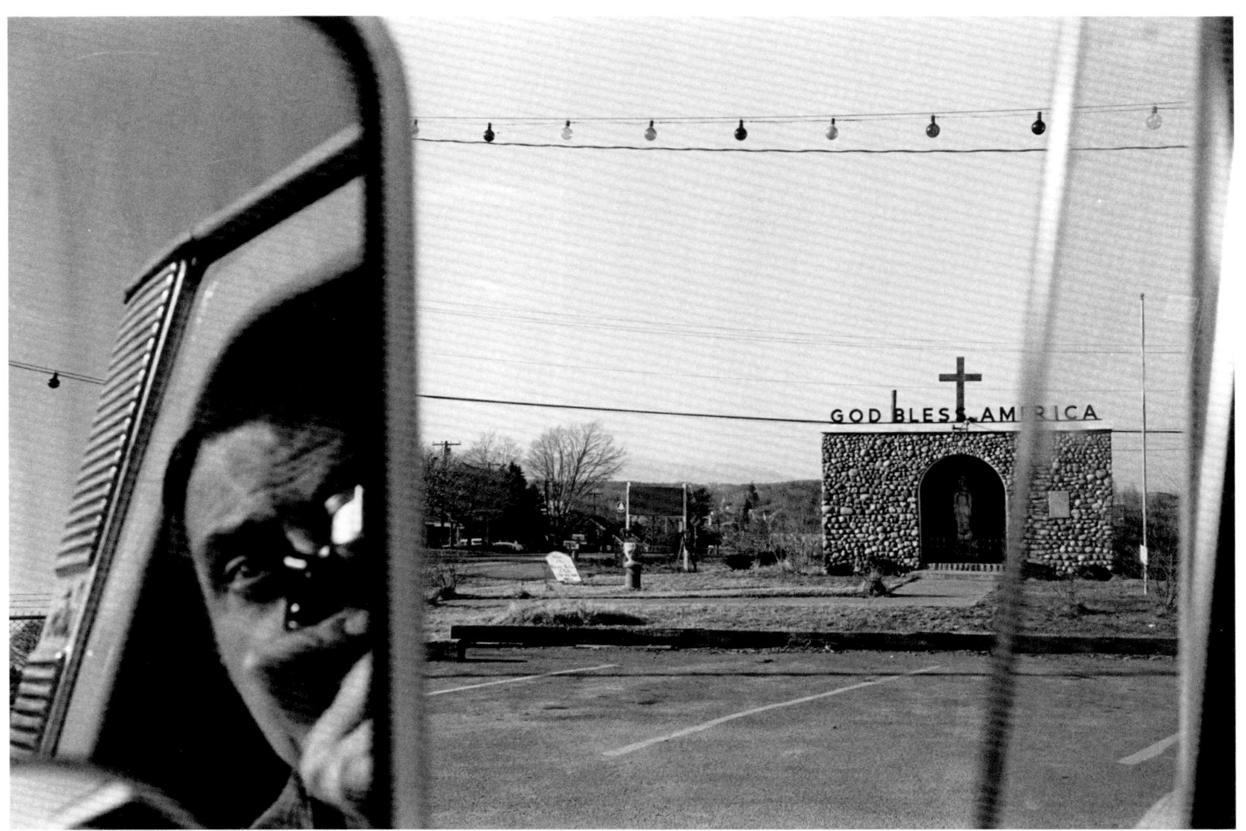

Lee Friedlander (American, born 1934). *Route 9W, New York*. 1969. Gelatin silver print, 6 5/16 × 9 7/16 in. (16 × 24 cm)

"They began as straight portraits," Lee Friedlander wrote in the introduction to his 1970 photobook, *Self Portrait*, "but soon I was finding myself at times in the landscape of my photography. I might call myself an intruder."

Time Travelers

Photographs from the Gayle Greenhill Collection

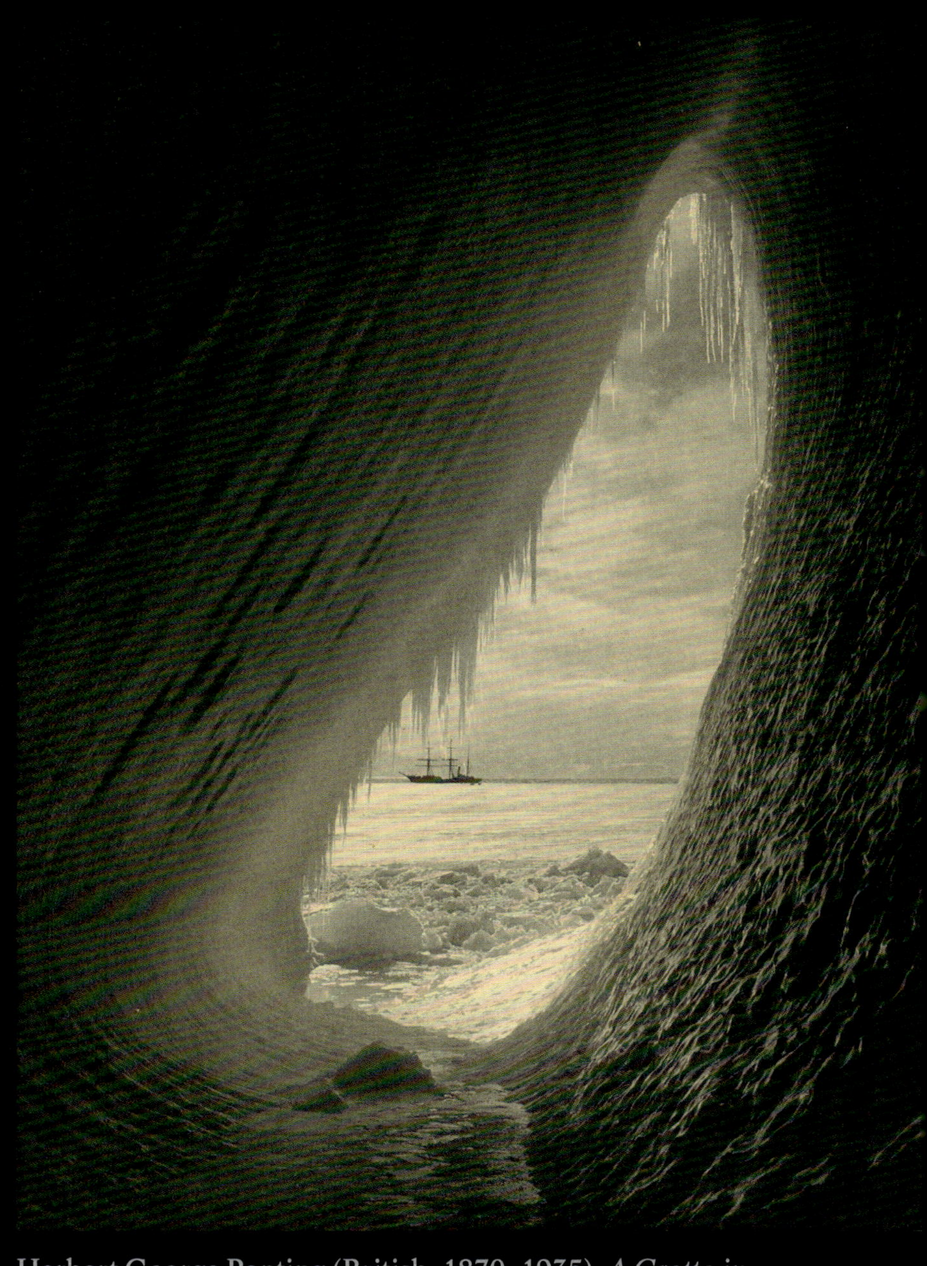

Herbert George Ponting (British, 1870–1935). *A Grotto in an Iceberg*. 1911. Carbon print, 16 × 12 in. (40.6 × 30.5 cm)

Time Travelers

Photographs from the Gayle Greenhill Collection

Lucy Gallun

With contributions by
Samuel Allen
Kaitlin Booher
Lee Ann Daffner
Casey Li
Rachel Rosin

The Museum of Modern Art, New York

This publication celebrates a donation of photographs to The Museum of Modern of Art made in 2019 by Robert F. Greenhill in memory of his wife, Gayle Greenhill. All illustrated works are part of this generous gift unless otherwise noted.

Contents

Time Travelers: Photographs from the Gayle Greenhill Collection presents a group of extraordinary photographs dating from the medium's earliest years to our present time and reflecting a multiplicity of styles, approaches, and processes. The exhibition and this catalogue share some of the stories and ideas these objects carry; in a similar spirit, this foreword tells of the remarkable couple whose generosity underpins *Time Travelers*: Gayle and Robert F. Greenhill.

As we read in this catalogue, for several years in the 1920s the photographer André Kertész printed his images on postcard paper. Decades later, one such photograph, *The Studio Cat* (1926–27; p. 9), would catch Bob Greenhill's eye. Knowing that his wife, Gayle, was an animal lover, he purchased it as a gift for her—a destiny fully in keeping with Kertész's choice to print the photograph on sturdy paper so that it could be readily exchanged with others. More recently, this cherished present has become a gift of a different nature. In 2019 Bob donated a large group of photographs, including *The Studio Cat*, to The Museum of Modern Art in memory of Gayle, who had passed away two years earlier. *Time Travelers* showcases a selection of these works, chosen from hundreds of objects by more than one hundred identified photographers and many more unknown.

A portion of this gift will remain at the Museum to form the Gayle Greenhill Collection; the remainder will be sold to establish the Gayle Greenhill Endowment Fund, supporting future photography exhibitions and acquisitions. Together, the Collection and Fund will form a lasting tribute to Gayle's relationship with MoMA's Department of Photography, an association that began in 1986 and encompassed more than two decades of service on the Committee on Photography.

Champions of the Department's curators and their collecting priorities, Gayle and Bob previously gave the Museum important groups of artworks by Robert Frank, Lucas Samaras, and William Wegman. Many of the nearly four dozen Samaras photographs, donated in 1992, immediately went on view at MoMA in a single-artist show, *The Photographs of Lucas Samaras: Selections from a Recent Gift* (1992–93). The Wegman photographs, gifted in 1994, have featured prominently in multiple exhibitions, including a presentation of studio-based works from the collection and one exploring photography's role in performance. Over the past two decades—from the inaugural installation of the new photography galleries in 2004 to a major exhibition in 2024—Museum audiences have had the opportunity to engage with photographs by Robert Frank that arrived at MoMA through the Greenhills' generosity.

At the time of *The Photographs of Lucas Samaras*, the exhibition's curator, Peter Galassi, then Chief Curator of

Photography, remarked in the press release that the "richness" of this artist's work lies in its "fusion of opposites." "The intimate is fused with the theatrical," Galassi observed, "the earnest with the satirical, the flagrantly vulgar with the exquisitely beautiful." A similar richness, deriving from the multitude of uses photography has found since its inception, characterizes *Time Travelers*. The exhibition and this catalogue, which mark the exciting first chapter of the Greenhill Collection's life at MoMA, reflect Gayle's wide-ranging curiosity about photography.

Each object from this lovingly assembled collection offers a point of entry into photography's histories and the worlds it describes. In photographs by Julia Margaret Cameron and Edward Steichen we encounter efforts to assert the medium as a means of artistic creation. Works by László Moholy-Nagy and Harold Eugene Edgerton explore photography's capacity to reveal modes of vision foreign to the human eye. Expeditions into unfamiliar realms—Antarctica and outer space—are recorded in images by Herbert George Ponting and Hiro. Still lifes such as Imogen Cunningham's bedscape and Karl Blossfeldt's botanical studies uncover profound significance in the everyday. Portraits, made under a broad range of circumstances, illuminate the complexities of photographing the self and others.

Time Travelers has been organized by Lucy Gallun, Curator in the Department of Photography, working with a team of talented collaborators that includes Samuel Allen, Curatorial Assistant, and Kaitlin Booher, former Beaumont and Nancy Newhall Curatorial Fellow. Lucy's introductory essay, which approaches the Greenhills' fascination with photography through the work of Ponting, is complemented by extended discussions of individual artworks written by Lucy, Kaitlin, and Samuel, as well as Lee Ann Daffner, Andrew W. Mellon Foundation Conservator of Photographs, and Rachel Rosin, Curatorial Assistant.

We are grateful to MoMA's Board of Trustees for its unwavering support and are particularly indebted to the Committee on Photography, led by Chairman Jon Lloyd Stryker, and to the lead donors of the Annual Exhibition Fund. Leadership support for the publication was provided by the Kate W. Cassidy Foundation; funding was also provided by the John Szarkowski Publications Fund. I thank Lucy for her skillful shepherding of the exhibition and this publication. My deepest gratitude goes to the Greenhill family, especially Bob and Gayle, who have done so much over many decades to enrich the stories we tell about and through photography, and whose imprint on the Museum will persist for decades to come.

Glenn D. Lowry
The David Rockefeller Director
The Museum of Modern Art

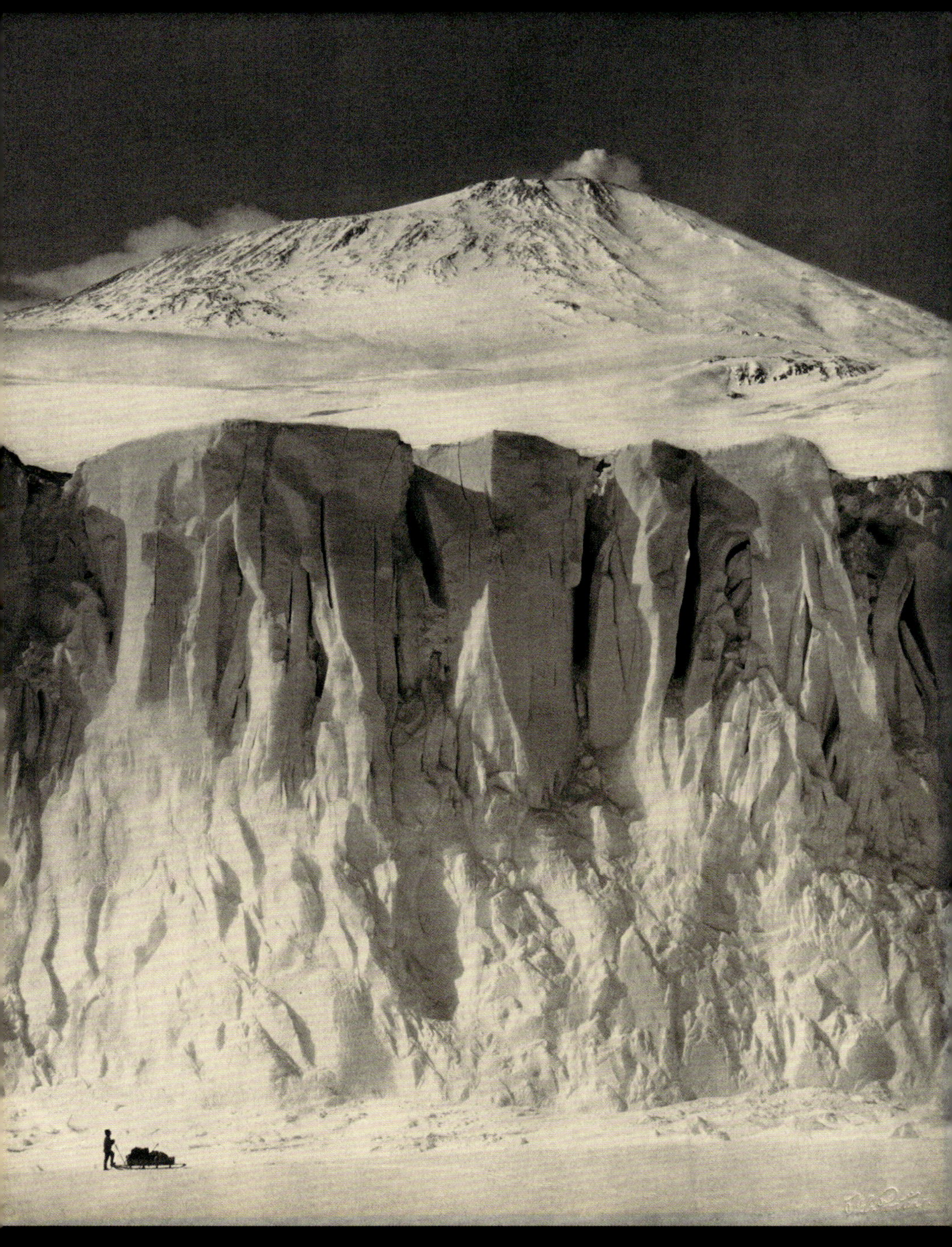

Herbert George Ponting (British, 1870–1935). *The Ramparts of Mount Erebus*. 1911. Gelatin silver print, 29⅞ × 23½ in. (75.9 × 59.7 cm)

“Some Photographing Episodes”: An Introduction

Lucy Gallun

The English photographer Herbert George Ponting set up a darkroom that doubled as his bunk on the *Terra Nova*, a Scottish whaling ship used for Walter Falcon Scott’s Antarctic expedition of 1910–13. He made another makeshift darkroom at the winter camp established by the expedition once they reached Cape Evans, Ross Island, Antarctica. This second darkroom was housed in the hut erected by the crew, and Captain Scott described it in a journal entry from April 13, 1911: “Such a palatial chamber for the development of negatives and prints can only be justified by the quality of the work produced in it, and is only justified in our case by the possession of such an artist as Ponting.”[1] It was from this base—at once temporary and meticulously constructed—that Ponting created several memorable pictures that he recounted in the chapter titled “Some Photographing Episodes” in his popular 1921 book *The Great White South*, a volume that was reprinted multiple times within his own lifetime. The episodes range from the planned to the unplanned, from the dangerous to the pleasant, and from the epically sublime to the intimately affecting. All of these were experienced by this acclaimed photographer during his participation in an expedition bankrolled by the Royal Navy and the Royal Geographic Society—an endeavor marketed as a heroic symbol of exceptionalism (with that effort being supported in no small way by Ponting’s photographs), and one that ultimately ended in tragedy and defeat.

It is through such a perspective—with an awareness of the unique circumstances in which every photograph is made—that we might attempt an introduction to the extraordinary collection of photographs assembled over many years by Robert F. and Gayle Greenhill, only a fraction of which is gathered within the pages of this book. Gayle Greenhill is often remembered for her keen curiosity. She was inspired to learn new skills—including how to fly a plane—and to learn about new subjects, like photography. The pictures in the Gayle Greenhill Collection reflect this quest. Through our encounters with these images, we enter different worlds. The Collection includes a diverse array of objects; some are impressively scaled prints that capture magnificent landscapes, others are cherished, intimate portraits. There are early photographic experiments in which practitioners painstakingly fixed a picture within a coating of silver nitrate on paper that had been sensitized with salt, and later experiments in which artists altered images that had automatically emerged in the emulsion of instant film, by then widely available. There are also significant differences in how each of these pictures initially reached audiences. Some were made by professionals hired for a specific job, and immediately reproduced on the printed page; others were made expressly to be displayed on the walls of a gallery or museum; and still others were made by amateurs and then tucked away in storage for many years. Fortunately for us, we can now encounter them in conversation with one another on the pages of this book and in the exhibition it accompanies.

In his own book, Ponting included a list of members of the expedition party, with his name next to the title "Camera Artist." This was a term used frequently in the nineteenth century and into the twentieth century to refer not only to Pictorialists, who imbued their works with personal expression, but to any photographer who made pictures meant to be understood as art. Ponting, for his part, was tasked with documenting the Antarctic expedition, but he was also recognized for the narrative that his images could convey. "He is an artist in love with his work," Scott wrote in his diary. "It is good to hear his enthusiasm for results of the past and plans of the future."[2] The photographs included in the Greenhill Collection were not all made by individuals who would call themselves artists, but they do conjure the sense of enthusiasm their makers had for the possibilities of image-making in the past and the future. Through photographs, we encounter people, things, and events from outside our own time. These images are portals through which we can transport ourselves, whether to geographical designations found on a map or into spatial constructions developed entirely within the boundaries of the photographic paper.

Photographing the Epic: Alone Under Mount Erebus

Mount Erebus, the southernmost active volcano on Earth, is located on Ross Island, an entirely volcanic island in Antarctica. In ancient Greek mythology, Erebus was the personification of the underworld, or the region through which souls pass to reach Hades. Ponting described the volcano, perched above the Barne Glacier, as a regal being: "Over this formidable rampart there were miles of icy slopes, above which Erebus, the King of the mountains of the South, monarch of all he surveyed, sat enthroned in all his majesty."[3] In one of his photographs, Ponting captured the mountain rising behind the glacier, and, in the bottom left corner of the composition, the small, dark silhouette of a person with a sleigh carrying their gear (1911; p. 22). The figure is dwarfed by the immense landscape, a scene that emphasizes their isolation in the environment. "It was not so much the austere beauty of the scene that so dominated me, as its utter desolation, and its intense and wholly indescribable loneliness," Ponting later wrote. "I stood awhile beneath the shivering stars, with every sense alert, striving to detect some sound; but the stillness about me was profound. . . . An eerie feeling crept over me in the presence of this majesty of silence: a feeling of exhilaration and awe."[4]

This epic landscape is typical of many of Ponting's photographs of Antarctica; his pictures capture the awe-inspiring ice sheets in all their grand scale and sublime beauty. Such a setting heightens the comparative insignificance of individual human lives, even as the perseverance of the human spirit appears ever more remarkable against its harshness. "Exploration is the physical expression of the intellectual passion," wrote Apsley Cherry-Garrard, one of Ponting's fellow expeditioners. "And I tell you, if you have the desire for knowledge and the power to give it physical expression, go out and explore."[5] The mission of the Scott expedition was foremost one of national supremacy: the attempt to reach a destination before others—particularly those hailing from other nations—have reached it, to plant a flag in the pristine white snow before another flag has been planted. Ponting posited, in the years following the Scott expedition, that explorers attempt heroic endeavors not so much for their own sense of accomplishment, but to share the magnificence with others. For him, this goal was achieved by making images to bring back and distribute to wider audiences (at least the ones that might have access to his publications). An explorer, Ponting said, "is not storing up experience for himself alone, but for all mankind."[6]

Photographing the Intimate: The Most Wonderful Place Imaginable

Even as he claimed to be making pictures for others, Ponting himself felt personally and inextricably bound to his role as a photographer. Describing an episode in which he sensed himself beginning to sink through the sea ice, he recounted this inseparable bind, at once metaphorical and literal: "For a moment the impulse was to save myself, by slipping out of the harness, at the expense of all my apparatus. But I went to the frozen South to illustrate its wonders, and without my cameras I was helpless. At all costs, therefore, my precious kit should be saved. I would save it, or go down with it. We would survive or sink together."[7] Ponting had recognized his devotion to his camera—his photographing tool—even before the polar expedition and the specific goals of that trip. "My camera," Ponting wrote in an earlier book about a journey to Japan, "has always been, to me, one of the things which made life most worth living."[8]

While in Antarctica, Ponting had one of those worthwhile personal experiences with his camera. He found himself in surroundings that he would later call "the most wonderful place imaginable," a grotto within an iceberg (1911; p. 16). The grotto was not far from the ship ("By almost incredible good luck," Ponting wrote, "the entrance to the cavern framed a fine view of the *Terra Nova* lying at the icefoot, a mile away."). But inside the grotto, it was another world, filled with exceptional color and changing light that Ponting later attempted to describe, calling it a "symphony." As words would not suffice to convey the feeling of being inside an interior of glistening ice, Ponting turned to photographs: "I made many photographs in this remarkable place—than which I secured none more beautiful the entire time I was in the South."[9] After making pictures, he went to tell the rest of the crew about being in a place of such beauty, and brought some of them back to experience it as well.

One of Ponting's most important tasks on the expedition was to train other members in photography. As he would not be present when they reached the pole, he had to teach those who would be part of that smaller group to record their experience. "Keep the photographic end up," he wrote in a letter to Frank Debenham, the expedition's geologist, once home.[10] A party of five individuals from the expedition finally arrived at the South Pole on January 17, 1912. There they found a flag and a note left by Roald Amundsen, leader of a Norwegian team that had arrived thirty-four days earlier, beating them to the record. In the face of this disappointment, they still fulfilled their responsibility to document the moment through photography. One of the party, Henry Robertson Bowers, made seven exposures at the pole using a camera on a tripod, with a line of twine attached to its trigger, which he could set using a stick.[11] The party never made it back to the hut at Cape Evans, perishing amid blizzards more than two months later, but their collective portrait remains, frozen into the film that was found with their bodies by a search party on November 12, 1912.

Time Travelers

When Ponting joined Scott's Antarctic expedition in 1910, he was already a renowned photographer. As a young person, he had lived and worked in California, where he first found success. After returning to England he went on to photograph extensively throughout Europe and Asia, publishing accounts of his travels (including images and texts, it must be underscored, from the perspective of an Englishman traveling abroad during a period of colonial expansion). During his time in Antarctica, Ponting shared this prior work with his fellow expeditioners through lantern slide lectures. In a diary entry of August 11, 1911, Scott admiringly described Ponting's dramatic lecturing style and the effective manner in which he moved from the impression of one place to that of another. The pictures themselves were made under varying conditions, and in Ponting's delivery the possible relationships among them—whether relationships of subject, form, or technique—could emerge over time, or remain mysterious.

Often when a person is delivering a photographic slide lecture, Scott wrote in his diary entry, they're "inclined to give too much attention to connecting links which join one episode to the other," but, he concluded, it "need not be a connected story; perhaps it is better it should not be."[12]

Readers of this book will also move from one photograph to the next, not following a prescribed path, though likely developing their own comparisons among the pictures—influenced, perhaps, by their own range of experiences—and in so doing finding their way into the Collection. The book's authors have contributed texts on a wide range of topics, each with their own distinctive approaches. Samuel Allen, Kaitlin Booher, and Casey Li have penned short texts that accompany a number of the images. Also interspersed among the plates are longer essays on a variety of subjects: Allen brings us into the prismatic patchwork of Lucas Samaras's panoramic views of his home and studio; Booher conveys how a portrait by Julia Margaret Cameron is at once a construction and "from life"; Lee Ann Daffner locates the places and processes through which Edward Steichen created photographs on the edges of painting; Rachel Rosin describes how László Moholy-Nagy experimented with novel photographic languages in the 1920s to create "new hidden worlds"; and I trace the manner in which photography was deployed to express the promise of aviation production. Like the circulation of images of new aircraft "up in the air" together (see p. 117, fig. 6), invigorating the imaginations of audiences, this book holds within its covers different photographic experiences, and the encouragement to travel among them.

(1) Walter Falcon Scott, quoted in Herbert G. Ponting, *The Great White South* (London: Duckworth, 1921), x.
(2) Scott, quoted in ibid., ix.
(3) Ponting, *The Great White South*, 59.
(4) Ibid., 149.
(5) Apsley Cherry-Garrard, *The Worst Journey in the World* (London: Constable & Co, 1922), 577.
(6) "To the South Pole with the Cinematograph: Film Records of Scott's Ill-fated Expedition," *Scientific American* 108, no. 25 (June 21, 1913): 560–61.
(7) Ponting, *The Great White South*, 70.
(8) Herbert G. Ponting, preface to *In Lotus-Land Japan* (London: Macmillan and Co., 1910), v.
(9) Ponting, *The Great White South*, 67.
(10) Ponting, quoted in Dennis Lynch, "The Worst Location in the World: Herbert G. Ponting in the Antarctic, 1910–1912," *Film History* 3, no. 4 (1989): 291–306.
(11) Ibid., 301.
(12) Scott, quoted in Ponting, *The Great White South*, xii.

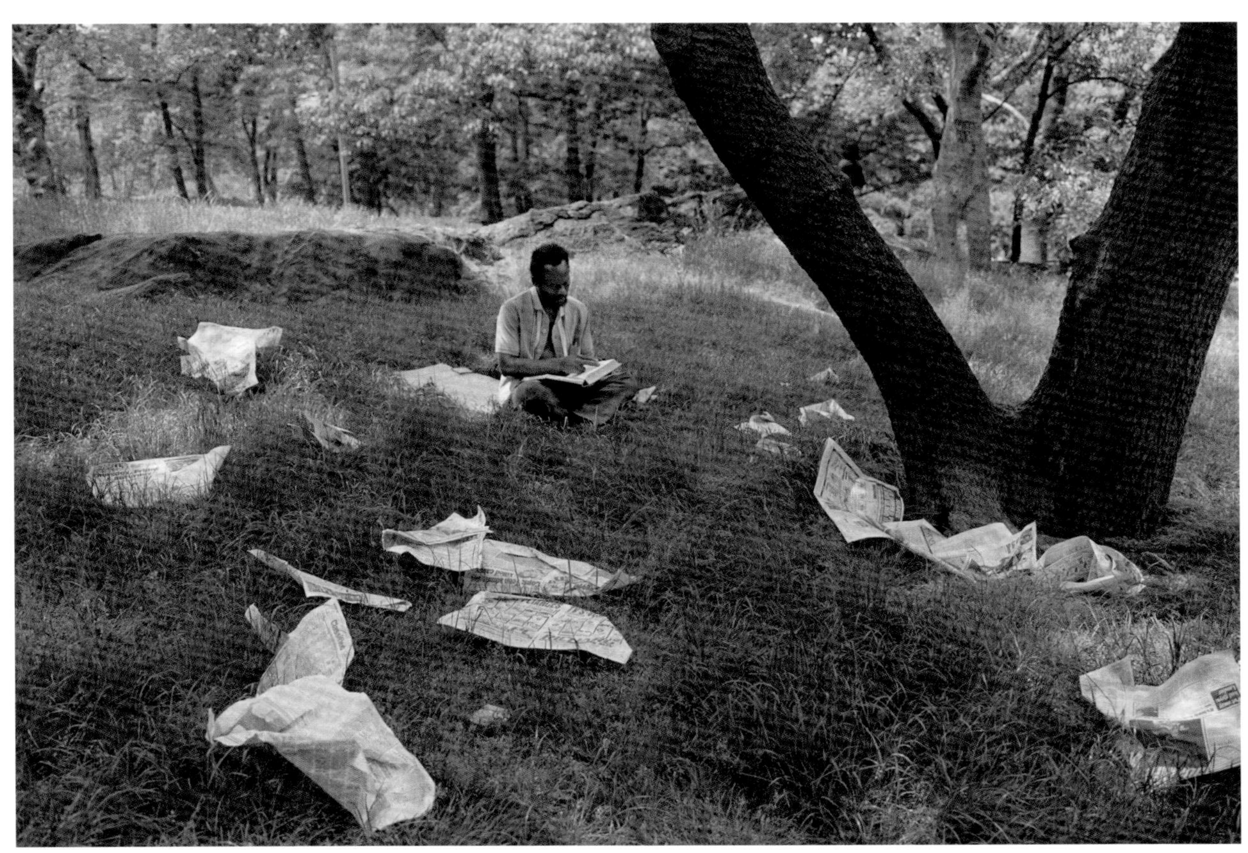

Tod Papageorge (American, born 1940). *Central Park*. 1989.
Gelatin silver print, 15 5/16 × 22 13/16 in. (38.9 × 57.9 cm)

Of the many photographs he made in Central Park over several decades, Tod Papageorge reflected, "We all carry our imaginary heavens around with us, and it was fortunate (although obviously not an accident) that, in my case, these elysian fields so literally resembled those I encountered in the park."

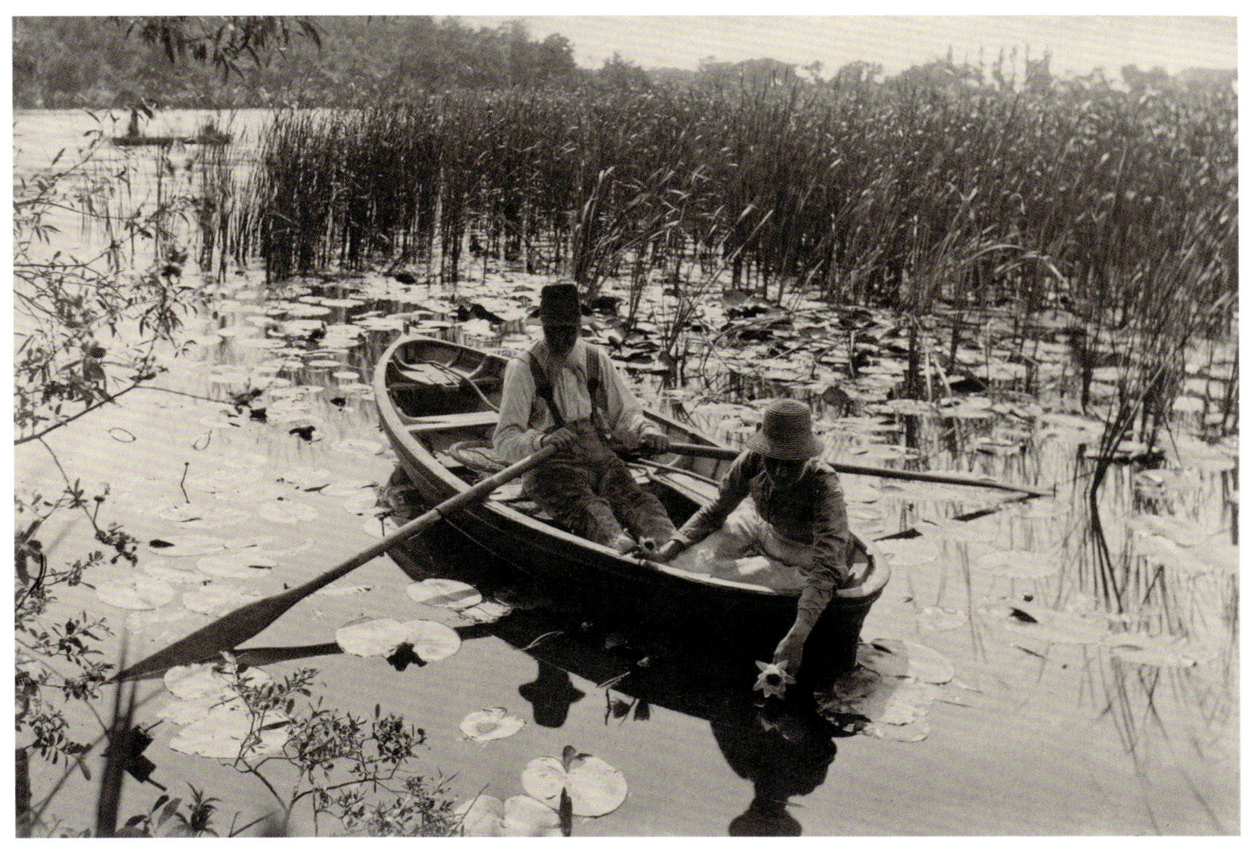

Peter Henry Emerson (British, born Cuba. 1856–1936). *Gathering Water-Lilies*. 1886. Platinum print, 7 11/16 × 11 1/2 in. (19.5 × 29.2 cm)

This bucolic picture, originally an illustration in Peter Henry Emerson and painter Thomas Frederick Goodall's 1886 publication, *Life and Landscape on the Norfolk Broads*, reenacts a scene of labor: collecting flowers as bait for fish traps. A staged photograph, its central figures are modeled by Goodall's fiancée and her father, who both hailed from the Norfolk Broads.

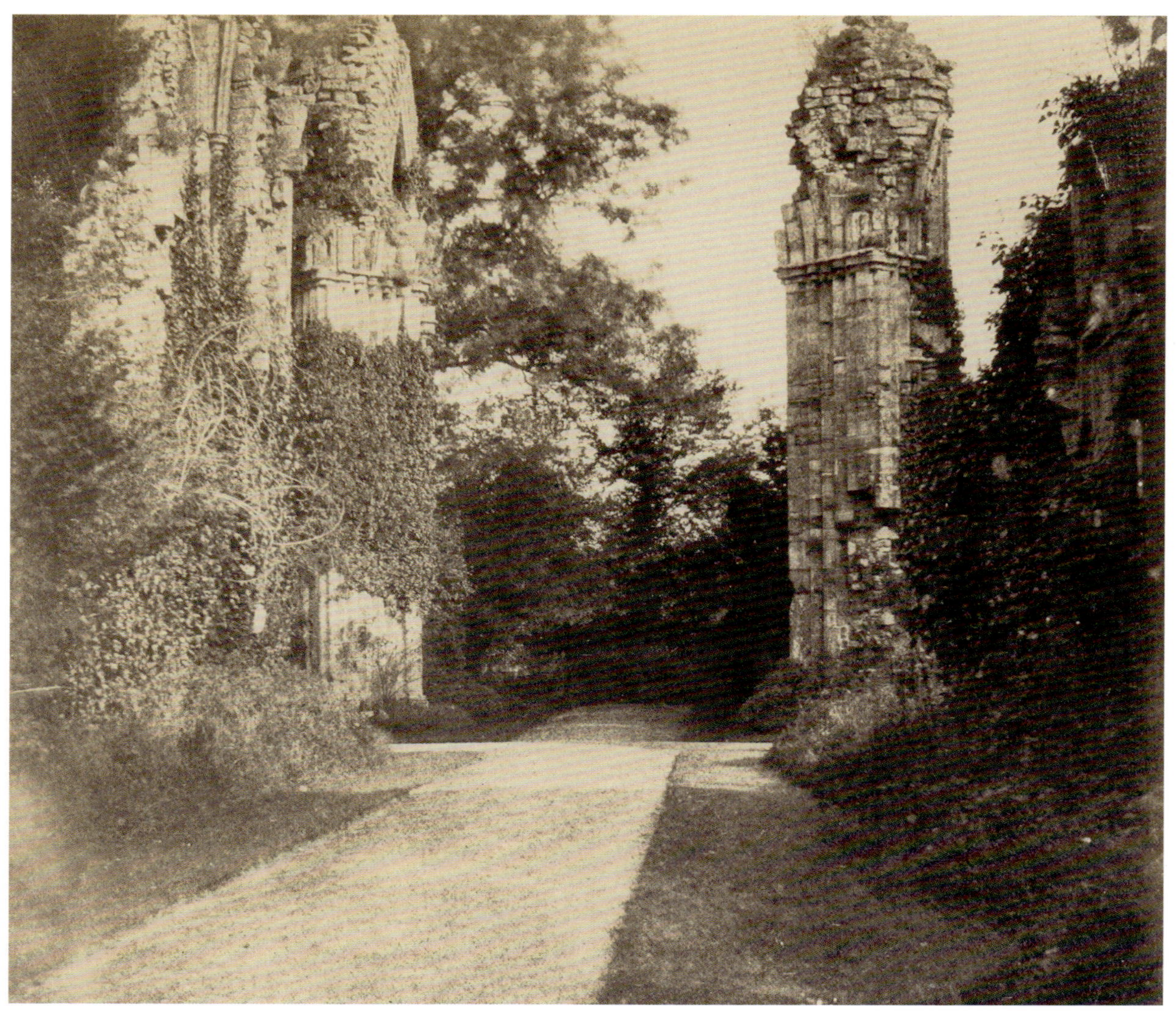

Henrietta Augusta Mostyn (British, 1830–1912). Untitled.
c. 1854. Salted paper print, 6⅝ × 7 13⁄16 in. (16.8 × 19.8 cm)

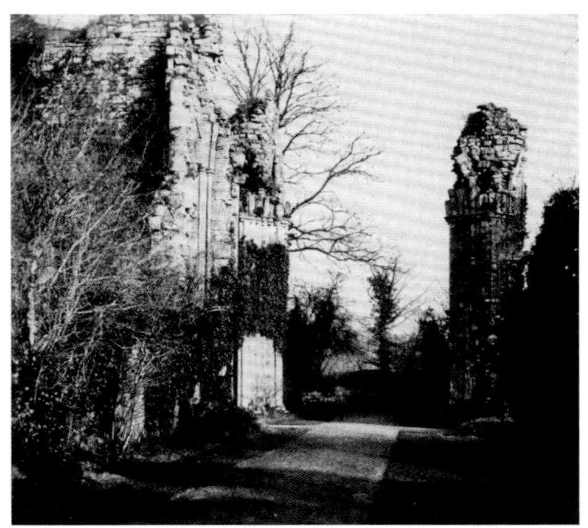

Fig. 1. Henrietta Augusta Mostyn (British, 1830–1912). *Pathway and Ruins, Bayham Abbey*. c. 1854–58. Albumenized salt print, 7½ × 8⅜ in. (19.1 × 21.3 cm). Solander Collection, Portland, OR

Lady Henrietta Augusta Mostyn (née Nevill) took up the camera amid the first flowering of amateur photography in England in the mid-nineteenth century. The Great Exhibition of Arts and Industry of 1851 had introduced a broad British public to the nascent technology, then scarcely a decade old. Soon after, numerous photographic societies formed as forums for sharing technical knowledge and aesthetic ideas; these included the Photographic Exchange Club, whose members, Mostyn among them, traded photographic prints twice a year. The club's participants, hailing predominantly from the aristocracy and landed gentry, modeled their camerawork after sketching and other established artistic pastimes. Created amid a period of social transformation, their images often depict subjects that suggest the endurance of upper-class values and traditional ways of life, such as pastoral scenes and timeworn monuments.

Hewing to this convention, Mostyn's photograph from the Gayle Greenhill Collection records a view among the ruins of Bayham Abbey, an ecclesiastical complex in southeastern England that had been active from the thirteenth through sixteenth centuries. The image is framed by the walls of the abbey church's former nave and punctuated by two of its massive piers. Such environments were a common trope of the picturesque, an aesthetic category that gained popularity in the late eighteenth century. The picturesque embraced rough surfaces and irregular proportions, qualities Mostyn's photograph magnifies through its fine-grained detail and subtly asymmetric framing. Settings like this one were highly sought after by Victorian tourists, as well, and this cultural fascination leaves its trace within the image. The remains of Bayham Abbey had been partially restored and opened to visitors in the early nineteenth century; the well-maintained gravel paths that intersect in the photograph's lower half testify to the Gothic ruins' second act as a public attraction.

Mostyn photographed the abbey on at least one other occasion, framing a similar view of the ruins amid a leafless landscape (fig. 1). Her work is replete with such rustic scenes, many encountered on her family's nearby estate of Eridge Park. She appears to have ceased photographing shortly after her marriage in 1855, which prompted a move to Wales, but her interest in art persisted. Several decades after participating in the Photographic Exchange Club, she helped to found another creative community, the Gwynedd Ladies' Art Society, in her adopted country. In 1901 she financed the construction of the Mostyn Art Gallery to serve as the society's home, establishing the world's first purpose-built gallery dedicated to women artists. **SA**

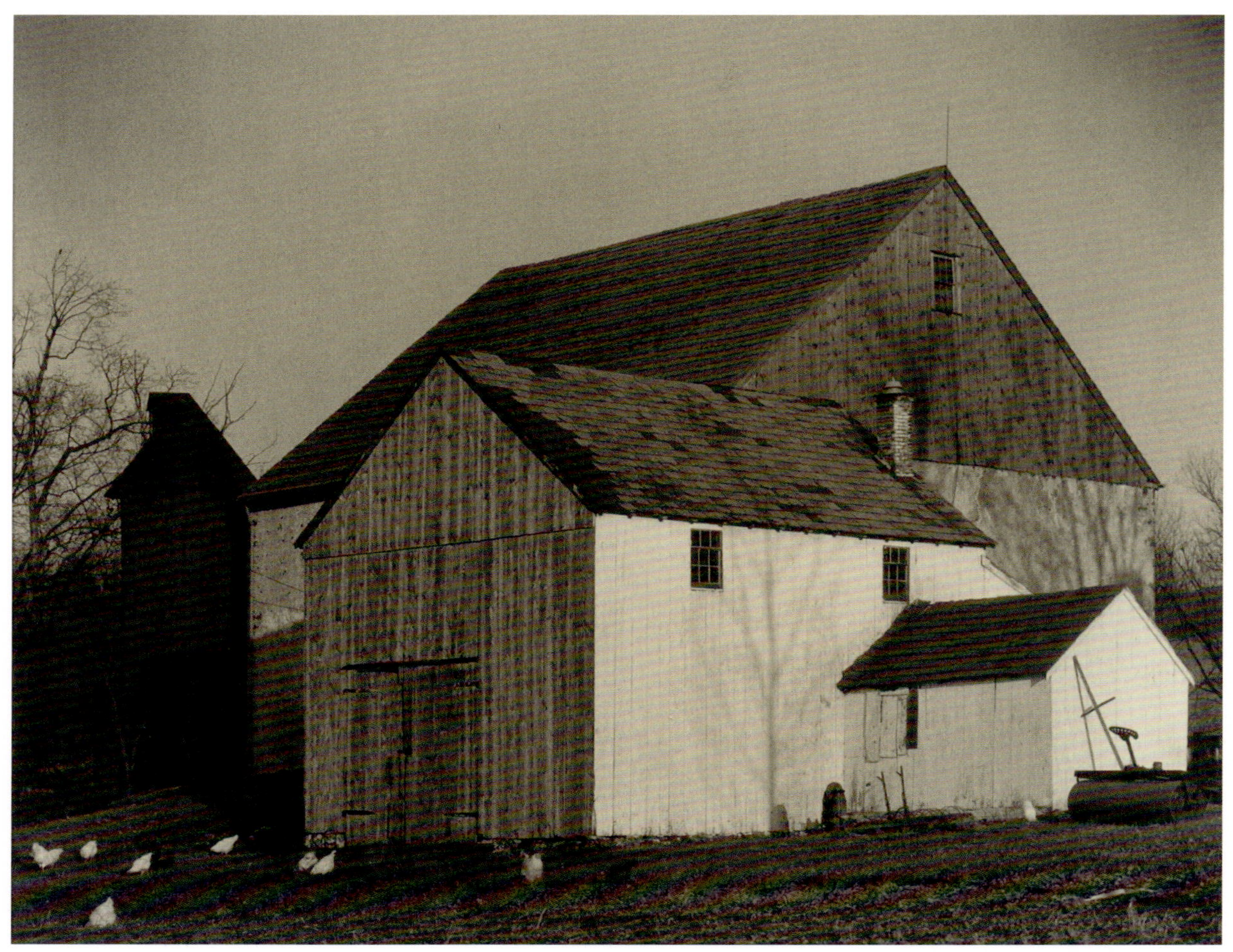

Charles Sheeler (American, 1883–1965). *Bucks County Barn with Chickens*. c. 1915–17. Gelatin silver print, 7 3/16 × 9 3/8 in. (18.3 × 23.8 cm)

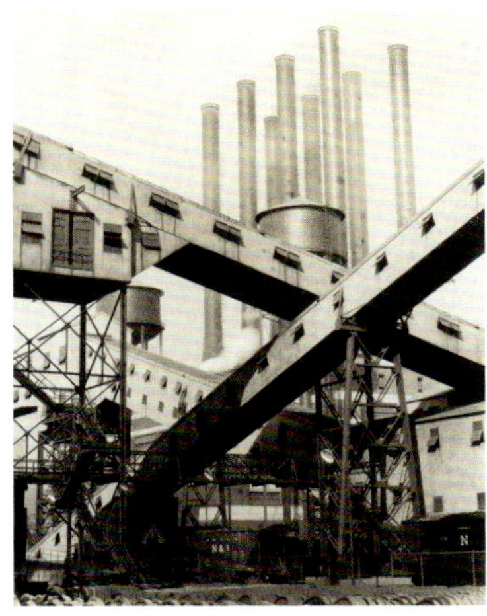

Fig 1. Charles Sheeler (American, 1883–1965). *Criss-Crossed Conveyors, River Rouge Plant, Ford Motor Company*. 1927. Gelatin silver print, 9¼ × 7½ in. (23.9 × 19 cm). The Museum of Modern Art, New York. Gift of Lincoln Kirstein, 1941

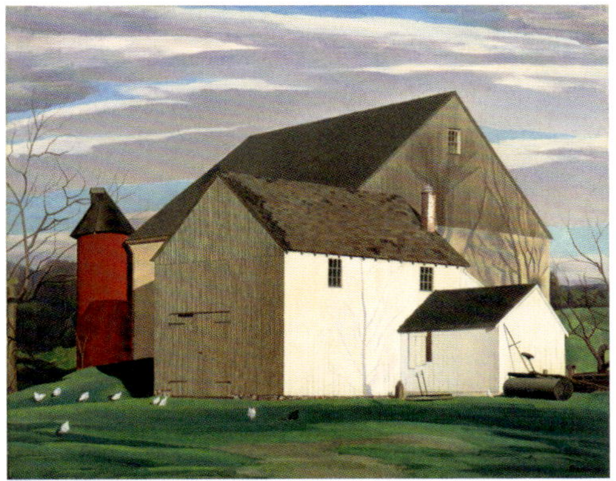

Fig. 2. Charles Sheeler (American, 1883–1965). *Bucks County Barn*. 1932. Oil on board, 23⅞ × 29⅞ in. (60.6 × 75.9 cm). The Museum of Modern Art, New York. Gift of Abby Aldrich Rockefeller, 1935

In 1909 Charles Sheeler—a recent graduate of the Pennsylvania Academy of the Fine Arts, trained in a by-then conservative Impressionism—traveled to Paris. There he experienced a decisive encounter with the groundbreaking modernism of Paul Cézanne, Pablo Picasso, and Georges Braque. Upon returning Stateside, he recast his painting practice in emulation of these artists. He also took up the camera, initially to support himself as a working photographer, producing photographic records of art and architecture.

Around 1916 Sheeler fused his recently adopted medium and vanguardist aesthetic commitments with a quintessentially American iconography. Working from a rented eighteenth-century farmhouse in Doylestown, Pennsylvania, he commenced a group of photographs that describe the region's vernacular architecture through the Post-Impressionist and Cubist idioms he had admired in Paris. *Bucks County Barn with Chickens* is one of several photographs Sheeler made at this time that centers on a barn's exterior. Depicting the three-building complex as a group of interlocking, tonally contrasting planes, its composition recalls the radically simplified geometries populating Cézanne's paintings and those of early Cubism.

Sheeler considered the Pennsylania barns' responsiveness to function to be analogous to his own engineer-like construction of a picture. The structures, the artist later reflected, present "forms created for the best realization of their practical use"; similarly, his own artmaking, he elaborated, pursued the "efficient work of the parts toward the consummation of the whole."[1]

For all their visual interest, Sheeler understood these barns to be sites of work. Their utilitarian nature links the images, despite stark differences in subject matter, to his subsequent photographs and paintings of a fast-modernizing America—including those depicting the Ford Motor Company's sprawling River Rouge factory in Dearborn, Michigan (fig. 1). As he did with many of his photographs, the artist later translated *Bucks County Barn with Chickens* into a painting, held in the collection of The Museum of Modern Art (fig. 2). Executed in 1932, its date indicates how traditional, agrarian architecture continued to hold Sheeler's interest even as he delved ever deeper into its Machine Age counterpart. **SA**

(1) Charles Sheeler, quoted in Karen Lucic, *Charles Sheeler in Doylestown: American Modernism and the Pennsylvania Tradition* (Allentown, PA: Allentown Art Museum, 1997), 61.

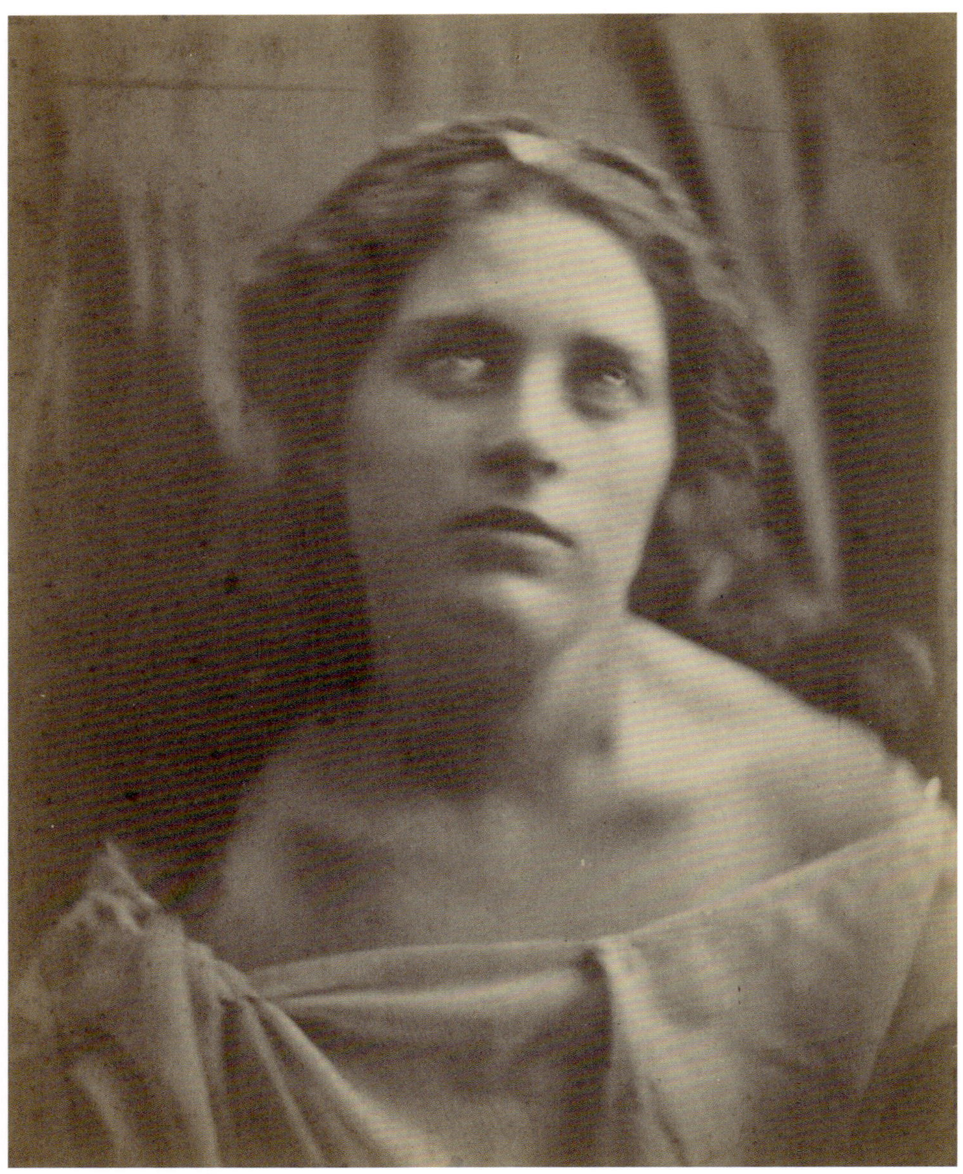

Julia Margaret Cameron (British, born India. 1815–1879). *Cyllena Wilson.* 1868. Albumen silver print, 13 × 10 11/16 in. (33 × 27.1 cm)

"From Life, Freshwater": Julia Margaret Cameron's Photograph of Cyllena Wilson

Kaitlin Booher

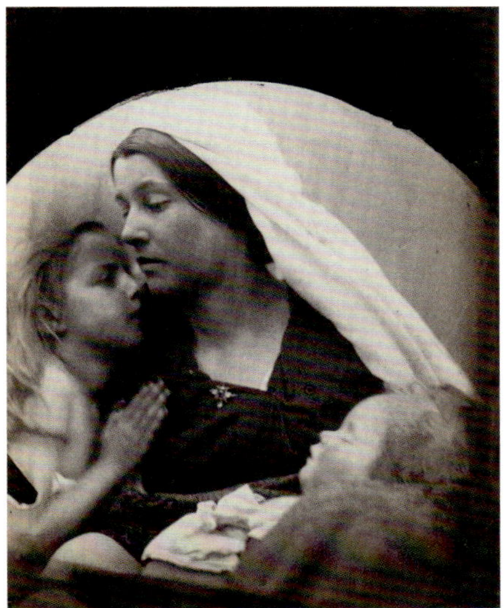

Fig. 1. Julia Margaret Cameron (British, born India. 1815–1879). *Madonna with Children*. 1864. Albumen silver print, 10½ × 8⅝ in. (26.7 × 21.9 cm). The Museum of Modern Art, New York. Gift of Shirley C. Burden, 1968

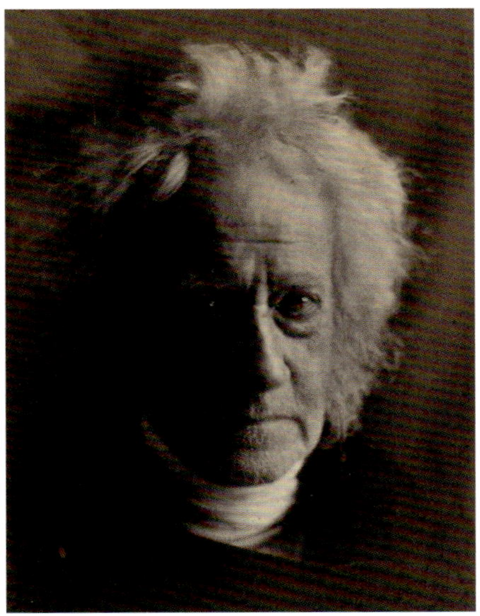

Fig. 2. Julia Margaret Cameron (British, born India. 1815–1879). *Sir John F. W. Herschel*. April 9, 1867. Albumen silver print, 14 × 10¾ in. (35.6 × 27.3 cm). The Museum of Modern Art, New York. Gift of Edward Steichen, 1952

Julia Margaret Cameron photographed her adopted daughter Cyllena Wilson, then seventeen years old, several times over the summer of 1868. The result of one such sitting shows Wilson before a simple cloth backdrop and possesses Cameron's hallmark techniques of soft focus, extreme close-up, and dramatic lighting (p. 36). In combination with Wilson's draped clothing and exposed shoulders, these qualities suggest that the image is of what Cameron would have called a "fancy subject," rather than a portrait of Wilson as an individual. Cameron used the term on a price list of works for sale at an exhibition in 1868 to describe photographs that depicted people or groups of people, often young women and children, posing as biblical, literary, or classical figures, with titles that direct their meaning.[1] Her 1864 photograph *Madonna with Children* (fig. 1) is an early work that would fall into the category, given its title and the costumes and poses of the sitters. But the print in the Gayle Greenhill Collection is simply annotated "From Life, Freshwater," a phrase that appears on many of Cameron's photographs of people—the enduring, nearly exclusive focus of her photographic career, which she forged primarily from her home studio in the village of Freshwater Bay on the Isle of Wight.

That Cameron distinguished her fancy subjects from her portraits, often of well-known men, thus created a divide in her work between what her grand-niece, writer Virginia Woolf, and art critic Roger Fry called "famous men and fair women."[2] Fry preferred the portraits, which he found to be distinguished and important in their look and approach.[3] Cameron's portrait of Sir John Herschel, one of her closest interlocutors about photography, is one such example (fig. 2). It features some similarities to the photograph of Wilson: an uncanny reflection in the eyes, a subtle blurriness, and dramatic lighting. Because of what we know about Herschel's life—he was, among other things, an astronomer and a chemist, and someone who played a major role in the invention of photography—it is easy to see his penetrating gaze and wild hair as signs of his intellect.[4]

Cameron rarely portrayed middle-aged or older women as established personalities, and she often portrayed young women as fancy subjects. For this reason, the fancy subjects present a number of problems: Cameron's reluctance to use the real names of young women suggests that although she made a name for herself, she did not necessarily extend her own privilege to other women.[5] Hand in hand with her portrayal of women are the connotations of the allegories and themes that she evoked in her representations. Born in India in 1815, Cameron was the daughter of an official for the East India Company, and she later married an owner of coffee and rubber plantations in present-day Sri Lanka. (She and her husband relocated to the Isle of Wight after her husband retired.) Her life was wholly enabled by England's colonization of India and

Sri Lanka. As historian Jeff Rosen has argued, Cameron and her contemporaries' idealization of classical antiquity in art and literature served to justify British imperialism.[6]

All of these issues come to the fore in Cameron's close-up of Wilson. Cameron made this image in the fourth year of her photographic career. By then, thanks to her professional approach of copyrighting images, holding exhibitions, and soliciting criticism, she had developed a reputation for her bold and unconventional approach to the medium. She had upgraded to a large-format camera that accommodated fifteen-by-twelve-inch glass plate negatives, allowing her to make intimate portraits. When contact printed from these negatives, Cameron's subjects would appear at life-scale. In format, presentation, and style, this technique was a departure from the more conventional types of portraits made in commercial photography studios at the time. Instead, Cameron produced albumen silver prints, such as the print in the Greenhill Collection, which measures thirteen by nearly eleven inches and is mounted to a sturdy paper support. This treatment is typical of the photographs that Cameron sold and distributed through the publishers and art dealers Paul and Dominic Colnaghi, who had a gallery in London and published prints under the imprint of Colnaghi & Co. The Greenhill Collection's print has the company's oval blind stamp at the lower center of the paper mount, identifying it as a "Registered Photograph Sold by Messrs Colnaghi," and features a thin gold border surrounding the image. The print's annotation and signature are not in Cameron's handwriting but in that of an unknown assistant, which is also typical of the prints that she sold through Colnaghi & Co.[7] The photograph's scale, as well as its stamp and mounting treatment, speaks to Cameron's professional intention: she produced the image to sell it, so that its owner could display it as a work of art.

In 1868, on the occasion of an exhibition at Colnaghi & Co., Cameron created her "Priced Catalogue," which listed the titles and costs of prints for sale.[8] Two photographs of Wilson appear in it: one is identified as *Cyllena study*, under the category "Fancy Subjects"; another, *Miss Cyllena Wilson*, appears under the category "Portraits," in the company of figures such as poet Alfred Tennyson, historian Thomas Carlyle, and Sir John Herschel.[9] It is not known whether either entry refers to the work in the Greenhill Collection, but because photographs of Wilson appear in both categories, it appears that Cameron considered her sessions with Wilson to produce both portraits and allegorical images. Other allegorical scenes for which Wilson posed include one where she represented the character of Rosalba from Sir Henry Taylor's play *The Virgin Widow* (fig. 3), and prints with titles referencing, among other roles, the Renaissance figure Beatrice Cenci and a follower of Bacchus, the Roman god of wine.

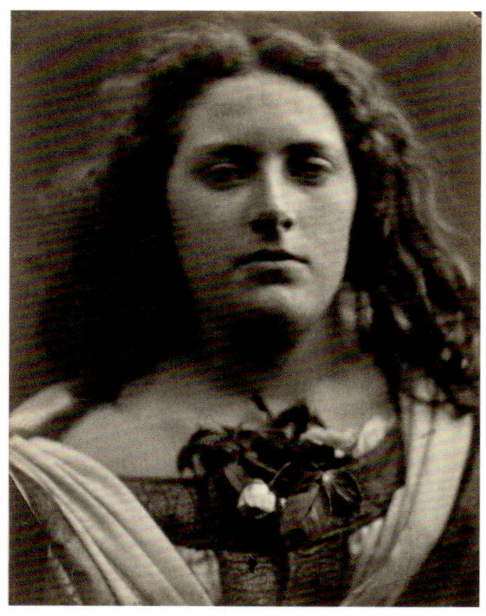

Fig. 3. Julia Margaret Cameron (British, born India, 1815–1879). *Rosalba (Cyllena Wilson)*. 1867. Albumen silver print, 14 × 11 1/16 in. (35.5 × 28.1 cm). The Museum of Fine Arts, Houston. Museum purchase funded by the Brown Foundation Accessions Endowment, The Manfred Heiting Collection, 2004.335

Also in 1868, Cameron registered five photographs of Wilson with the Copyright Office of the Stationers' Company, with descriptive titles including *Photograph of Cyllena Wilson, bust, full face. No* 6.[10] Perhaps one of these photographs refers to the print in the Greenhill Collection, in which Wilson appears with her face illuminated by a light source from above, head tilted to the right edge of the photograph. Her eyes, turned upward, catch the light in such a way that they seem to glow, and Wilson's collarbone and shoulders stand out against the muted backdrop. The slightest overall blur of the image, a result of Cameron's camera techniques and the long exposure time of the wet collodion negative, further adds to the work's mysterious effect.

Wilson and her two younger siblings were orphaned in 1866, and the Camerons, who had been friends of the family, adopted them. According to historian Helmut Gernsheim, Wilson disliked modeling; in his biography of Cameron he relates a visceral anecdote during which Cameron locked Wilson in a closet in order to evoke emotional responses.[11] Gernsheim and Colin Ford both wrote that Wilson "ran away" from Freshwater in 1870, speculating that it was due to her dislike of modeling for Cameron.[12] When Wilson left the Camerons, she chose a particularly adventurous path and went to work as a stewardess on an ocean liner with a route to Argentina.[13] Wilson's photo shoots with Cameron may have represented the meeting of two strong wills; historians and biographers convey Cameron's imperiousness, eclecticism, and disregard for social mores, suggesting she was willing to solicit anyone she found interesting to sit for her camera.[14]

As Cameron worked through different ideas about portraiture and allegory, she corresponded with fellow artists and photographers. Chief among them was Herschel, who was engaged in the artistic qualities of Cameron's photographs. While Cameron drew upon a panoply of contemporary and art historical references for her subjects, including Pre-Raphaelite works of her friends, such as painter G. F. Watts, she and Herschel shared a particular focus on her photography's relationship to sculpture, and she may have had this in mind when photographing Wilson in 1868. Through letters, and the photo albums that Cameron would ultimately create for Herschel, the two compared her photographs to sculptures many times. Herschel called *The Mountain Nymph Sweet Liberty* (fig. 4) "really a most astonishing piece of high relief— She is absolutely alive and thrusting her head from the paper into the air."[15] Curator Julian Cox has speculated that the sitter for this photograph, whose identity is unknown, may be Cyllena's sister.[16] Cameron inscribed Herschel's copy of her portrait of philosopher Thomas Carlyle "Carlyle Like a Rough Block of Michel Angelo's Sculpture" (fig. 5). Sculpture was also an ideal subject for early photographic experiments. William Henry Fox Talbot's photograph *The Bust of Patroclus*

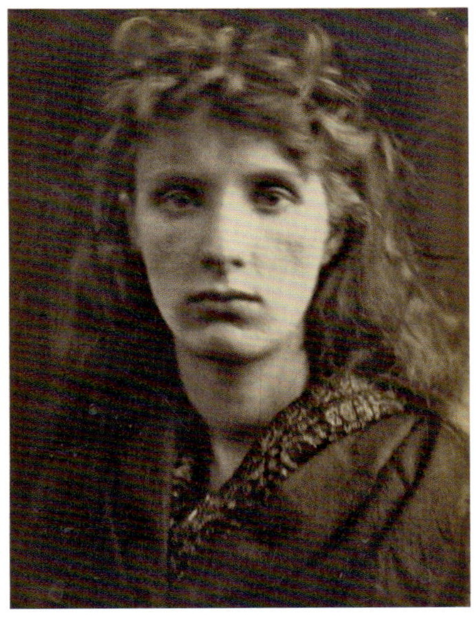

Fig. 4. Julia Margaret Cameron (British, born India, 1815–1879). *The Mountain Nymph Sweet Liberty*. 1866. Albumen silver print, 14¼ × 11⅛ in. (36.2 × 28.3 cm). The J. Paul Getty Museum, Los Angeles, 1984

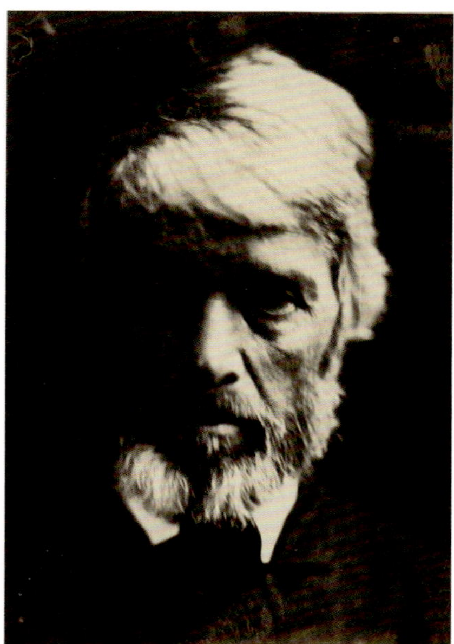

Fig. 5. Julia Margaret Cameron (British, born India. 1815–1879). *Thomas Carlyle*. 1867. Albumen silver print, 14 7/16 × 10 3/16 in. (36.7 × 25.9 cm). The J. Paul Getty Museum, Los Angeles, 1984

(p. 1), featuring one of Talbot's plaster casts, displays an expression not dissimilar to Wilson's. For Talbot, the bright, matte surface of the bust made it an ideal subject for his long exposures.[17]

As Cameron and Herschel considered photography's relationship to more traditional art forms, including sculpture, Herschel was also working through the medium's inability to represent a spectrum of color beyond tones of black to white. In 1866 Cameron wrote to Herschel seeking advice for how to advance her photographs aesthetically. Herschel demurred and said he could not offer her guidance, beyond one suggestion:

> Have you ever tried the effect of draping all the figures of a group in pure white—whitening their faces, hands and hair and then photographing your group as sculpture—the background also and all of the appendages being white or grey. I cannot help thinking it might have a good effect—colour being so very great an obstacle to good photography at present. With your system of working slightly out of focus the texture of the white would not betray the material used (whether flour or simply whitewash!).[18]

In 1867, perhaps in response, Cameron posed Wilson along with another frequent model, Mary Hillier, to emulate two of the figures on the Parthenon frieze, often referred to as the Elgin Marbles, which had arrived in London in 1813. In one resulting image, *2d. Version of Study after the Elgin Marbles*, Rosen has identified their pose as that of the Fates from the frieze's west pediment (fig. 6).[19] Although she does not appear to have added any substance to the surfaces of their bodies, by presenting the two against a light backdrop, wearing all white, Cameron seems to have partly taken up Herschel's prompt. Cameron and Herschel may indeed have been thinking foremost about stylistic and artistic innovation, but their idealization of whiteness serves as an example of white Victorian supremacy and photography's role in constructing notions of race.[20]

In Victorian-era art and photography, allegory often signified nostalgia for what were presumably simpler times. As Rosen has elucidated, classical references provided Victorian artists with a way to express their national identity and colonial ambitions.[21] They also served as a means of connecting contemporary Britain to ancient Greek civilization. This sense of cultural continuity helped justify Britain's colonial project and positioned the empire as the inheritor of the ideals of classical antiquity. By dressing Wilson in muslin, Cameron may have been subtly referencing her own relationship to imperial power structures of the day, while at the same time drawing on the fabric's classical

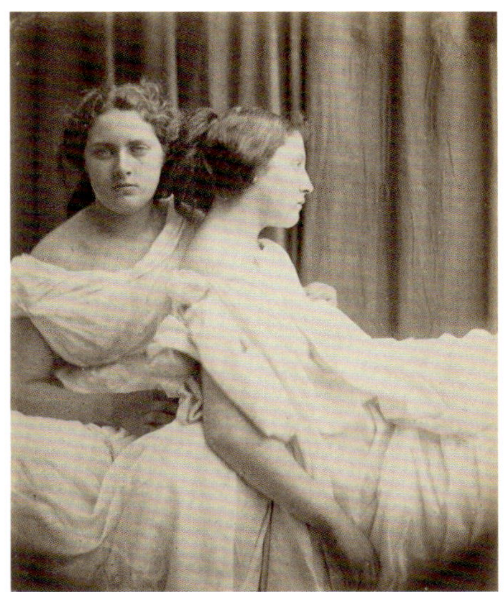

Fig. 6. Julia Margaret Cameron (British, born India. 1815–1879). *2d. Version of Study after the Elgin Marbles*. 1867. Albumen silver print, 11⁵⁄₁₆ × 9½ in. (28.8 × 24.1 cm). Victoria and Albert Museum, London. Nevinson Bequest, 1990

connotations. Wilson's family history may have also inspired the artist's choice to associate her subject with ancient Greek sculpture. Wilson's grandfather, Reverend Samuel Sheridan Wilson, had been a missionary in Greece and translated the New Testament into modern Greek.[22] Cameron's *2d. Version of Study after the Elgin Marbles* lacks the extreme close-up, blur, or sfumato effects seen in the artist's other portraits or fancy subjects, often emphasized with darkroom manipulation and gold toning to achieve rich, deep browns and blacks. If Cameron was unhappy with the results of these studies—only a few prints exist—perhaps she sought to improve upon them when she photographed Wilson the following summer.

Cameron wrote that taking up photography allowed her to "arrest all beauty" that she encountered.[23] While that may indeed have been her primary goal, by making a photograph of Wilson that recalls classical antiquity, she inevitably also made a portrait of a young woman on the brink of adulthood, as she was soon to travel far abroad herself. In the Greenhill Collection photograph, Wilson's expression and her simple dress suggest a blank slate, a person ready to define her own identity. Her photograph is "from life," and she is on the brink of living her own.

(1) Sylvia Wolf, "'Mrs. Cameron's Photographs, Priced Catalogue': A Note on Her Sales and Process," in Sylvia Wolf, ed., *Julia Margaret Cameron's Women* (New Haven, CT: Yale University Press, 1998), 208.
(2) Virginia Woolf and Roger Fry, *Victorian Photographs of Famous Men and Fair Women* (London: Hogarth Press, 1926), 13–14.
(3) Ibid., 10.
(4) For more on Sir John Herschel's role in the invention of photography, see Kelly Wilder, "A Note on the Science of Photography: Reconsidering the Invention Story," in Tanya Sheehan and Andrés Mario Zervigón, eds., *Photography and Its Origins* (New York and London: Routledge, 2015), 208–21.
(5) Anne McCauley, "Brides of Men and Brides of Art," *Études photographiques* 28 (November 2011), http://journals.openedition.org/etudesphotographiques/3469.
(6) Jeff Rosen, *Julia Margaret Cameron: The Colonial Shadows of Victorian Photography* (London: Paul Mellon Centre for Studies in British Art, 2024), 5–11.
(7) See "Appendix B: Inscriptions, Stamps, and the Business of Photography," in Julian Cox and Colin Ford, *Julia Margaret Cameron: The Complete Photographs* (Los Angeles: Getty Publications, 2003), 499–501.
(8) For a detailed analysis and image of Cameron's Priced Catalogue, see Wolf, "'Mrs. Cameron's Photographs, Priced Catalogue,'" 208–9.
(9) Stephanie Lipscomb, "Sitters' Biographies," in Wolf, ed., *Julia Margaret Cameron's Women*, 227. As Lipscomb has noted, the spelling of Wilson's name varied considerably: historian Helmut Gernsheim spelled it "Cyllene" and some of Cameron's copyright registers spell it "Selina." Lipscomb and Wolf decided to use "Cyllena," as Cameron wrote it in her Priced Catalogue. Wolf, "'Mrs. Cameron's Photographs, Priced Catalogue,'" 208.
(10) Julia Margaret Cameron, copyright paperwork, The National Archives, Kew, August 3, 1868.
(11) Helmut Gernsheim, *Julia Margaret Cameron: Her Life and Photographic Work*, 2nd ed. (Millerton, NY: Aperture, 1975), 78.
(12) See Ford, *Julia Margaret Cameron*, 61; and Gernsheim, *Julia Margaret Cameron*, 78.
(13) Lipscomb, "Sitters' Biographies," 227.
(14) For other accounts of the experience of sitting for Cameron, see Colin Ford, *Julia Margaret Cameron: A Critical Biography* (Los Angeles: J. Paul Getty Museum, 2003), 56 and 61; and Victoria Olsen, *From Life: Julia Margaret Cameron and Victorian Photography* (New York: Palgrave Macmillan, 2003), 152.
(15) Herschel to Cameron, September 25, 1866, The Royal Society Archives, London.
(16) Julian Cox, *Julia Margaret Cameron, In Focus: From the J. Paul Getty Museum* (Los Angeles: J. Paul Getty Museum, 1996), 52.
(17) Larry Schaaf, *The Photographic Art of William Henry Fox Talbot* (Princeton, NJ: Princeton University Press, 2000), 148. Herschel and Cameron would have been familiar with Talbot's photography through his 1844 book *The Pencil of Nature*, but Talbot also sent Herschel photographs that included the sculpture in 1839. See Talbot to Herschel, December 7, 1839, the Royal Society Archives, London.
(18) Herschel to Cameron, February 5, 1866, The Royal Society Archives, London.
(19) Rosen, *Julia Margaret Cameron*, 115.
(20) For more on this, see Stephanie Polsky, *The Photographic Invention of Whiteness: The Visual Cultures of White Atlantic Worlds*, Routledge History of Photography (New York: Routledge, Taylor & Francis Group, 2024).
(21) See Jeff Rosen, *Julia Margaret Cameron's "Fancy Subjects": Photographic Allegories of Victorian Identity and Empire* (Manchester, UK: Manchester University Press, 2016), 19–23, 125.
(22) Lipscomb, "Sitters' Biographies," 227.
(23) Cameron, quoted in Violet Hamilton, ed., *Annals of My Glass House: Photographs by Julia Margaret Cameron* (Claremont, CA: Ruth Chandler Williamson Gallery, 1996), 12.

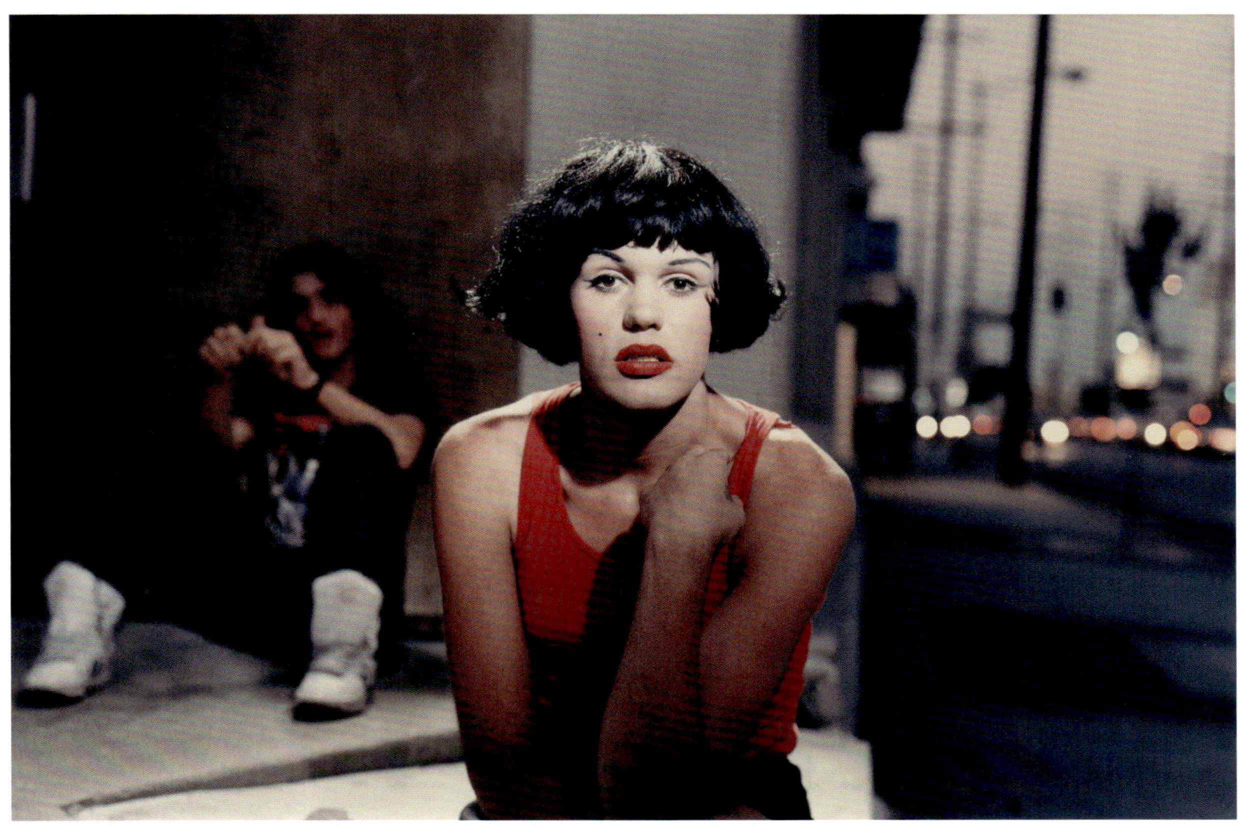

Philip-Lorca diCorcia (American, born 1951). *Marilyn; 28 Years Old; Las Vegas, Nevada; $30* from the series Hustlers. 1990–92. Chromogenic print, 25 3/16 × 37 13/16 in. (64 × 96 cm)

Philip-Lorca diCorcia's series Hustlers presents stylized images of sex workers encountered around Hollywood's Santa Monica Boulevard. Each artwork's title records the sitter's name, age, place of birth, and the fee they received to be photographed, roughly equivalent to what they would have charged for paid sex. Funded by a grant from the National Endowment for the Arts, diCorcia began the series shortly after a cadre of right-wing politicians, led by Senator Jesse Helms, accused the federal agency of supporting "obscene" art. diCorcia's titles were meant partly as a riposte to these culture warriors—"a report to the government," he disclosed, "of its well-spent dollars."

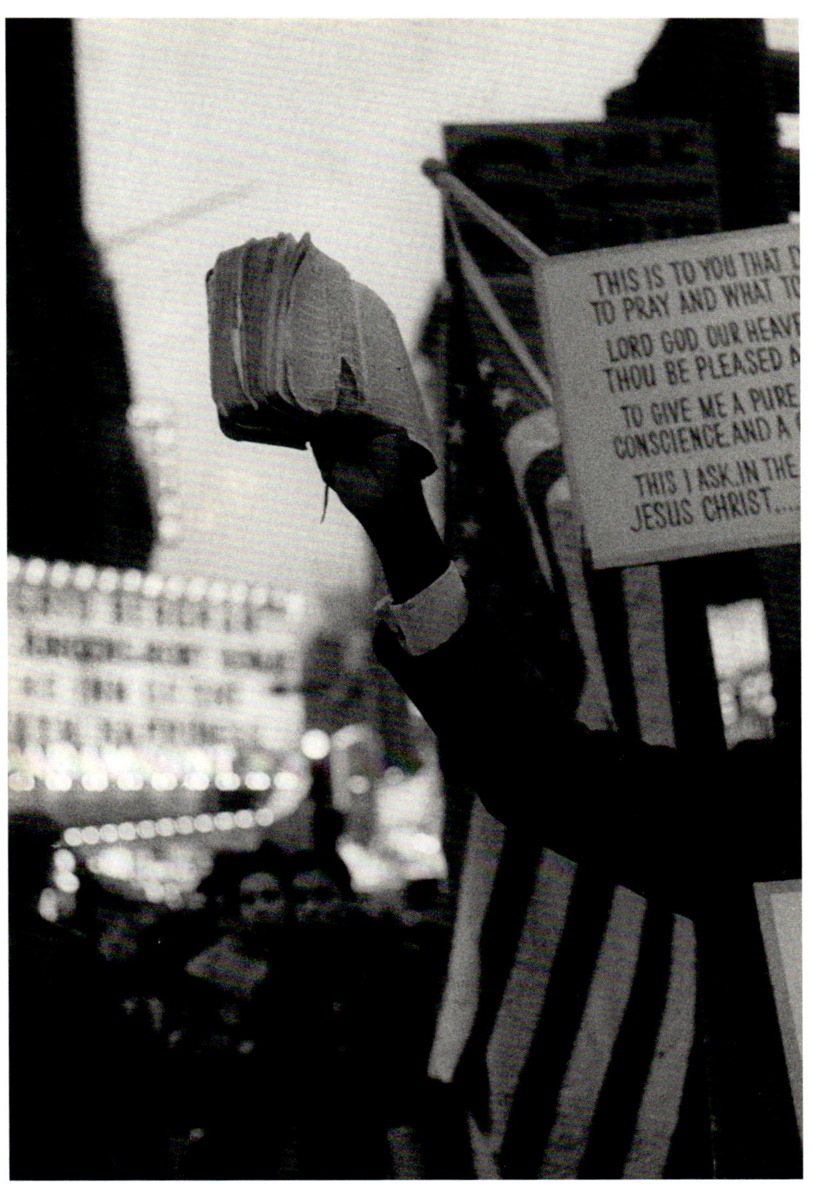

Robert Frank (American, born Switzerland. 1924–2019). *New York City*. 1958. Gelatin silver print, $16\frac{5}{8} \times 11\frac{7}{16}$ in. (42.2 × 29.1 cm)

Robert Frank made this image the same year that he published *Les Américains* (*The Americans*). Like many of the photographs in that book, this shot of a street preacher in New York City, wielding a Bible before an American flag and a marquee, shows the United States as a place of converging realities. It later appeared in *Show* magazine, illustrating a story by American journalist Gay Talese titled "42nd St.–How It Got That Way."

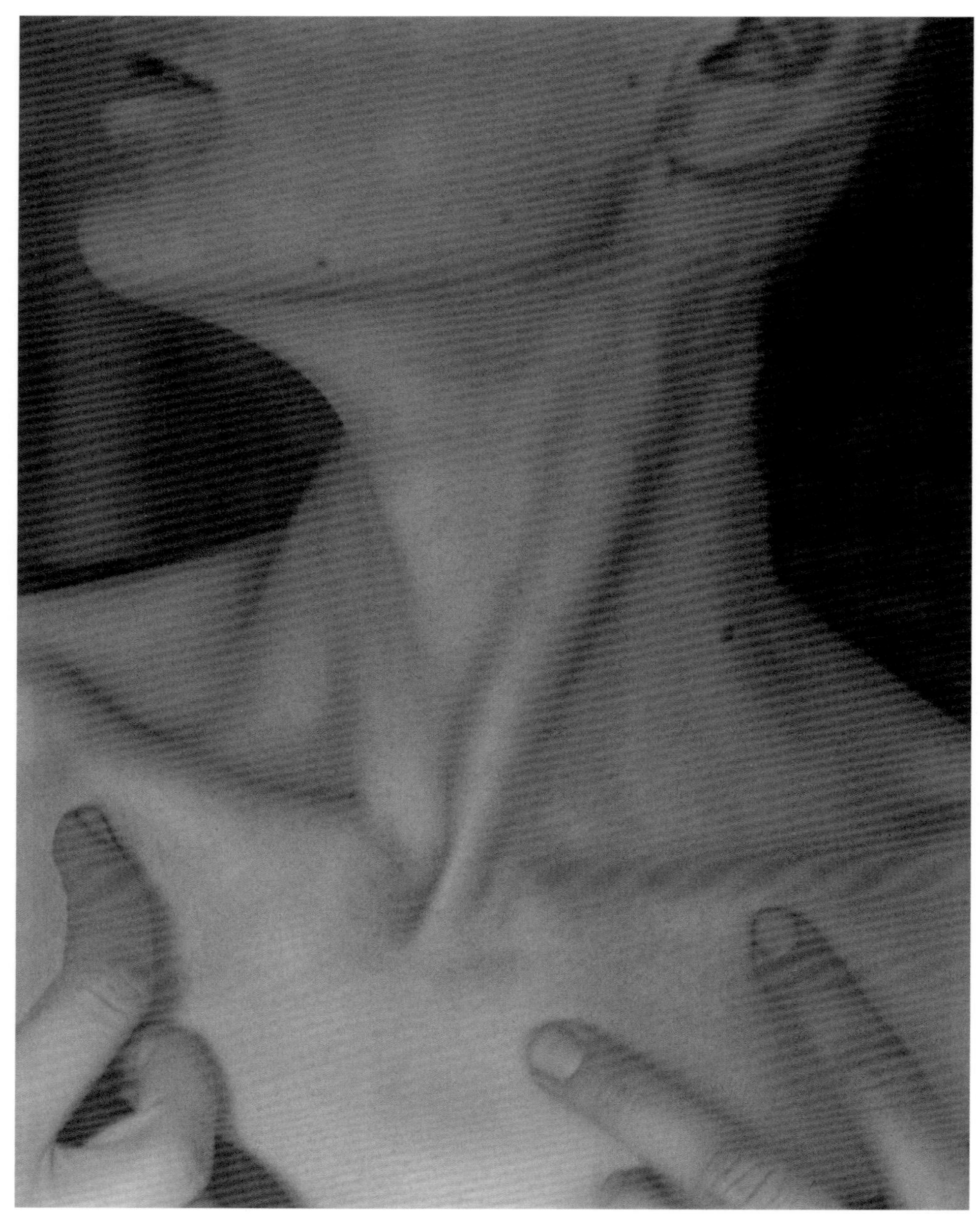

Alfred Stieglitz (American, 1864–1946). *Georgia O'Keeffe–Neck*. 1921. Gelatin silver print, 9 9/16 × 7 5/8 in. (24.3 × 19.4 cm)

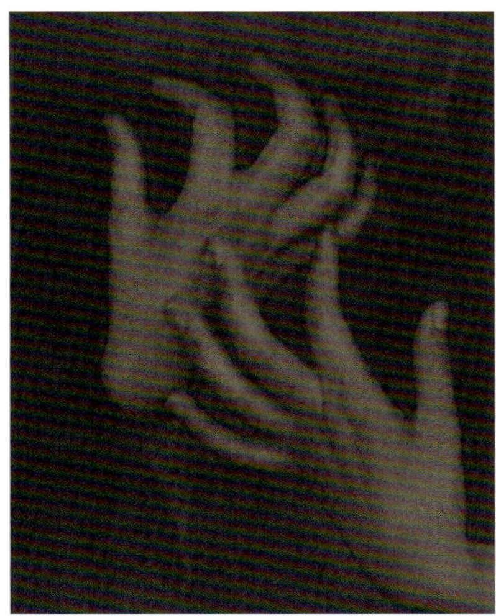

Fig. 1. Alfred Stieglitz (American, 1864–1946). *Georgia O'Keeffe—Hands*. 1919. Palladium print, 9½ × 7¹³⁄₁₆ in. (24.2 × 19.9 cm). The Museum of Modern Art, New York. Alfred Stieglitz Collection. Gift of Georgia O'Keeffe, 1984

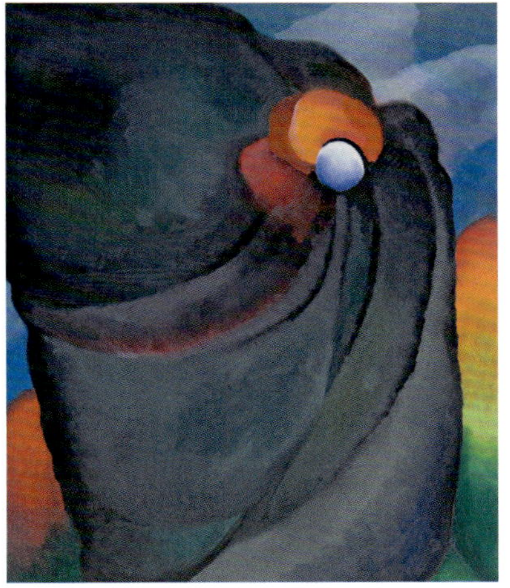

Fig. 2. Georgia O'Keeffe (American, 1887–1986). *Lake George, Coat and Red*. 1919. Oil on canvas, 27⅜ × 23¼ in. (69.6 × 59 cm). The Museum of Modern Art, New York. Gift of The Georgia O'Keeffe Foundation, 1994

Alfred Stieglitz's *Georgia O'Keeffe—Neck* depicts the neck, shoulders, and hands of Georgia O'Keeffe in a compressed space. By cropping the top of the image just above her mouth, Stieglitz avoids more identifying features traditionally included in a portrait, instead making a study of freckles and flexed tendons. The picture is one of more than three hundred that Stieglitz made of O'Keeffe, which he considered to be parts of a greater, composite portrait that began before the two were romantically involved and continued through their marriage in 1924, ending only when old age prevented Stieglitz from working.

Stieglitz was a pioneering photographer and editor who promoted modernist experimentation in the United States through his galleries and publications. Many of his portraits of O'Keeffe were made at their summer home in Lake George, New York, and show her hands in dramatic poses (fig. 1), perhaps a reference to O'Keeffe's own artistic production. O'Keeffe's 1919 painting *Lake George, Coat and Red* (fig. 2) might be interpreted as a portrait of Stieglitz, its sweeping dark forms depicting his black coat with red lining at a place of lifelong significance to him.[1]

Stieglitz's and O'Keeffe's respective works oscillate between abstraction and representation, reflecting the kaleidoscopic dynamics of their artistic identities over time. As O'Keeffe wrote in 1978 in a preface to a book of Stieglitz's photographs of her, "When I look over the photographs Stieglitz took of me—some of them more than sixty years ago—I wonder who that person is. It is as if in my one life I have lived many lives. If the person in the photographs were living in the world today, she would be quite a different person—but it doesn't matter—Stieglitz photographed her then."[2] KB

(1) For more on Georgia O'Keeffe's approaches to portraiture, see Samantha Friedman, *Georgia O'Keeffe: To See Takes Time* (New York: The Museum of Modern Art, 2023), 136.

(2) Georgia O'Keeffe, "Introduction," in Maria Morris Hambourg, ed., *Georgia O'Keeffe: A Portrait by Alfred Stieglitz* (New York: The Metropolitan Museum of Art, 1997), n.p.

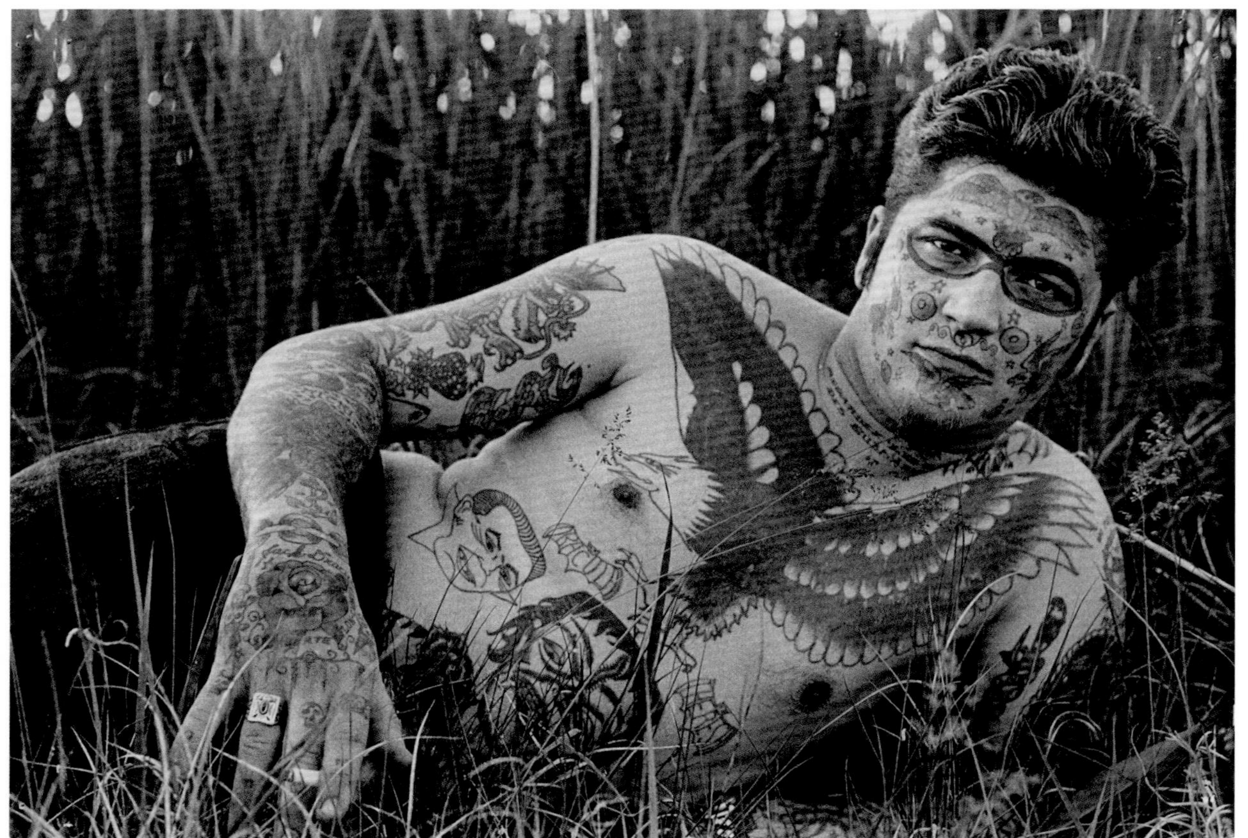

Diane Arbus (American, 1923–1971). *Jack Dracula, the Marked Man, N.Y.C., 1961.* 1961. Gelatin silver print, 7 15/16 × 10 3/4 in. (20.2 × 27.3 cm)

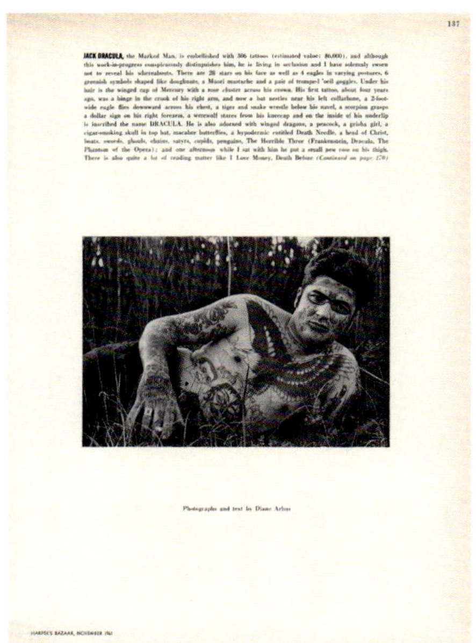

137

JACK DRACULA, the Marked Man, is embellished with 306 tattoos (estimated value: $6,000), and although this work-in-progress conspicuously distinguishes him, he is living in seclusion and I have solemnly sworn not to reveal his whereabouts. There are 28 stars on his face as well as 4 eagles in varying postures, 6 greenish symbols shaped like doughnuts, a Maori mustache and a pair of trompe-l 'oeil goggles. Under his hair is the winged cap of Mercury with a rose cluster across his crown. His first tattoo, about four years ago, was a hinge in the crook of his right arm, and now a bat nestles near his left collarbone, a 2-foot-wide eagle flies downward across his chest, a tiger and snake wrestle below his navel, a scorpion grasps a dollar sign on his right forearm, a werewolf stares from his kneecap and on the inside of his underlip is inscribed the name DRACULA. He is also adorned with winged dragons, a peacock, a geisha girl, a cigar-smoking skull in top hat, macabre butterflies, a hypodermic entitled Death Needle, a head of Christ, boats, swords, ghouls, chains, satyrs, cupids, penguins, The Horrible Three (Frankenstein, Dracula, The Phantom of the Opera); and one afternoon while I sat with him he put a small new rose on his thigh. There is also quite a lot of reading matter like I Love Money, Death Before *(Continued on page 170)*

Photographs and text by Diane Arbus

HARPER'S BAZAAR, NOVEMBER 1961

Fig. 1. *Jack Dracula, the Marked Man, N.Y.C., 1961*, published in Diane Arbus, "The Full Circle," *Harper's Bazaar* (November 1961). Hearst Magazine Media, Inc., New York

"There are 28 stars on his face as well as 4 eagles in varying postures, 6 greenish symbols shaped like doughnuts, a Maori mustache and a pair of trompe-l'oeil goggles."[1] This was how Diane Arbus introduced some of the many tattoos adorning Jack Dracula's face in a text that accompanied his portrait in a 1961 issue of *Harper's Bazaar* (fig. 1).

Dracula's portrait appeared in an article titled "The Full Circle," which featured five people Arbus had photographed because of their idiosyncratic dress, lifestyle, or profession. Dracula, who owned a tattoo parlor in Connecticut for a brief period before working as a performer, satisfied all of these criteria for a 1960s audience. The article included an extended text by Arbus, in which she detailed not only Dracula's tattoos, but also his interests and assumed identity. The gelatin silver print in the Gayle Greenhill Collection, printed full-bleed on standard eight-by-ten-inch photo paper and mounted to board, has edges that show its handling over time. This print may be the very one used to create the duotone plate printed on the page, as its verso bears a *Harper's Bazaar* stamp. Arbus's portrait of Dracula, published at the start of her career, is representative of the intense, focused interactions the photographer would have with many of her portrait subjects. KB

(1) Diane Arbus, "The Full Circle," *Harper's Bazaar*, November 1961, 137.

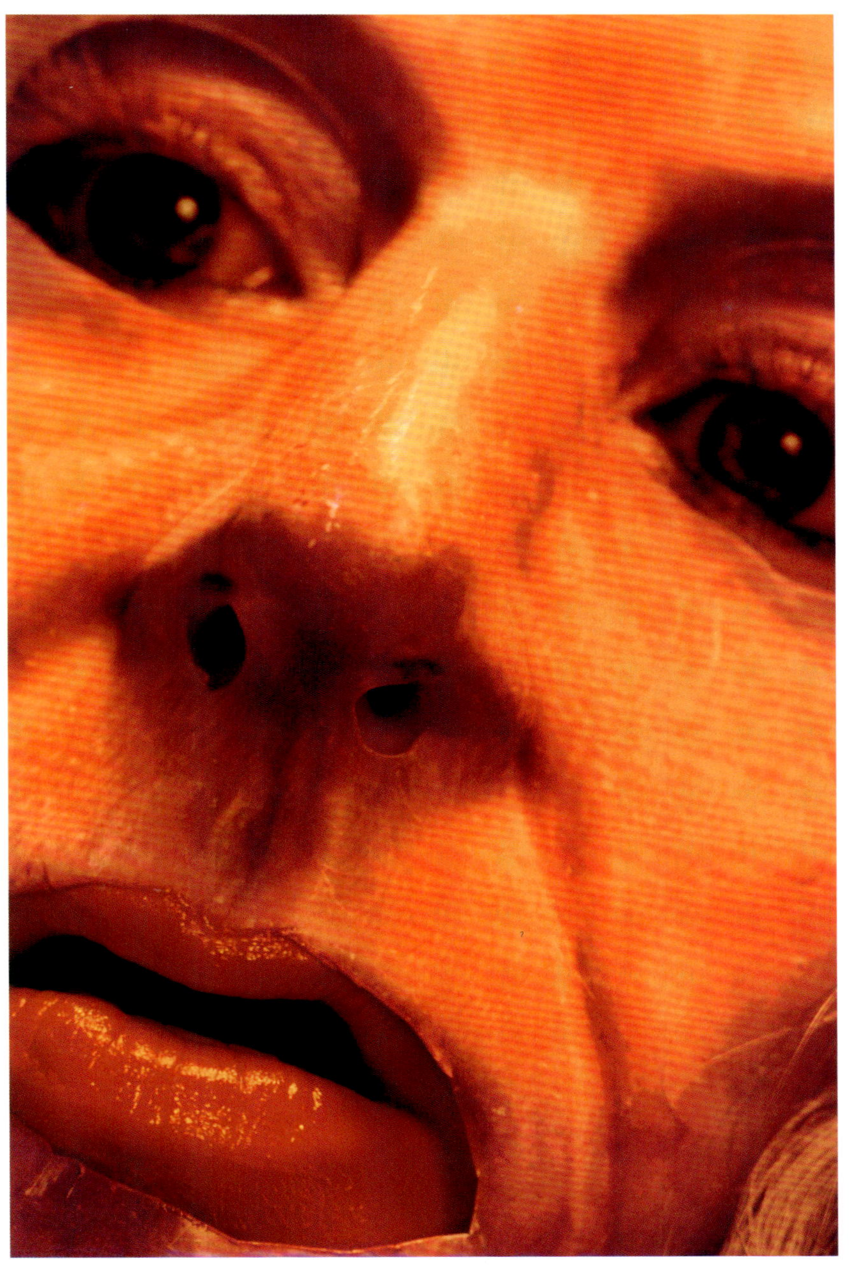

Cindy Sherman (American, born 1954). Untitled #325. 1996. Chromogenic print, 57⅞ × 39¼ in. (147 × 99.7 cm)

Throughout her critiques of female stereotypes and explorations of the grotesque, masks are an essential part of Cindy Sherman's process. This extreme close-up of the artist's face, partially covered by a mask, conjures imagery of a person recovering from an accident or cosmetic surgery.

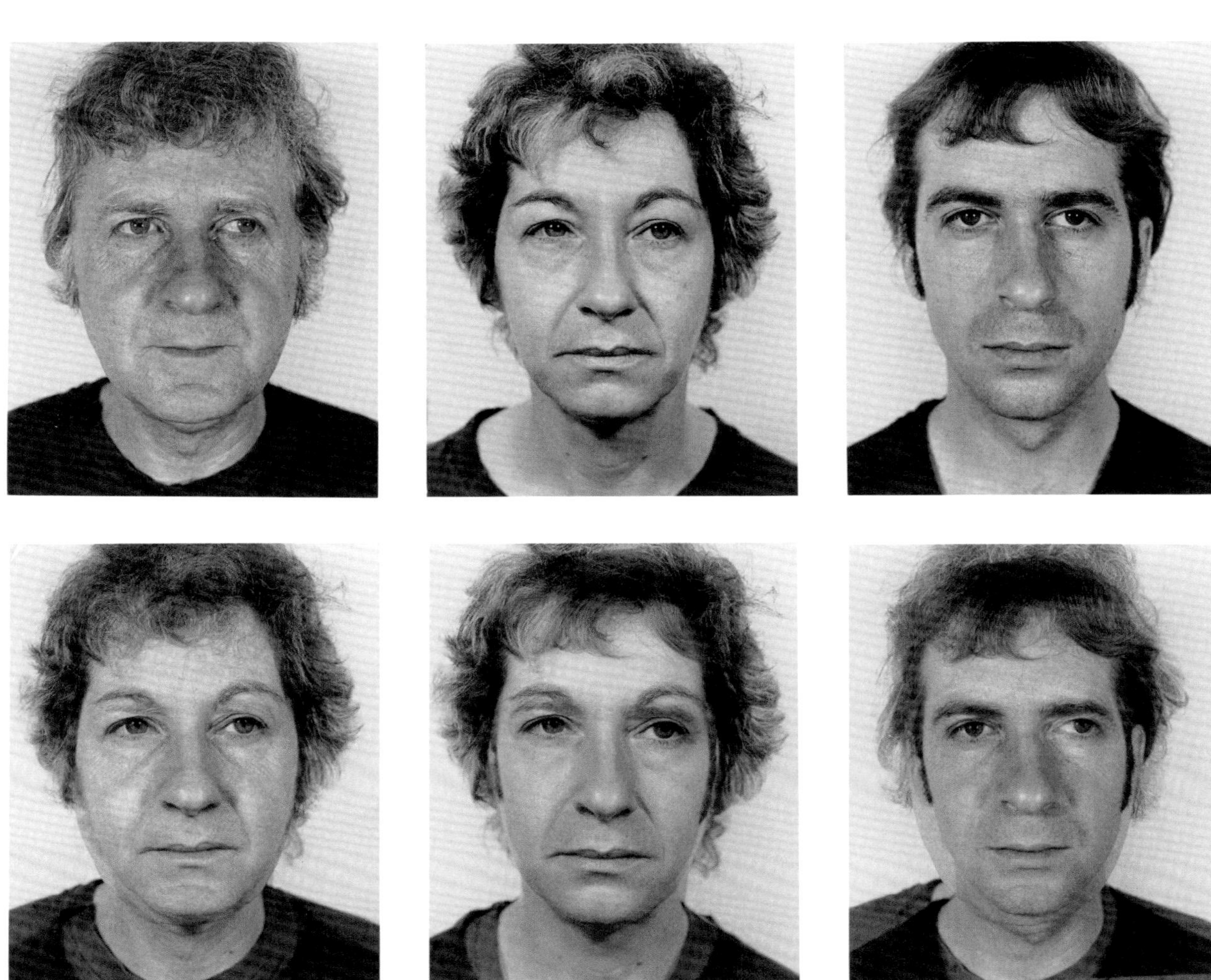

William Wegman (American, born 1943). *Family Combinations*. 1972.
Six gelatin silver prints, each 12 7/16 × 10 3/16 in. (31.6 × 25.9 cm).
The Museum of Modern Art, New York. Acquired through the generosity of Robert and Gayle Greenhill, 1994

Across its top row, *Family Combinations* displays frontal photographs of William Wegman's father, his mother, and the artist himself. The second row presents every possible combination of any two of these three portraits, printed from pairs of superimposed negatives.

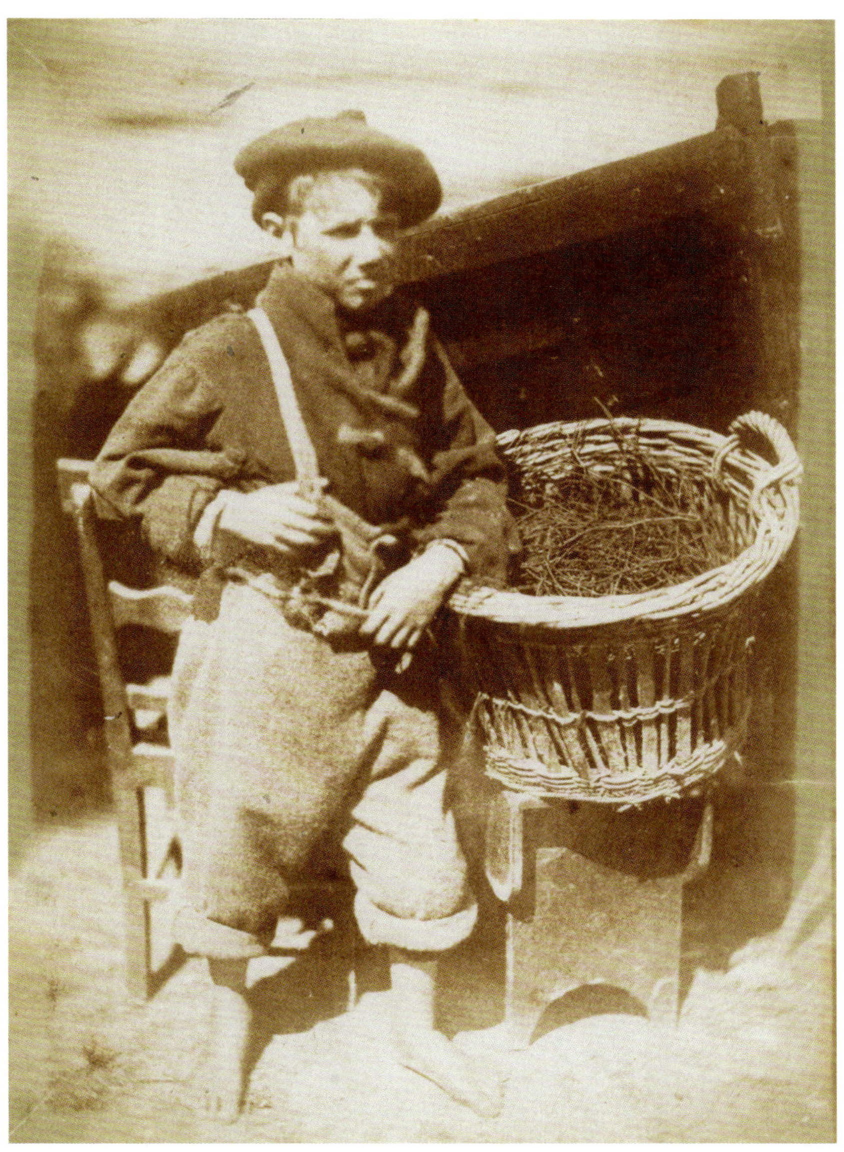

David Octavius Hill (British, 1802–1870) and Robert Adamson (British, 1821–1848). *Newhaven Boy ("King Fisher" or "His Faither's Breeks").* 1843–47. Salted paper print, 7⅞ × 5 11/16 in. (20 × 14.4 cm)

This image belongs to a series of more than one hundred photographs David Octavius Hill and Robert Adamson created documenting life in the fishing community of Newhaven, outside Edinburgh. Hill inscribed another print of the image with the words: "His faither's breeks he hath girded on," suggesting, by way of the boy's oversized trousers, that this youth has followed his father into the fishing profession—possibly in the aftermath of the parent's death at sea.

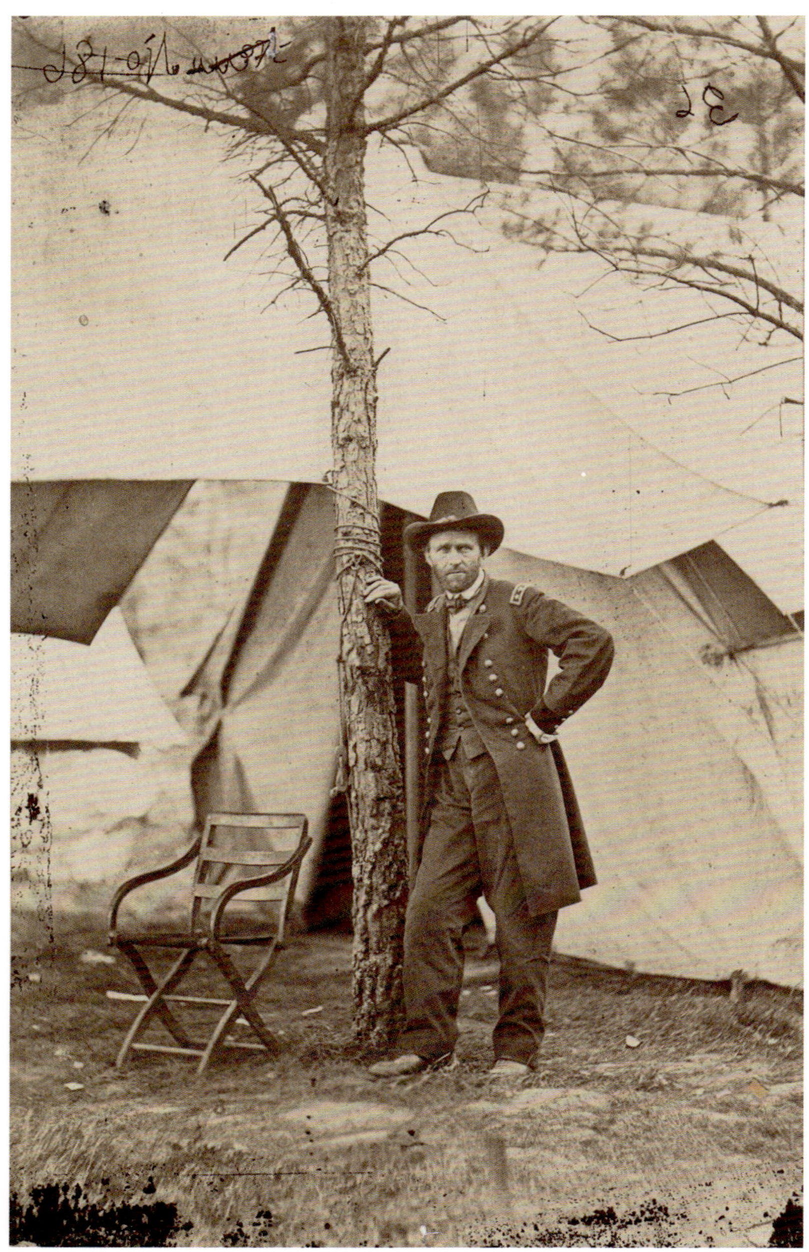

Mathew B. Brady (studio, active 1844–c. 1875). *Ulysses S. Grant at Headquarters in Cold Harbor, Virginia*. June 1864. Albumen silver print, 6 7/16 × 4 1/16 in. (16.4 × 10.3 cm)

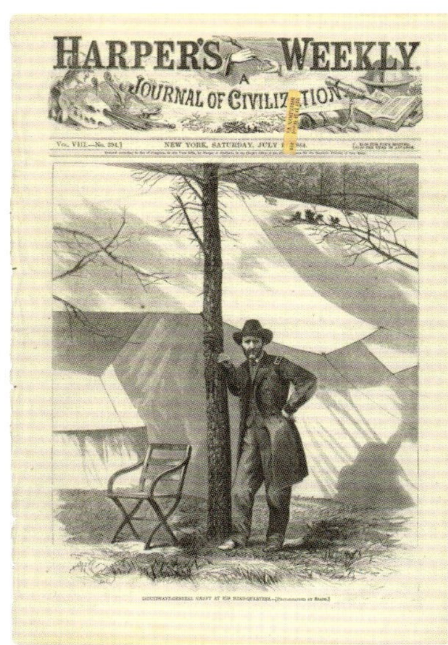
HARPER'S WEEKLY
A JOURNAL OF CIVILIZATION

Fig. 1. *Lieutenant-General Grant at his Head-quarters*, in *Harper's Weekly* (July 16, 1864). Wood engraving after a photograph, $15\frac{13}{16}$ × 11 in. (40.5 × 27.9 cm). The Metropolitan Museum of Art, New York. Harris Brisbane Dick Fund, 1928

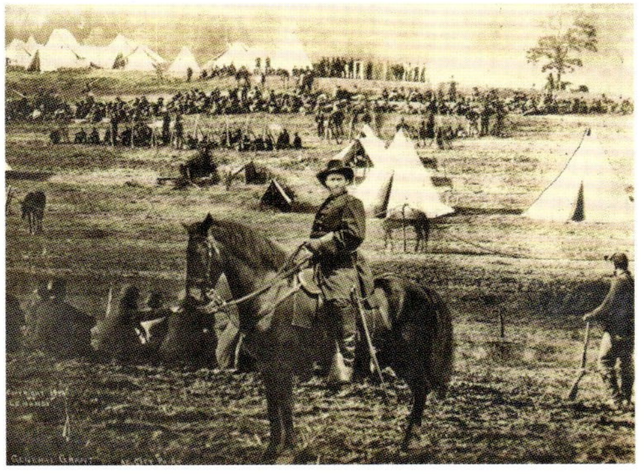

Fig. 2. Levin Corbin Handy (American, 1855–1932). *General Grant at City Point*. c. 1902. Gelatin silver print, $9\frac{13}{16}$ × $13\frac{3}{8}$ in. (25 × 34 cm). Prints & Photographs Division, Library of Congress, Washington, DC

This portrait of Ulysses S. Grant, leaning against a tree with his arm akimbo, was taken by a photographer associated with the studio of Mathew Brady. Grant, who would later become the eighteenth president of the United States, was at his temporary headquarters in Cold Harbor, Virginia, in early June 1864, as the American Civil War continued to grind on. At the time, Grant was in command of the Union Army of the Potomac as it advanced toward Richmond; Cold Harbor, located about ten miles north, was a significant site of battle.

Having gained permission to photograph behind Union Army lines in 1864, Brady coordinated other professional photographers to make images at Cold Harbor that he purchased, signed, and distributed. Historian Susan E. Williams attributes this particular portrait of Grant to the photographer Egbert Guy Fowx, citing the dimensions of his other glass plate negatives at the National Archives.[1] In the Gayle Greenhill Collection's albumen silver print, Brady's plate numbering system is visible in reverse at the top of the image, having been etched into the negative.

This image was used as an engraving on the cover of the July 16, 1864, issue of *Harper's Weekly,* presented as an image by Brady (fig. 1). It later appeared in yet another act of transformation, in a photomontage created by Brady's nephew, Levin Corbin Handy, in 1902 (fig. 2). Having inherited Brady's negatives, Handy reassembled them into new images for viewers interested in heroic pictures of the Civil War.[2] Handy's photomontage *General Grant at City Point* takes Grant's head from this 1864 portrait, combines it with the body of another general on horseback, and places it before a view of Confederate prisoners of war from a different Virginia battle. In each iteration of the image, Grant's weary yet steadfast gaze telegraphs the high stakes of the war, which would last for another year. KB

(1) Susan E. Williams, "Richmond Again Taken: Reappraising the Brady Legend through Photographs by Andrew J. Russell," *Virginia Magazine of History and Biography* 110, no. 4 (2002): 449.

(2) Mia Fineman, *Faking It: Manipulated Photography before Photoshop* (New York: The Metropolitan Museum of Art, 2012), 60.

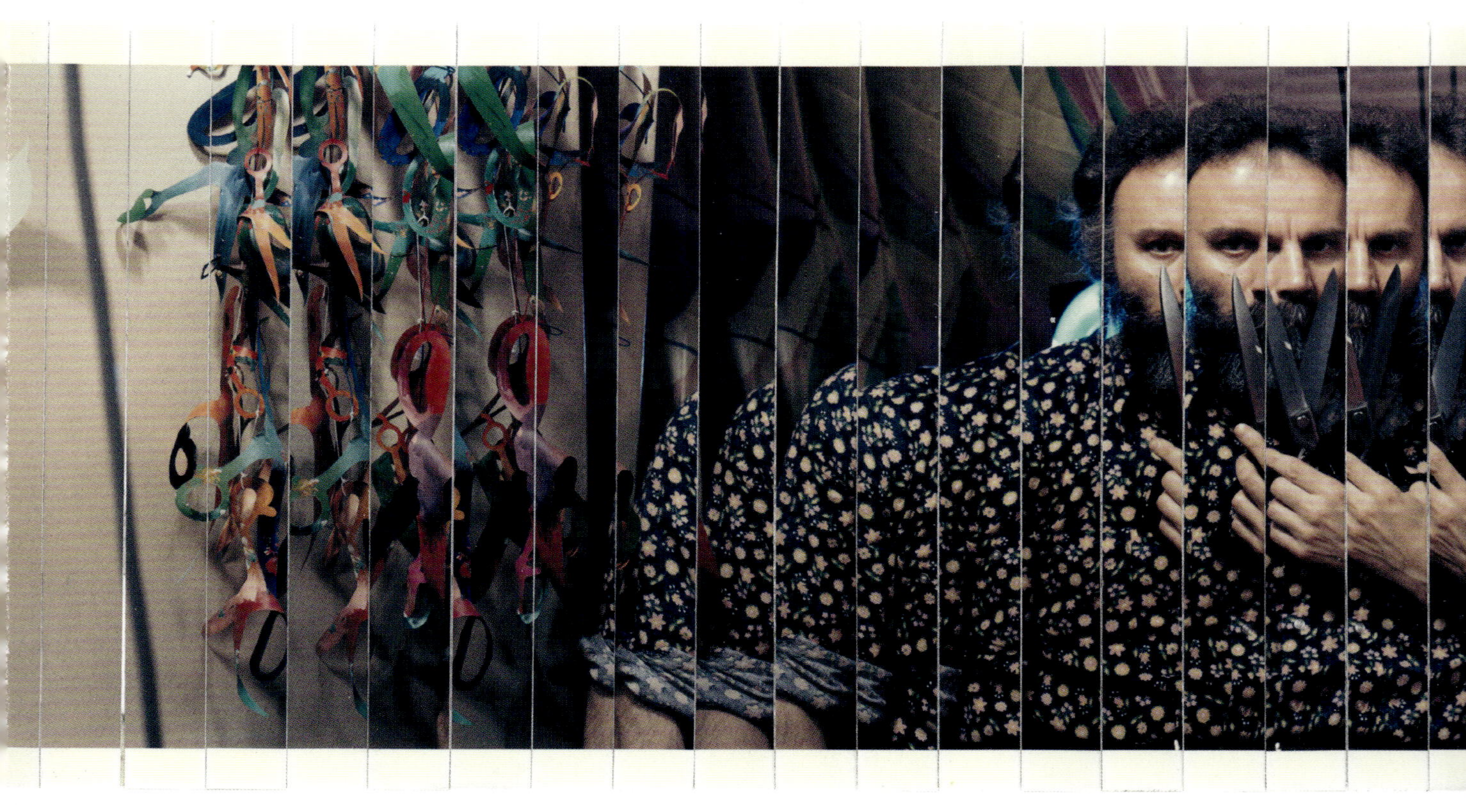

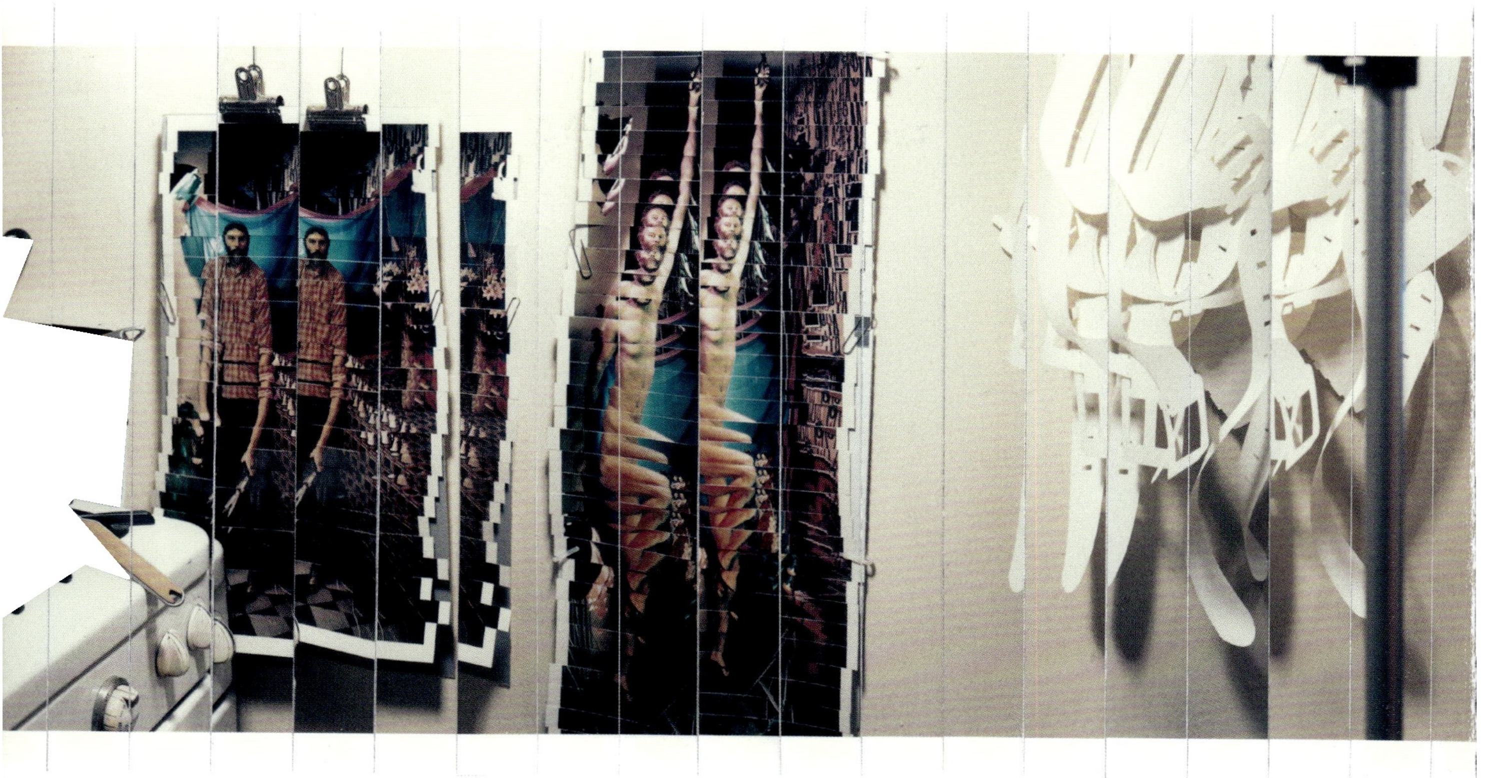

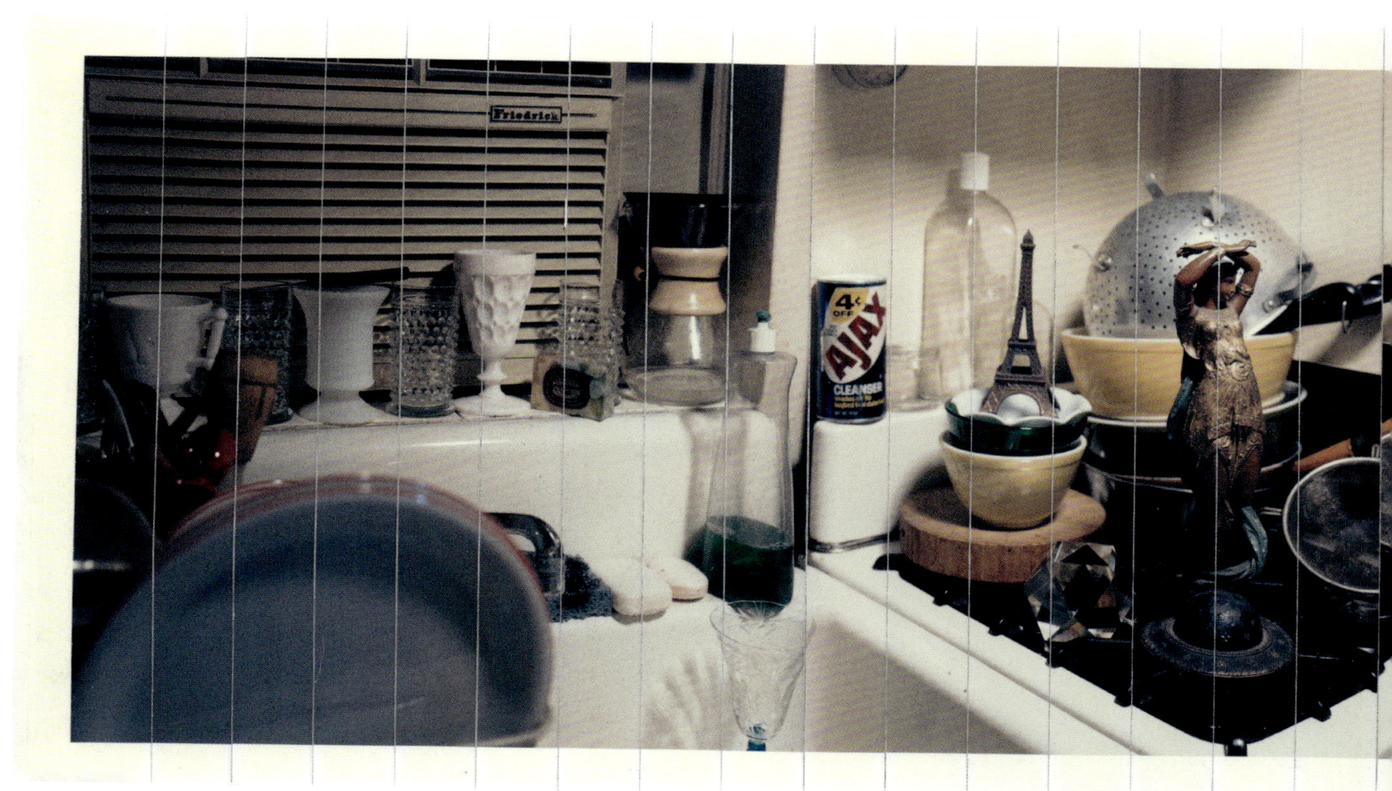

Lucas Samaras (American, born Greece. 1936–2024). *Panorama*. March 9, 1983. Collage of color instant prints, 7⅜ in. × 7 ft. 10⅛ in. (18.8 × 239.1 cm). The Museum of Modern Art, New York. Gift of Robert and Gayle Greenhill, 1992

Lucas Samaras's Tesseract Self-Portrait: On Seams and Stitches in *Panorama*

Samuel Allen

Lucas Samaras's *Panorama* (March 9, 1983; pp. 60–65) offers a prismatic view into the one-bedroom Manhattan apartment that, from 1967, served as the artist's home and studio for twenty-two years. "The place is like an enchanter's workshop," the journalist Janet Malcolm once observed, noting how it abounded with mesmerizing fabrics, strange figurines, rows of dangling trade beads, and jars whose contents seemed intended for occult ends.[1] A similar inventory populates *Panorama*'s horizontally elongated frame, within which such beguiling objects are joined by domestic items and art-making tools—X-Acto blades, tripods, boxes of film—to crowd the walls and surfaces of a kitchen and adjoining living room. Punctuating this agglomeration of the mundane and the fantastic are objects issued from Samaras's hand: artworks ranging in medium from painted tondos to cut-paper renditions of belts, arms, and scissors to photographic assemblages that resemble *Panorama* in their facture.

These photo works, like *Panorama* itself, belong to the artist's Panorama series of 1982–86, a group of objects composed from multiple eight-by-ten-inch Polaroid-brand instant prints that have been sliced into strips and pieced together. In them, Samaras treats the instant photograph as a bearer of images, which he manipulates into deft illusions, as well as a physical material to cut and recombine. If his handling of the Polaroid recalls the textile-based practice of patchwork, this affinity is reinforced throughout the series by the recurrence of colorful, ornately patterned fabrics that hang as backdrops, drape tables, and cluster in odd corners. Underscoring his technical dialogue with this non-photographic form of making, Samaras appears at *Panorama's* center, set off by a billowing, multicolored sheer fabric, wielding a pair of shears.

By reworking the Polaroid print, Samaras taps into a preternatural power of the panoramic photograph, a format whose roots can be traced to Robert Barker's inaugural painted panorama of 1787. The genre established by Barker's room-sized, three-hundred-sixty-degree representation of the Edinburgh cityscape, which eschewed the reassuring frame and single vanishing point of traditional landscape painting, bewitched its earliest audiences, eliciting feelings of unease—gasping, seasickness, even fainting—as well as spiritual ecstasy.[2] Upon photography's introduction in 1839, the sweeping vistas encountered in these immersive environments were transposed to a new medium, with the camera performing the rotation previously delegated to the painted panorama's viewers. To create early panoramic photographs, the camera was turned on a tripod between exposures, generating sequences of prints that, placed side by side, form a near-seamless prospect in several directions simultaneously. Wrangling these competing views into one frame, panoramic photography explodes the camera's built-in

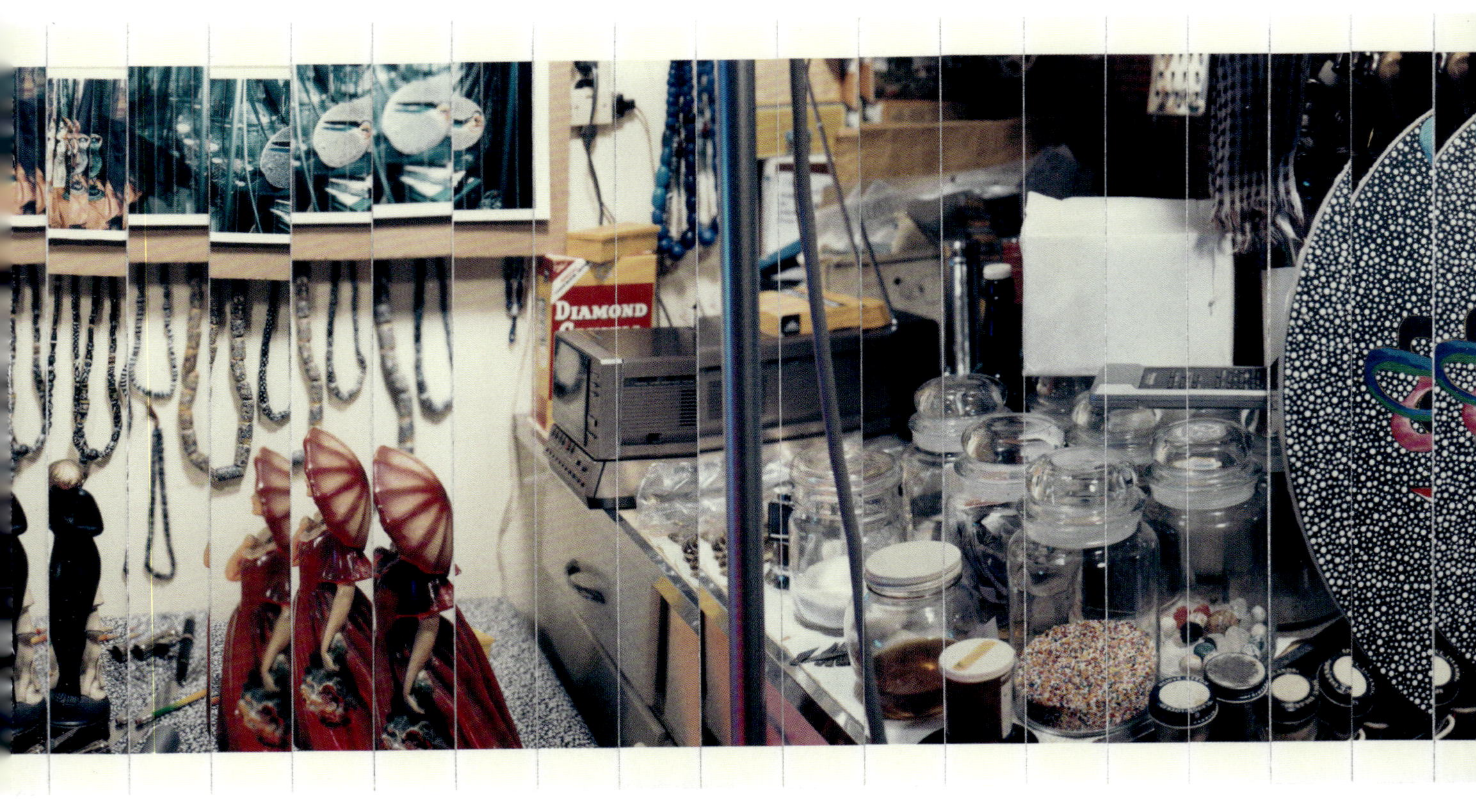
DIAMOND

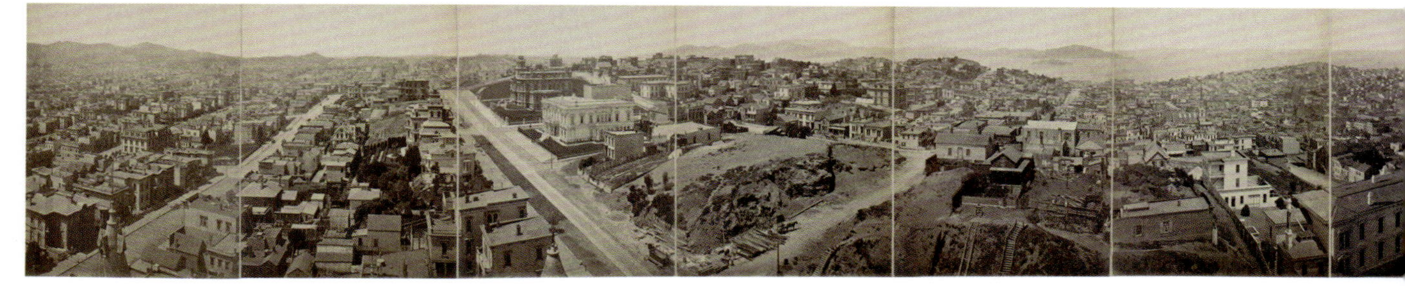

Fig. 1. Eadweard Muybridge (American, born England. 1830–1904). *Panorama of San Francisco taken from the tower of the house of Mrs. Mark Hopkins*. 1878. Thirteen albumen silver prints, 21 in. × 17 ft. ¾ in. (53.3 × 520.1 cm). The Miriam and Ira D. Wallach Division of Arts, Prints and Photographs, The New York Public Library

single-point perspective. Likewise, it compresses images made over an extended period into an object that can be beheld all at once, transgressing photography's conventional relationship to time, which associates the medium with instants—the click of the shutter—rather than durations.

The panoramic photograph's distinctive spatio-temporal dimensions amount to a kind of magic, as Eadweard Muybridge's famed 1878 panorama of San Francisco (fig. 1) evidences. This object, emblematic of early photography's ingenuity in exploring the camera's pictorial possibilities, comprises thirteen albumen prints that together convey a panoptic view from the city's California Street Hill (today, Nob Hill). As Muybridge had required five hours to complete his full suite of negatives, each of the panorama's components records a unique point in the day. Thus, as an outcome of its unfurling north, south, east, west, and all intermediate directions into a single, flat picture plane, the object also depicts a span of time that runs from morning through afternoon. The filmmaker Hollis Frampton, writing in *Artforum* in 1973 (a decade before Samaras created *Panorama*), deemed this simultaneous presentation of distinct moments "at once completely plausible and perfectly impossible." Frampton argued that Muybridge's San Francisco panorama constituted a "tesseract," a four-dimensional object possessing temporal as well as spatial extension.[3]

Samaras's Panoramas, as plausible and as impossible as this forerunner, exploit the format's tesseract nature. In many instances from the series, the artist, like a traditional panoramic photographer, rotated his tripod-mounted camera between exposing the prints that compose his artworks. Yet, unlike Muybridge's panorama, which progresses sequentially in time as it proceeds from left to right (with one print an outlier), Samaras's works superimpose several moments upon one another. Cutting his Polaroids into strips proliferates the seams across which disparate times can conjoin, permitting effects that resemble those achieved, more conventionally, through techniques of combination printing or multiple exposure. Another work from the Panorama series (fig. 2) puts this capacity on ostentatious display, representing the artist in

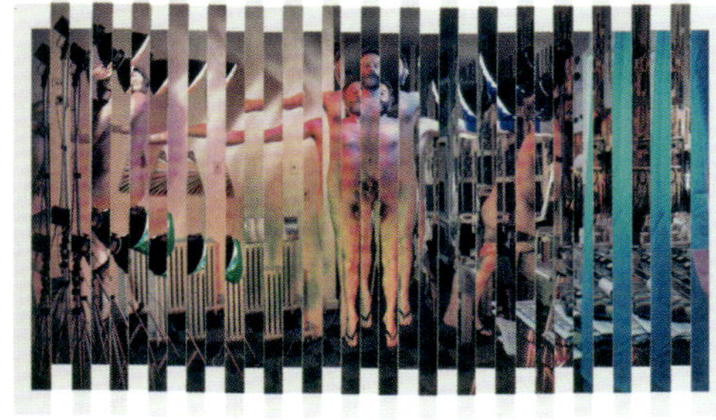

Fig. 2. Lucas Samaras (American, born Greece. 1936–2024). *Panorama*. April 8, 1983. Collage of color instant prints, approx. 11⁷⁄₁₆ × 18⁷⁄₁₆ in. (29 × 47 cm). Art Institute of Chicago. Gift of Robert and Gayle Greenhill, 1991

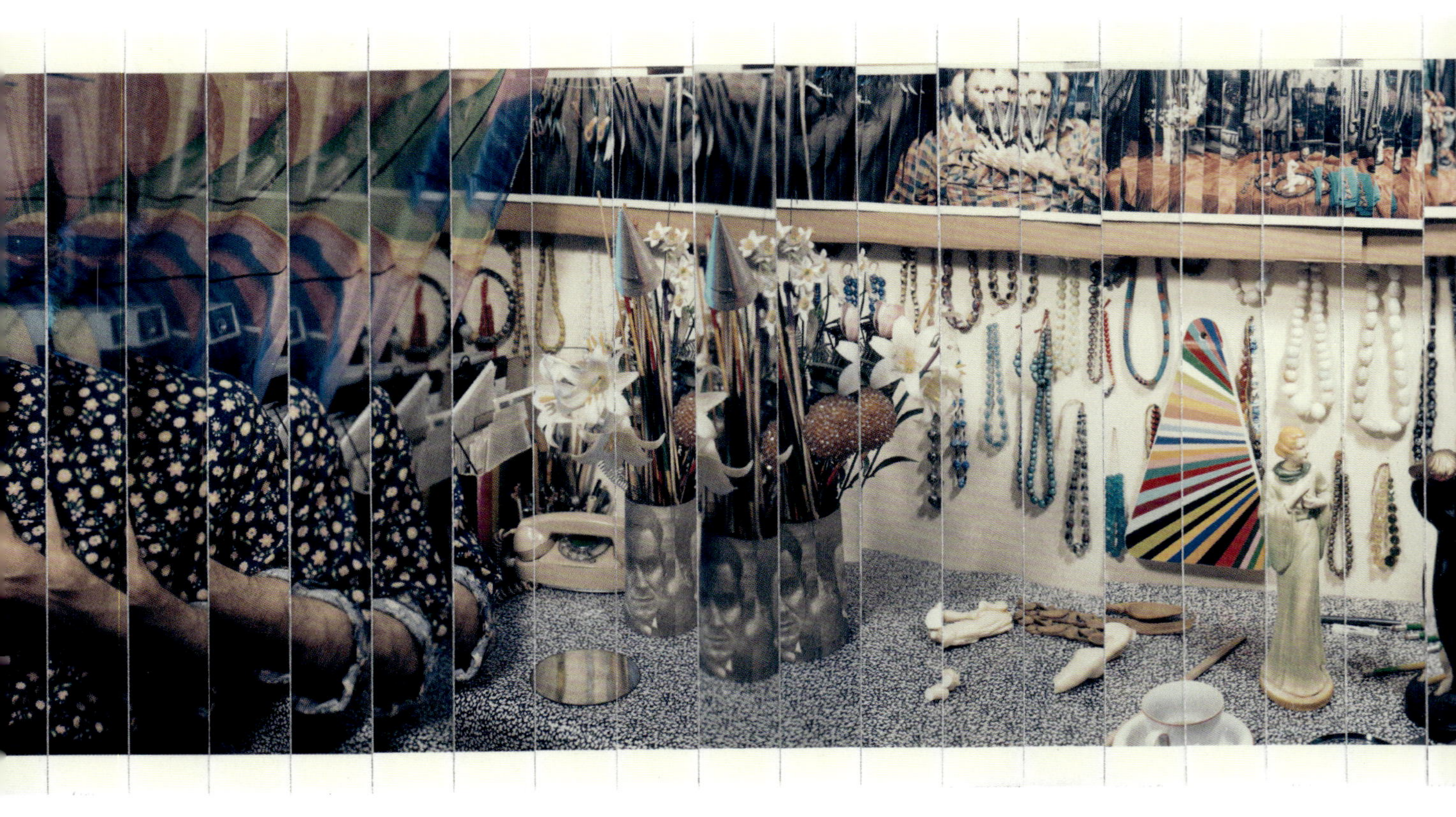

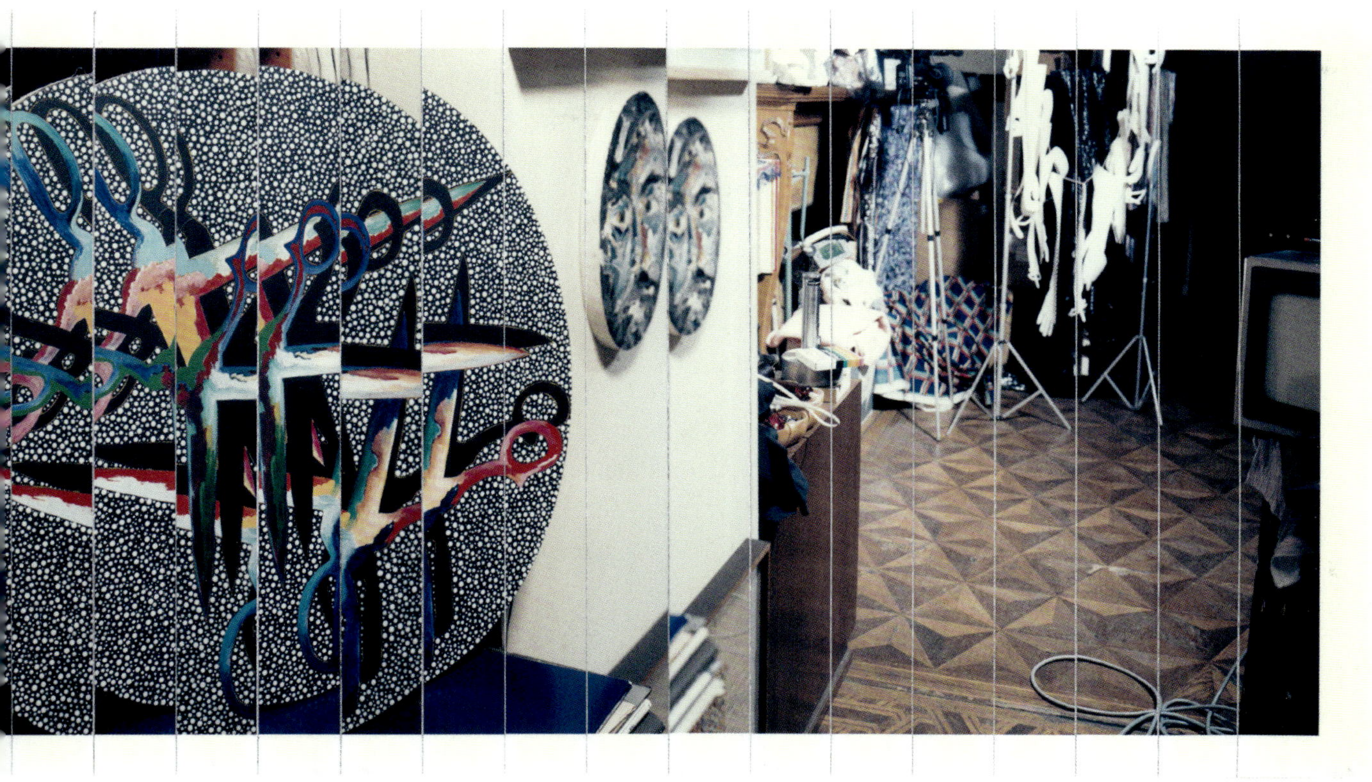

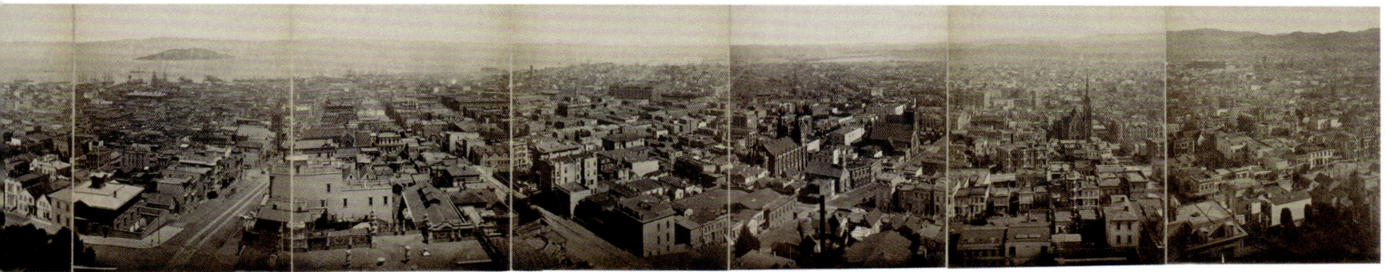

four positions at once: Samaras recoils at left, rests his knee upon a counter at right, and hangs midair at two elevations in its center.

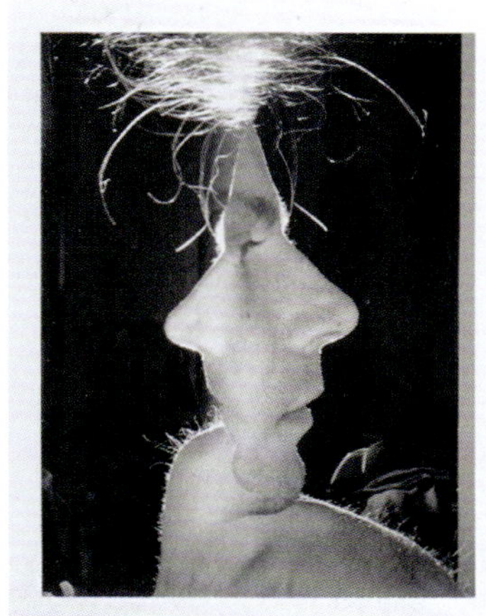

Fig. 3. Lucas Samaras (American, born Greece. 1936–2024). Detail of *AutoPolaroids*. 1969–71. Twelve black-and-white instant prints, overall 9½ × 24¾ in. (24.1 × 62.9 cm). The Museum of Modern Art, New York. Gift of Robert and Gayle Greenhill, 1992

"Discovering Unknown Territories of My Surface Self"

From the outset of his engagement with instant photography, a medium he adopted in 1969, Samaras experimented with visual languages of rupture and reassembly. Certain works from his AutoPolaroids series of 1969–71 (fig. 3) present surreal fusions of the artist's head and other body parts, made by masking portions of his negatives and exposing them multiple times. Later, in his Splits series of 1973 (fig. 4), the artist drew upon a stockpile of his recently made Polaroid prints, bisecting them along the diagonal and pairing the resulting halves into surprising combinations. Anticipating the working method of the Panoramas, these artworks illuminate the artist's attraction to how photography could disrupt surface appearances and generate transformations across seams.

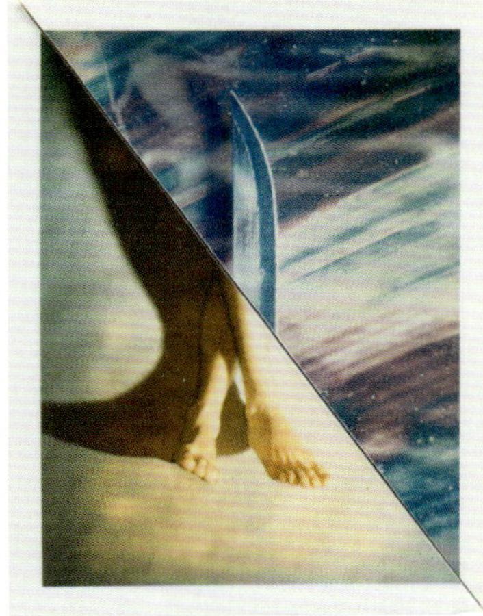

Fig. 4. Lucas Samaras (American, born Greece. 1936–2024). *Split*. 1973. Two color instant prints, 4¼ × 3⅜ in. (10.8 × 8.6 cm). The Museum of Modern Art, New York. Gift of Robert and Gayle Greenhill, 1992

The mutability of surfaces—those of the photograph as well as the body—factors centrally in the extended project of photographic self-portraiture Samaras initiated with his AutoPolaroids. This series, which Samaras characterized as an enterprise in "discovering unknown territories of my surface self," plumbs the artist's understanding of himself as multiple and changeable via the manifold, even contradictory presentations a single body can inhabit in a photograph.[4] Within the Polaroid's white border, the artist contorts this body, colors it in non-naturalistic hues, and adorns it with costumes, among other modifications. In certain AutoPolaroids, he also deposits dots and lines of ink directly on the surface of the print, often first removing areas of emulsion to clear a ground for the marks. One such artwork (fig. 5), in which swirling patterns have been inscribed upon both body and background, demonstrates how this technique saps the photograph of illusionistic space, conflating the body with the material that bears its image.

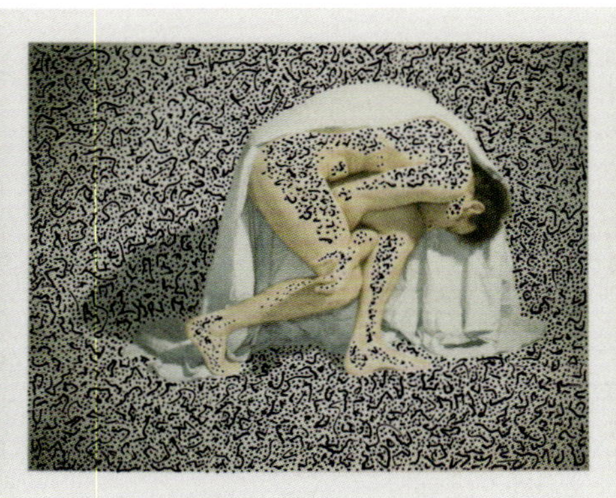

Fig. 5. Lucas Samaras (American, born Greece. 1936–2024). *AutoPolaroid*. 1969–71. Color instant print with hand-applied ink, 3⅜ × 4¼ in. (8.6 × 10.8 cm). The Museum of Modern Art, New York. Gift of Robert and Gayle Greenhill, 1992

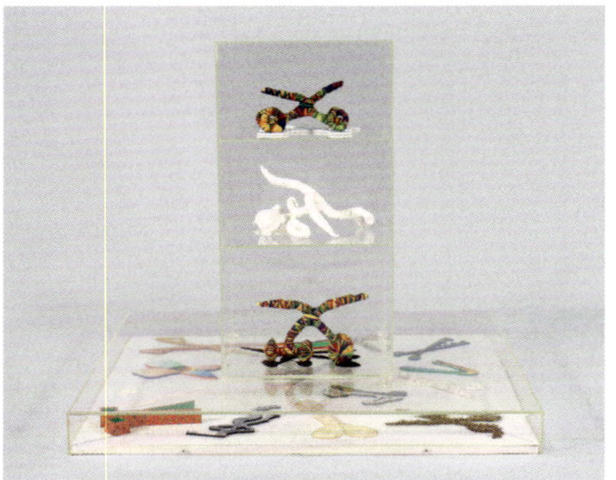

Fig. 6. Lucas Samaras (American, born Greece. 1936–2024). *Transformation: Scissors*. 1968. Mixed media, 31⅝ × 36⅝ × 36 9/16 in. (80.3 × 93 × 92.9 cm). Whitney Museum of American Art, New York. Purchase, with funds from Frances and Sydney Lewis in honor of the Museum's 50th Anniversary, 1980

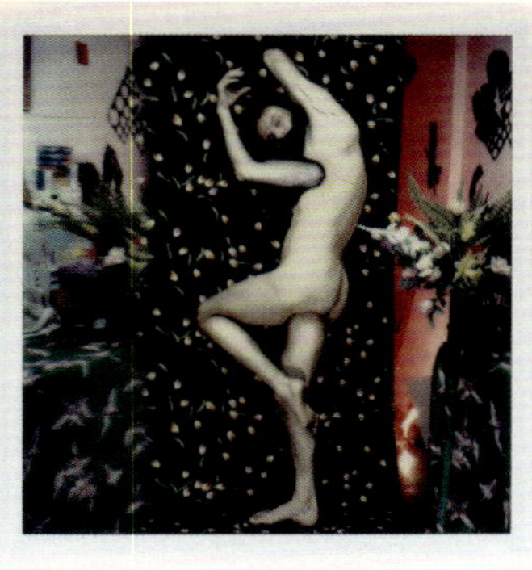

Fig. 7. Lucas Samaras (American, born Greece. 1936–2024). *Photo-Transformation*. August 17, 1976. Color instant print, 4¼ × 3½ in. (10.8 × 8.9 cm). The Museum of Modern Art, New York. Gift of Robert and Gayle Greenhill, 1992

The AutoPolaroids, which explode the unitary self into a riot of personae, followed immediately upon an effort by Samaras to explore multiplicity through sculpture. In 1968 the artist had exhibited several multipartite artworks bearing the title "Transformation" in the solo show *Boxes/Transformation* at The Pace Gallery, New York. Museums in miniature, these works display within acrylic cases polyglot collections of objects that refract a single, everyday item—a plate, flower, or knife, to name three examples from the exhibition—through an array of visual languages. *Transformation: Scissors* (fig. 6), featured in the Pace show, contains over a dozen renditions of scissors, each obliquely recalling the lexicon of pointillism, biomorphism, Cubism, or another artistic movement while subverting expectations concerning the tool's function, form, and materiality.

The Transformations, the artist explained, "negate the possibility of a single Platonic ideal acting as measure for any physical thing."[5] Bringing this negation to bear upon himself in the AutoPolaroids, he would subsequently push it into hallucinatory terrain in his Photo-Transformations of 1973–76. The Photo-Transformations relied upon technology introduced in 1972: Polaroid's SX-70 camera, which employed a novel print package containing, as a single unit, the negative and all chemistry required to develop a positive (the print format that has since become synonymous with the company). These prints' emulsion, Samaras learned, remains soft for several hours after an exposure; thus, it could be pushed with a stylus or the tip of a pen into startlingly reformulated images.

The Photo-Transformations extend the AutoPolaroids' merger of the body's surface with that of the print, revealing both to be pliable. Throughout this series of self-portraits, Samaras's image is stretched and squeezed into improbable forms or melted into chromatic pools from which ears, eyes, teeth, and fists emerge. In one work (fig. 7), the body has been incised at the joints where the limbs meet the torso, this dissection echoed by a similar fragmentation of the surrounding space. Via an in-camera technique—the exact method is unclear, but Samaras may have masked the negative or modified the camera's lens—the image's rightmost quarter, with its arranged flowers and emerald tablecloth, has been mirrored along the print's left edge. Like the multiple-exposure AutoPolaroids, this image's division into vertical bands presages the Panoramas' compositions. Such explorations of surface selves would culminate in *Panorama*'s fractured picture plane as a bold declaration of multiplicity: the artist representing himself, in a visual pun on the pronoun "I," with five eyes (fig. 8).

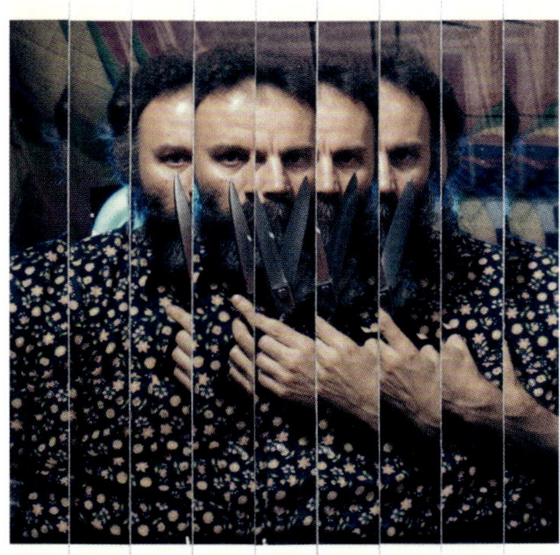

Fig. 8. Lucas Samaras (American, born Greece. 1936–2024). Detail of *Panorama*. March 9, 1983. Collage of color instant prints, 7⅜ in. × 7 ft. 10 in. (18.8 × 239.1 cm). The Museum of Modern Art, New York. Gift of Robert and Gayle Greenhill, 1992

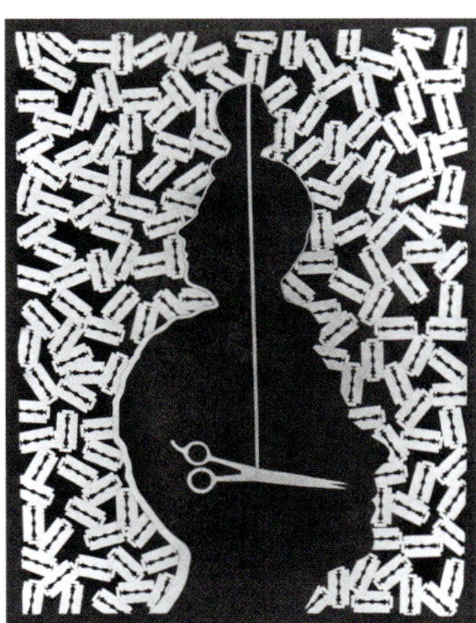

Fig. 9. Lucas Samaras (American, born Greece. 1936–2024). *Cut Paper Drawing #65*. 1968. Graphite on paper, 23 × 18 in. (58.4 × 45.7 cm). The Estate of Lucas Samaras

Stitched

"I fantasize how beautiful and calm it would be if I could erase all portions of my memory in which my parents appear," Samaras mused in an autobiographical text dated 1968, "but where would I be then, an unstitched Greek up a shit creek without language, direction or self. When I say I, more than one person stands up to be counted. If only memory had spatial extension."[6]

This passage, authored shortly before Samaras began his Polaroid works and later printed in a 1971 publication of his AutoPolaroids, articulates the notion of selfhood that would guide the artist's use of instant photography. Notably, it describes a multiplicity that is defined, in part, as ancestry; the "more than one person" that inhabit his "I," Samaras suggests, encompasses a lineage extending through his parents to include Greek culture writ large. Familial and cultural inheritance find expression in *Panorama* in several ways, answering Samaras's stated desire for spatialized memory. These include, among the artworks, ornaments, and domestic items that seed the image with personal and creative autobiography, certain objects—such as the can of Ajax (a product sharing its name with a hero of ancient Greek mythology) and the figurine of Selene (the Greek goddess of the moon) placed on a stovetop near the artwork's left boundary—that nod to the artist's Mediterranean roots.

The artwork alludes to kinship in a more material way, too: family history speaks through Samaras's technique of slicing and piecing together his Polaroids. The artist recalled childhood afternoons spent in his cousin's dress shop, in the city of Kastoria, Greece, where he was raised, cutting paper in imitation of the dressmakers, who admonished him not to touch their fabrics.[7] This form of play later resurfaced in his Cut Paper Drawings, a group of works, begun in 1967, incised by X-Acto knife to form intricate webs of patterning and imagery (often, silhouette portraits of the artist or his friends). Responsive to the tradition of paper-cutting, the Cut Paper Drawings also resemble, in terms of materials, dressmakers' patterns; this connection is reinforced by the series's recurrent iconography of cutting tools, which gathers the cousin's fabric shears into a shared genus with the artist's own instruments.[8] *Cut Paper Drawing #65* (fig. 9), for instance, ensconces a triple self-portrait within a lattice of razor blades, while suspending a pair of scissors inside the lowermost head. The shears' placement just behind Samaras's lips calls to mind the artist's translation of childhood memory into his use, throughout the series, of another blade.

The Cut Paper Drawings anticipate an aesthetic strategy that would gain prominence in the 1970s and, under the banner of Pattern and Decoration (P&D), would issue a collective critique of the Western canon's exclusions. P&D,

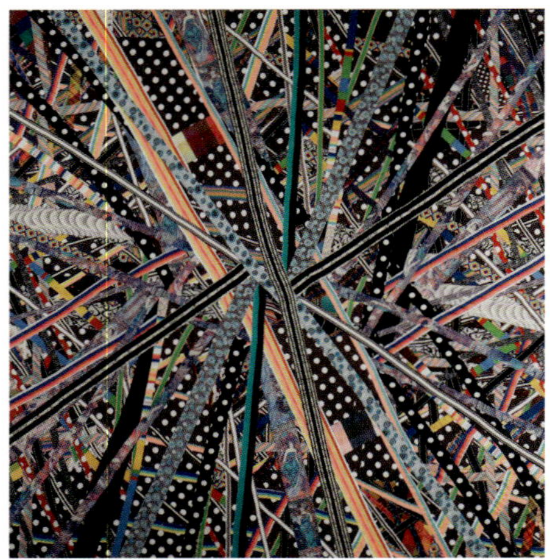

Fig. 10. Lucas Samaras (American, born Greece. 1936–2024). *Reconstruction #20.* 1977. Sewn fabric, 7 ft. 3 in. × 7 ft. 1 in. (221 × 215.9 cm). Denver Art Museum. National Endowment for the Arts Museum Purchase Grant, Dayton Hudson Foundation, Alliance for Contemporary Art, Joyce and Ted Strauss, Mr. & Mrs. Donald S. Graham, and anonymous donor, 1971.1

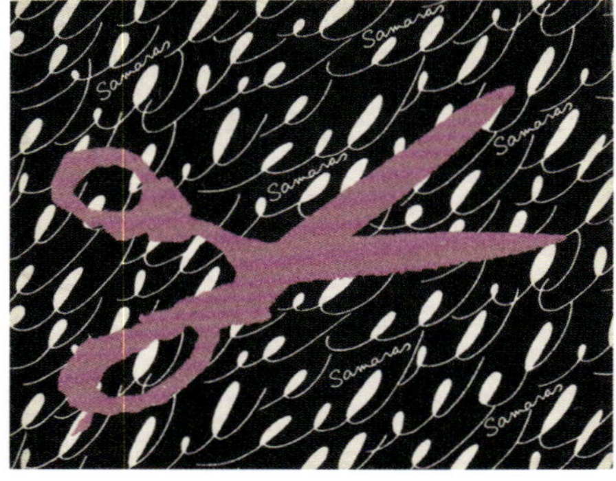

Fig. 11. Cover of *Samaras: Reconstructions* (New York: The Pace Gallery, 1980)

animated to a significant degree by the demands of second-wave feminism, adopted motifs, techniques, and materials from folk art, non-Western art, and creative traditions conventionally coded as feminine. Works from Samaras's Reconstructions series of the late 1970s (fig. 10) were included in two of the numerous group exhibitions through which P&D coalesced into a common cause.[9] The Reconstructions, which resemble patchwork quilts, generate dizzying abstractions via an iterative process: begun by dividing a large piece of fabric and sewing a second fabric between its halves, this composite is progressively cut at new angles and reconnected with further fabrics.[10] The resulting objects carry a memory of their making in their fractured and intersecting strips of textile, and Samaras attributed further mnemonic qualities to them. When the series debuted at The Pace Gallery in 1978, the artist characterized the works as mantles and shrouds for his recently deceased mother, whose "wonderful, lousy taste" their kitsch colors and patterns commemorate. He added, in a rebuttal to the dressmakers of his childhood, "I can cut the fabric."[11]

Beyond sharing the materials and techniques of artists more closely aligned with P&D—including Howardena Pindell's stitched-canvas paintings and Miriam Schapiro's fabric-incorporating "femmages" (both featured alongside Samaras's Reconstructions in the 1981 exhibition *Five on Fabric* at the Laguna Gloria Art Museum, Austin)—the Reconstructions also echo P&D's championing of female forerunners' creative labor and aesthetic worlds.[12] Lest the series's relationship to domestic and professional forms of textile work be overlooked, the catalogue for Pace's second exhibition of the Reconstructions, in 1980, contains no fewer than eight photographs of the artist operating a Singer sewing machine, and its cover is emblazoned with a pair of fabric shears (fig. 11). Similar shears, reappearing three years later in *Panorama* (where the tool itself is joined by representations in paint and cut paper), link Samaras's Panorama series to such textile-based practices as well. If the artist's procedure of cutting and connecting Polaroid prints transforms *Panorama* into a tesseract, this technique, furthermore, lends the work's temporality a specific historical content. Working like a seamster, Samaras has stitched his prismatic self-portrait into a personal and creative matrilineage.

(1) Janet Malcom, "A Girl of the Zeitgeist—II," *New Yorker*, October 27, 1986, 47.
(2) See Katie Trumpener and Tim Barringer, "Introduction," in *On the Viewing Platform: The Panorama Between Canvas and Screen* (New Haven, CT: Yale University Press, 2020), 3-5.
(3) Hollis Frampton, "Eadweard Muybridge: Fragments of a Tesseract," *Artforum* 11, no. 7 (March 1973): 51.
(4) Lucas Samaras, quoted in Marla Prather, "Introduction and Acknowledgements," in *Unrepentant Ego: The Self-Portraits of Lucas Samaras* (New York: Whitney Museum of American Art, 2003), 8.
(5) Lucas Samaras, *Lucas Samaras* (New York: Whitney Museum of American Art, 1972), n.p.
(6) Lucas Samaras, "Autobiography: Part 1—Autobiographic Preserves," in *Samaras Album: Autointerview, Autobiography, Autopolaroid* (New York: Whitney Museum of American Art, 1971), 9.
(7) "Barbara Rose Interviews Lucas Samaras," in *Samaras: Reconstructions* (New York: Pace Gallery, 1978), n.p.
(8) Artist and critic Kim Levin has previously noted the similarities shared between the Cut Paper Drawings' materiality and that of dressmakers' patterns. Kim Levin, *Lucas Samaras* (New York: Harry N. Abrams, 1975), 79.
(9) Samaras's Reconstructions appeared alongside work by other Pattern and Decoration artists in the exhibitions *The Decorative Impulse* (Institute of Contemporary Art, University of Pennsylvania, June 13-July 21, 1979) and *Five on Fabric* (Laguna Gloria Art Museum, Austin, TX, August 28-October 11, 1981). For more on Samaras and Pattern and Decoration, see Anna Katz, ed., *With Pleasure: Pattern and Decoration in American Art, 1972-1985* (Los Angeles: The Museum of Contemporary Art, 2019), 296.
(10) For all their affinities with quilts, the Reconstructions differ meaningfully from those craft objects, as Kim Levin has observed: they lack sandwiched layers and symmetrical blocks of patterning, and their seams abut rather than overlap. Kim Levin, "Lucas Samaras: The New Reconstructions," in *Samaras: Reconstructions*, n.p.
(11) "Barbara Rose Interviews Lucas Samaras," n.p.
(12) For a text that was foundational in theorizing Pattern and Decoration's uplift of creative techniques historically assigned to women, see Melissa Meyer and Miriam Schapiro, "Waste Not Want Not: An Inquiry into What Women Saved and Assembled—FEMMAGE," *Heresies* 1, no. 4 (Winter 1977-78): 66-69.

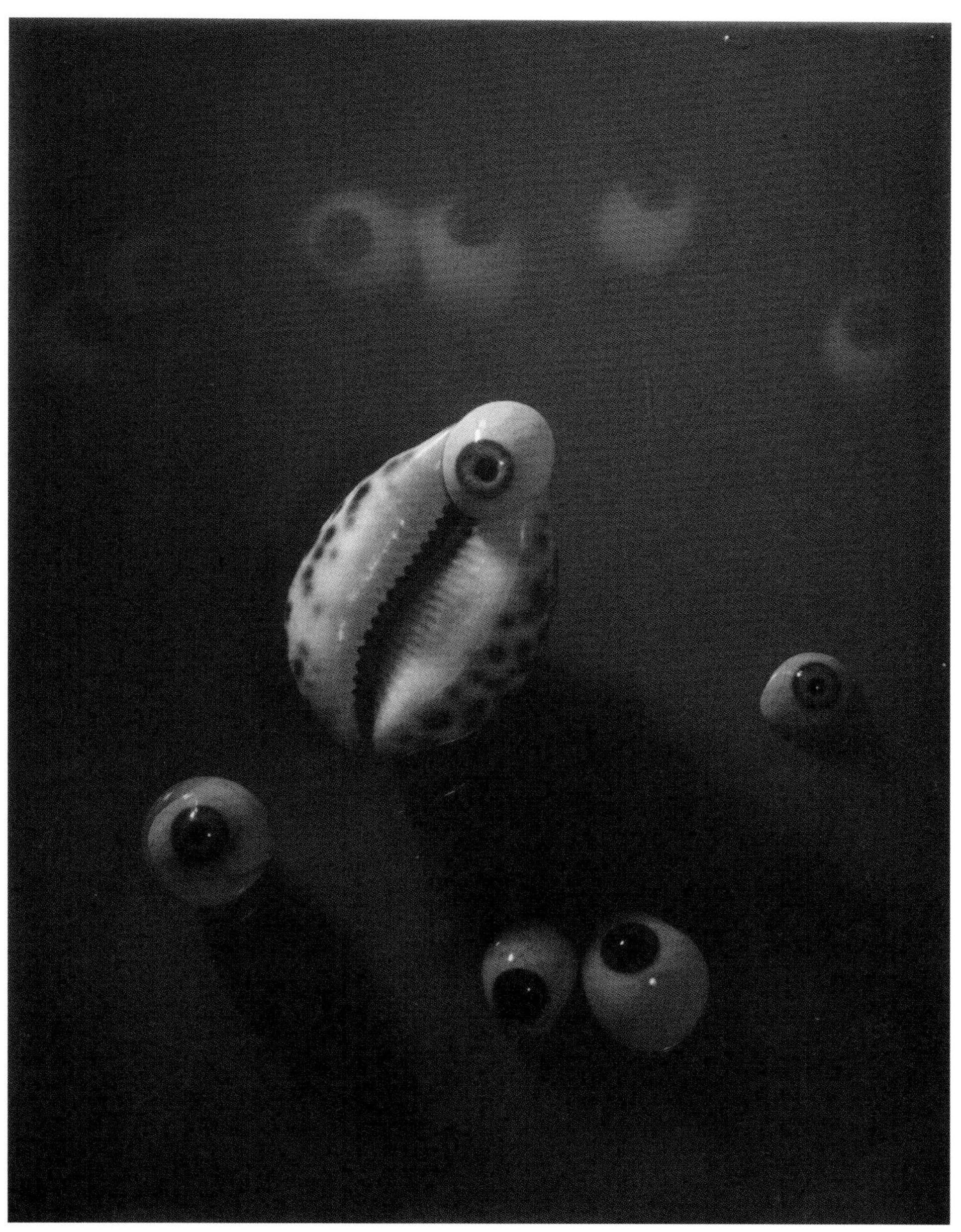

Josef Sudek (Czech, 1896–1976). Untitled from the series Milenci (Lovers). 1953. Gelatin silver print, 11⅜ × 8⅞ in. (28.9 × 22.5 cm)

During the Nazi occupation of Prague, which lasted from 1939 through 1945, Josef Sudek mainly worked within the confines of his studio, recording the changing views through its window and composing still lifes from objects in his home—practices he sustained, as this photograph evidences, even after the end of World War II.

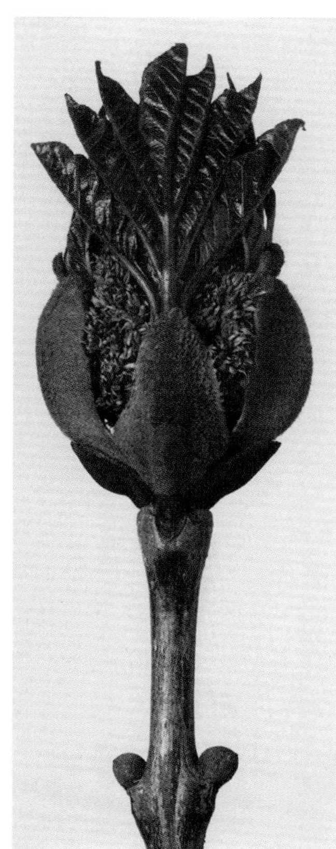

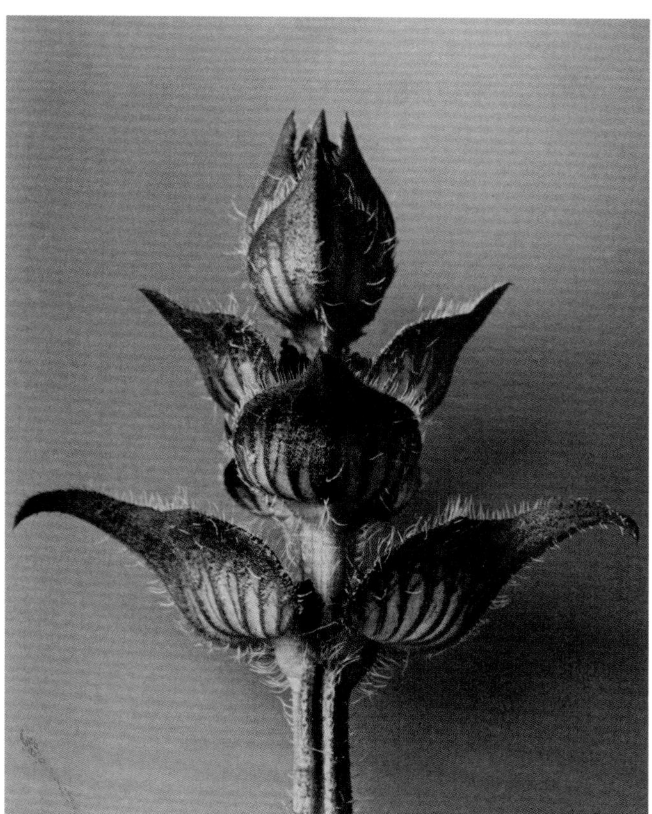

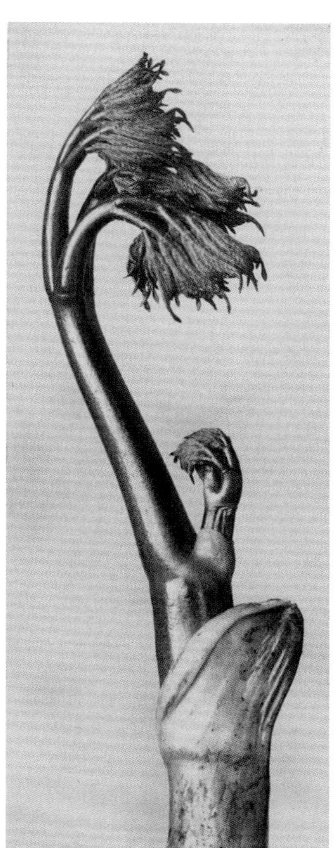

Karl Blossfeldt (German, 1865–1932). Left: *Fraxinus ornus*. 1898–1932. Gelatin silver print, 11¾ × 4¾ in. (29.8 × 12.1 cm). Center: *Salvia pratensis*. 1898–1932. Gelatin silver print, 11¾ × 9⅜ in. (29.8 × 23.8 cm). Right: *Acer pseudoplatanus*. 1898–1932. Gelatin silver print, 11⅞ × 4⅝ in. (30.2 × 11.7 cm)

Over a period of more than three decades, Karl Blossfeldt created a major suite of botanical photographs, initially to use as teaching aids at an applied arts academy in Berlin. Drawn to the simple forms of wild plants—this trio of images depicts species of ash, meadow sage, and maple readily found in Central Europe—Blossfeldt ventured out of the city seeking prime specimens that, once discovered, he would revisit and observe almost daily for several months.

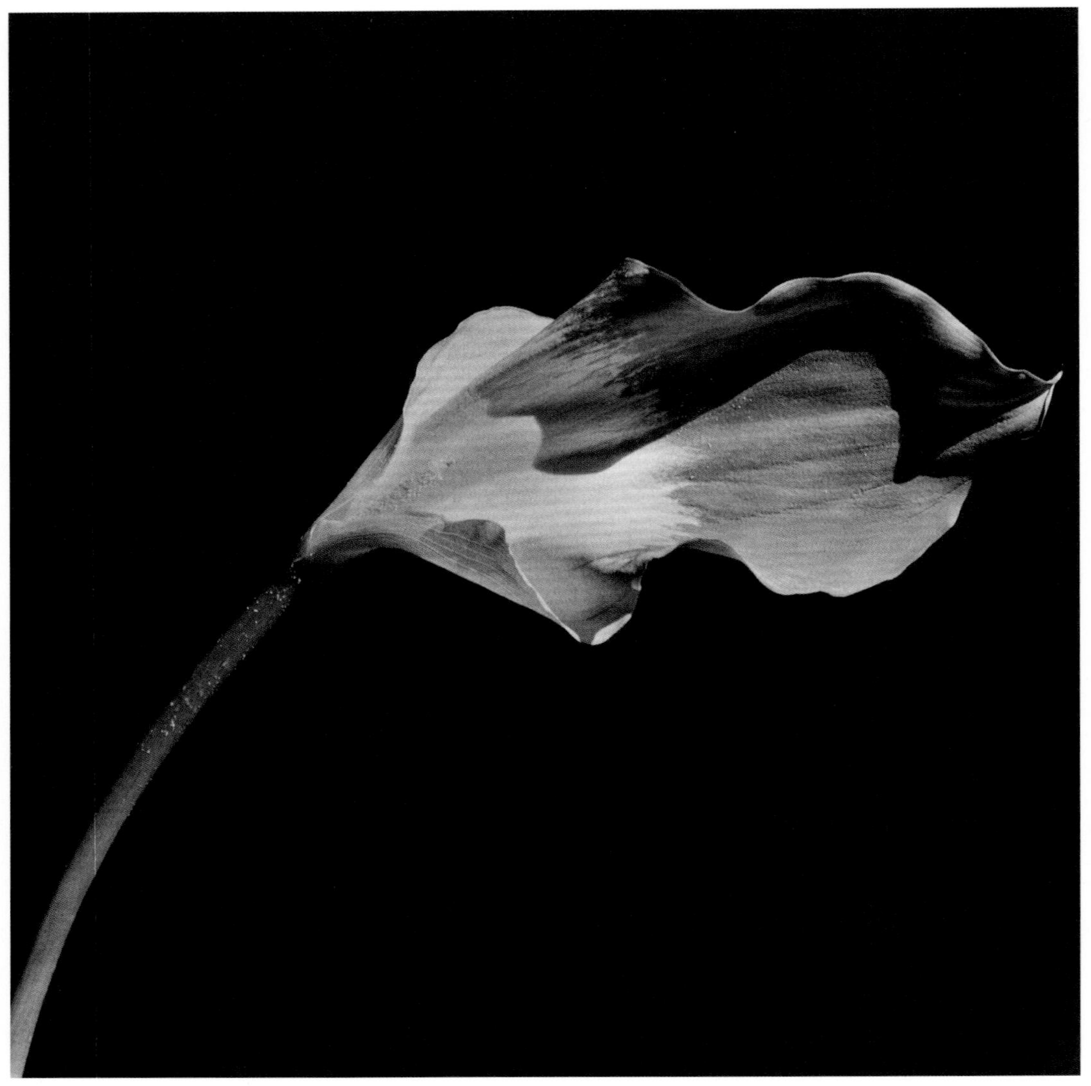

Robert Mapplethorpe (American, 1946–1989). *Calla Lily*. 1986. Gelatin silver print, 19¼ × 19¼ in. (48.9 × 48.9 cm)

In his photographs of flowers, Robert Mapplethorpe typically recorded his subjects at peak bloom, immortalizing transient moments of perfection; this image and four others from 1986, however, track a calla lily's transformation as it wilts.

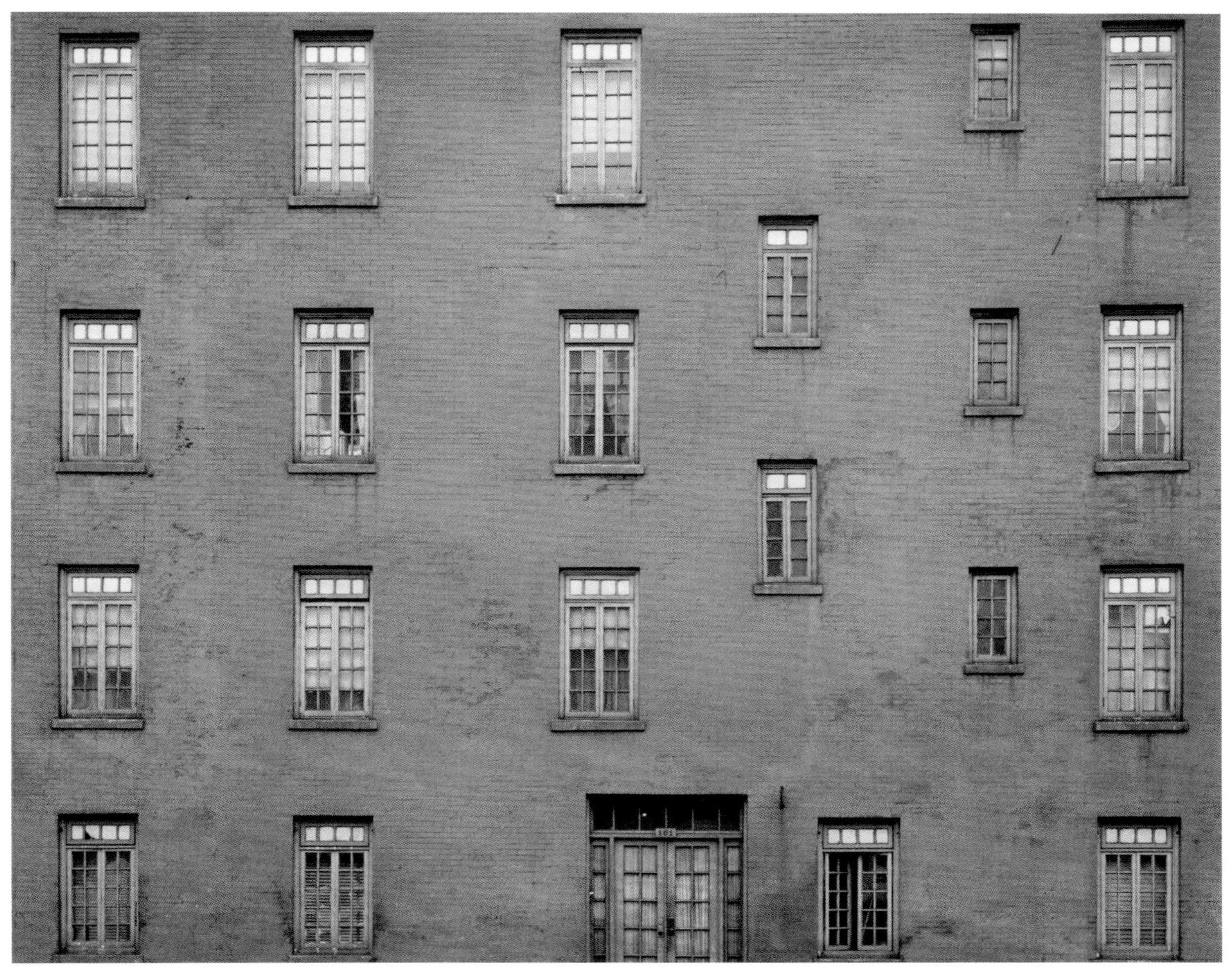

Harry Callahan (American, 1912–1999). *New York*. 1945.
Gelatin silver print, 6⅝ × 8 7/16 in. (16.8 × 21.4 cm)

Harry Callahan created this photograph during an attempt at living in New York, which lasted only three months. Returning to the Midwest in 1946, he would be hired by László Moholy-Nagy (see pp. 84–91) to join the faculty of Chicago's Institute of Design, then America's preeminent training ground for modernist photographers.

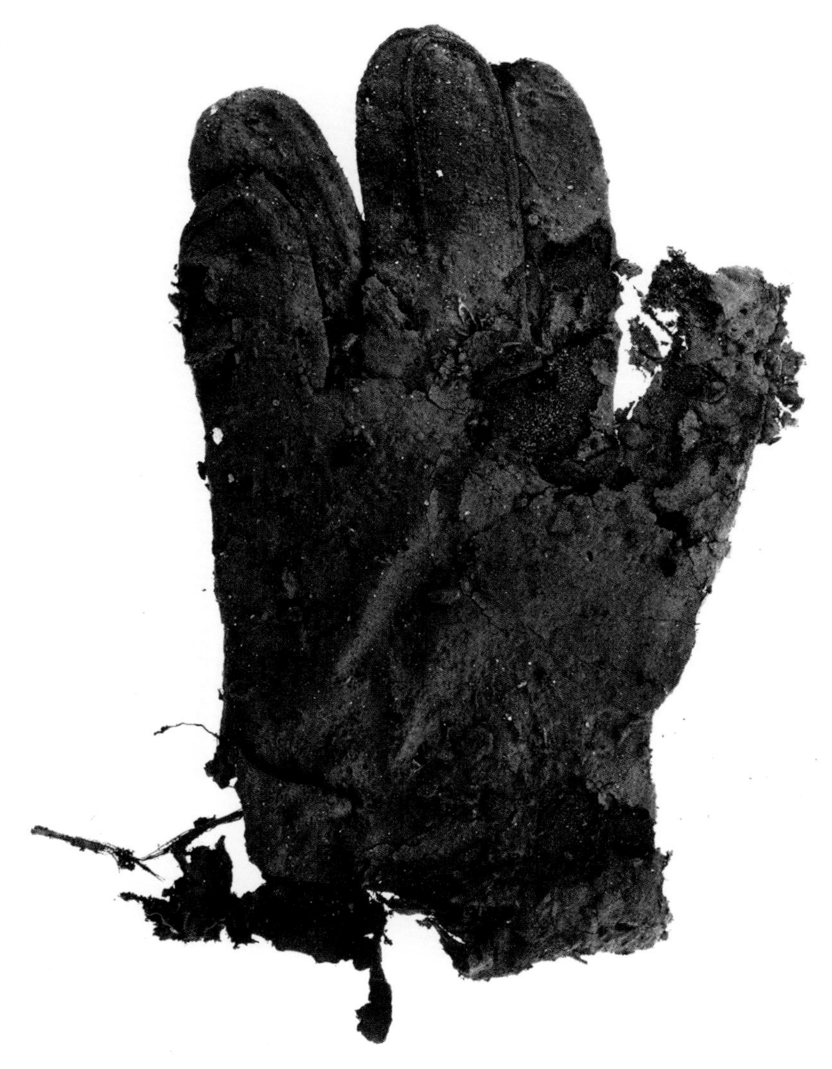

Irving Penn (American, 1917–2009). *Mud Glove, New York*. 1975. Platinum/palladium print, 30 × 22 in. (76.2 × 55.9 cm)

Irving Penn's platinum/palladium prints required several days to complete. To create one, he coated his paper with successive layers of light-sensitive platinum and palladium salts, exposing each coating separately to a distinct negative that bore the same image in a different tonal range.

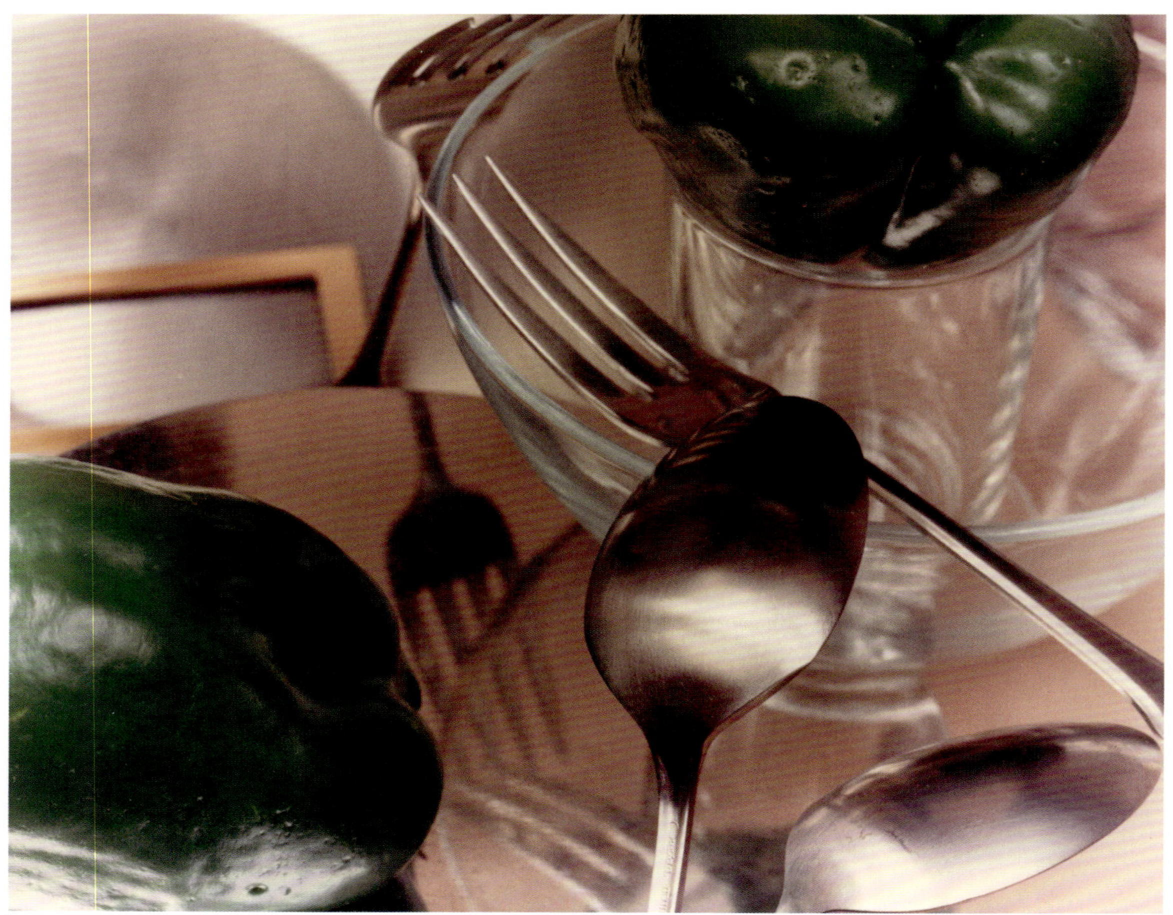

Jan Groover (American, 1943–2012). Untitled. c. 1979.
Chromogenic print, 14¾ × 19$^{1}/_{16}$ in. (37.5 × 48.4 cm)

To embrace a genre as traditional as still life, like Jan Groover did, represented a divergence from the more experimental photographic trends predominating in the late 1970s. Yet Groover, as much as her contemporaries who worked in a Conceptualist vein or appropriated the visual language of mass media, undertook her own analysis of the camera's production of reality. The artist's chromatically rich, formally complex photographs explore how interactions between surfaces and light, when enclosed within a frame, generate spaces that exist nowhere else but in the picture. "I had some wild concept that you could change space," the artist recounted, "which you can."[1]

In 1978, following several years of working outdoors in cities and suburbs to create conceptually driven diptychs and triptychs, Groover shifted her practice indoors. Turning her lens to the interior of her kitchen sink, she photographed cutlery, glassware, and other domestic articles in arrangements that, for all their seeming haphazardness, were often exactingly plotted in advance. Her prints render these objects, chosen for their transparency, reflectiveness, and linear clarity, at a size that is larger than life. Their nuanced registration of texture and tone stems from her use of a four-by-five-inch view camera, a device that had fallen out of favor as photographers gravitated toward handheld cameras.

By adopting the view camera, Groover revisited the working methods of early modernist photographers such as Paul Strand and Edward Weston. Her still lifes reference these photographers' landmark images by way of the bowls and peppers that reappear across her work. The still lifes also address the legacies of these early advocates of "straight" photography through their unapologetic formalism. Yet, unlike the images of her forebears, who championed the camera's capacity for objective description, hers destabilize their subjects' integrity as objects, refracting them across one another's mirrored surfaces. In this, Groover issues a tacit rebuttal of the tradition that "straight" photography initiated. Her images insist that photography does not reveal the world in its true nature, but rather presents it as it appears within the camera's perception. SA

(1) Jan Groover, quoted in *Jan Groover: Tilting at Space*, directed by Mark Trottenberg (1994; New York: Checkerboard Film Foundation).

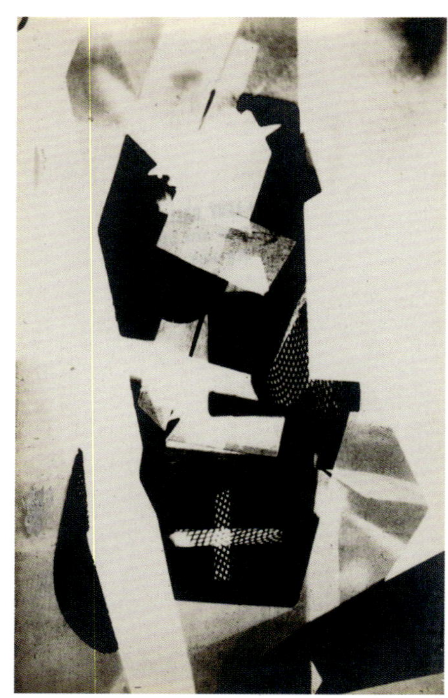
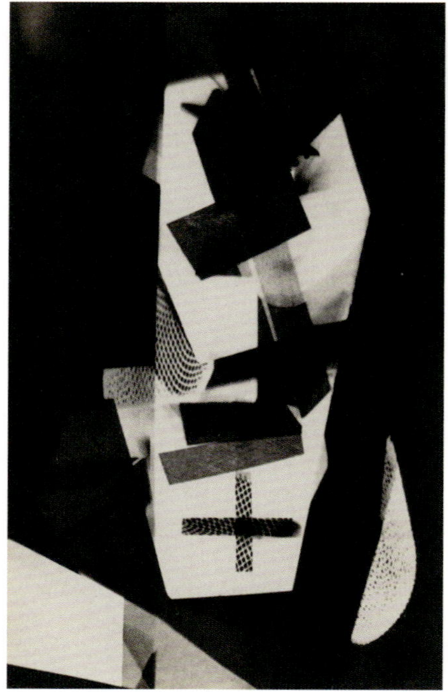
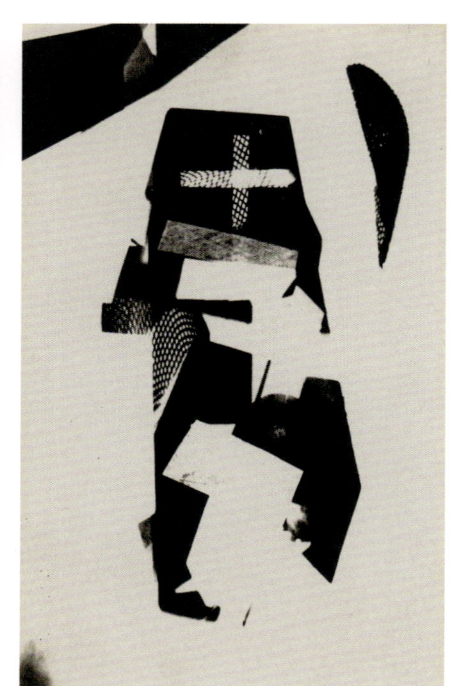

László Moholy-Nagy (American, born Hungary. 1895–1946). Untitled. 1925–30, from a 1922 photogram. Three gelatin silver prints, each approx. 7 11/16 × 4 7/8 in. (19.5 × 12.4 cm)

László Moholy-Nagy's Hidden Worlds

Rachel Rosin

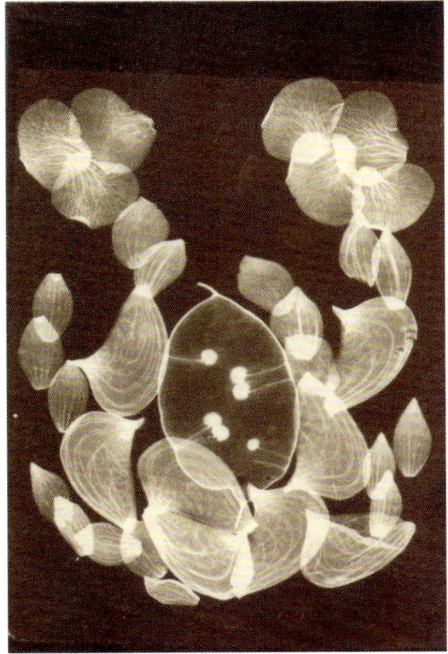

Fig. 1. Bertha Günther (German, 1894–1975). Untitled. c. 1920–22. Photogram, 5 7/16 × 3 11/16 in. (13.9 × 9.4 cm). Loheland-Stiftung Archiv, Künzell, Germany

In the summer of 1922, before their arrival at the Bauhaus, László Moholy-Nagy and Lucia Moholy traveled to the Rhön region of Germany, where they visited the Loheland School for Physical Education, Agriculture, and Crafts, an art school for women. There the two met Bertha Günther, a student at the school, who showed the couple her photograms of arboreal and floral pieces, among other natural elements sourced in the region (fig. 1). Moholy-Nagy was impressed by the young artist's simple process of placing objects on unexposed photographic paper, blocking the light of exposure to create silhouette shadows, and how she achieved a seemingly infinite array of tonalities without the use of a darkroom. Later, Moholy-Nagy wrote that it was on this trip he learned of the photogram technique in part through an unnamed "Loheländerin"—whom we now know to be Günther.[1] Back in Berlin, Moholy-Nagy immediately (and vigorously) began to produce small photograms.

Just before he and Lucia Moholy came across Günther's floral photograms, Moholy-Nagy had published an essay titled "Production-Reproduction" in the journal *De Stijl*.[2] In the article, Moholy-Nagy argues that the artist should produce "new, so far unknown relations" between the familiar and the unfamiliar, in photography and in other media, too, such as film or music.[3] A "reproductive" work repeated already-known relationships, whereas a "productive" work produced new, experimental relationships in an already-known technical process. In Günther's photograms, Moholy-Nagy had found a means to create productive work—and it would initiate a period of wide-ranging experimentation that carried him through the 1920s. The decade marked the beginning of Moholy-Nagy's ceaseless experimentation with the inherent, and oft-unexplored, peculiarities of the camera—or, in fact, the camera-less. Though the Hungarian-born artist traversed the realms of painting, sculpture, film, and other media throughout his prolific career, it was in this decade that photography became his most urgent site of experimentation. He worked against traditional photographic models and invented his own radical visual language, seeking to cast light on what he believed to be the unquestionable interrelationship between all facets of modernism: in life, art, and technology.

One of Moholy-Nagy's earliest experiments with the photogram technique can be traced back to 1922, and provides the foundation for a triptych now in the Gayle Greenhill Collection (p. 84). To make his initial photograms, Moholy-Nagy began with unexposed printing-out paper (at the time known as "daylight" paper, which did not require any chemical development, only exposure to light), upon which he placed an array of materials to create textural areas, ranging from pieces of paper cut into geometric shapes, patterned scraps of translucent paper, stencils, or small objects such as pinions, cogs, or drawing pins.[4] In a 1922 photogram,

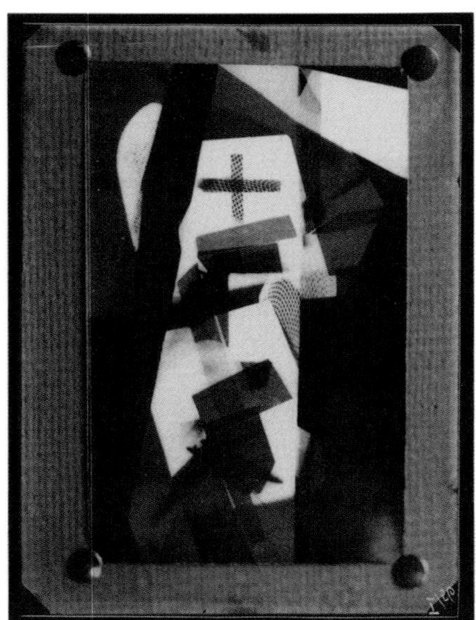

Fig. 2. Contact copy of Lucia Moholy's glass plate negative I/56 depicting the 1922 photogram by László Moholy-Nagy, 9⁷⁄₁₆ × 7¹⁄₁₆ in. (24 × 18 cm). The Estate of Hattula Moholy-Nagy

transparent, mutually penetrating forms give the impression of space and depth, and produce an example of what Moholy-Nagy referred to as "light compositions."[5] The artist would later reflect upon the negative of the photogram, "where black becomes white and white becomes black," as a process that "reverses the habitual way of selecting photographic views for their black and white values"; as such, he poetically observed, "a new hidden world arises."[6]

The whereabouts of this original photogram are unknown, however Lucia Moholy and Moholy-Nagy returned to the motif multiple times throughout the decade. Lucia Moholy secured a copy of the photogram onto a board using metal thumbtacks in all four corners and then photographed it using a glass plate negative, which she catalogued "I/56" (fig. 2).[7] The triptych in the Greenhill Collection was made sometime between 1925 and 1930 and consists of three prints, one presumably made from the glass plate negative, and two that could be referred to as "revaluations," Moholy-Nagy's term to describe the reversal of values.[8] Whereas the 1922 photogram was made under the sun on printing-out paper, the triptych in the Greenhill Collection was made in a darkroom on developing-out paper—an approach crucial to Moholy-Nagy's process of production-reproduction. To make the revaluations, an interpositive, which would yield inverted tones when printed in the darkroom, was required. Each print was inscribed on the verso with two distinct sets of numbers—perhaps to determine the arrangement of their display or, alternatively, to delineate the order in which they were made.[9] They also each include a stamp by Julien Levy, the New York–based art dealer who first acquired the triptych; Levy visited Moholy-Nagy in Berlin in 1931 and described viewing the photograms in a memoir published years later.[10] The triptych in the Greenhill Collection is one of two known sets produced; a second triptych has been traced to the German-Swiss art historian Carola Giedion-Welcker, whose home was an artistic and intellectual hub for modernists, such as artists Kurt Schwitters, Hans Arp, and Moholy-Nagy himself.

Far from new, the photogram process was at the forefront of photographic invention in the 1830s, when British scientist and photographic pioneer William Henry Fox Talbot exposed light-sensitive paper to the sun.[11] The technique was newly explored almost one hundred years later by the avant-garde for the abstract, formal possibilities it offered, and used by others within Moholy-Nagy's milieu: Christian Schad made his "schadographs" around 1918, and Man Ray made his "rayographs" beginning in 1922 (an example of which is held in the Greenhill Collection, see p. 10). Two of Man Ray's rayographs were reproduced alongside Moholy-Nagy's own 1922 photogram in the latter's inventive volume *Malerei, Photographie, Film* (*Painting, Photography, Film*), published in 1925. It was also in this publication that Moholy-Nagy

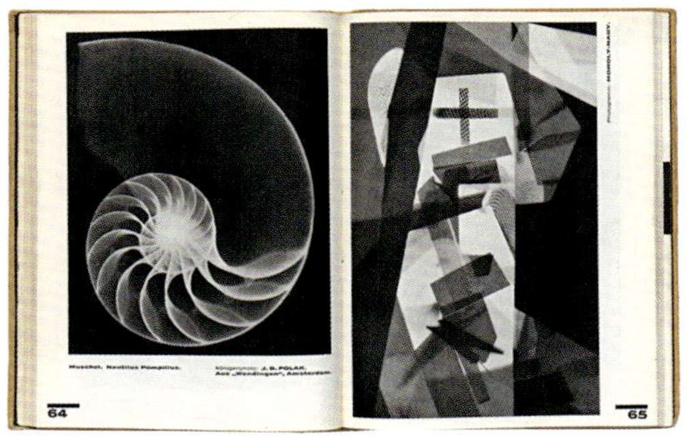

Fig. 3. Illustrations of an undated X-ray by J. B. Polak and the 1922 photogram by László Moholy-Nagy. Published in *Malerei, Photographie, Film* (Munich: Albert Langen Verlag, 1925), pp. 64–65. The Museum of Modern Art Library, New York

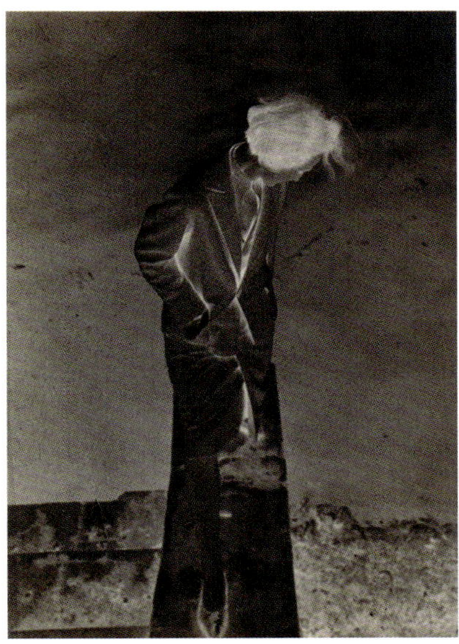

Fig. 4. László Moholy-Nagy (American, born Hungary. 1895–1946). *Negativ* (*Negative*). Before 1927. Gelatin silver print, 11 11/16 × 8 7/16 in. (29.7 × 21.4 cm)

first used the term "photogram," remarking upon how this method of working could lead "to new possibilities of light-composition, in which light must be treated as a new creative means, like color in painting and sound in music."[12]

Moholy-Nagy saw the revaluation process of the photogram in close relation to scientific photography, and especially X-ray photography, which he saw as "one of the greatest visual experiences" of the new age.[13] The dematerialization of objects into pure light and shadow was an aesthetic characteristic inherent to both the photogram and the X-ray photograph. In *Malerei, Photographie, Film*, Moholy-Nagy returns to his 1922 essay "Production-Reproduction" to cite new ways of expanding the possibilities of vision and perception. He concludes with the suggestion that one should consider the predecessors of this type of composition to be "astronomical, x-ray, and flash photography," and directs readers to the many illustrations of X-ray photographs he includes in the publication, shown side-by-side with reproductions of photograms, including his own 1922 work (fig. 3).[14] For Moholy-Nagy, the X-ray allowed for the intermingling of disparate photographic elements, without one obstructing the other. He later reflected that the technique provided "a transparent view of an opaque solid, the outside and inside of the structure."[15] Much like the photogram, the X-ray disrupts a linear spatial schema, challenging traditional modes of visual organization. Moholy-Nagy's interest in the reversal of tones is evident in his photographs from later in the decade, including the gelatin silver print *Negativ* (*Negative*), dated before 1927 (fig. 4). The photograph shows a skirt-suited central figure in motion, stepping forward, with just one pointed heel visible amid a darker swath of the print, towering before a murky, atmospheric sky.

Moholy-Nagy included *Negativ* in an article he wrote for *Bauhaus* magazine titled "Photography Is Creation with Light." In that article he also coined a term for his own experiments in photomontage, which he called "*fotoplastiken*," or "photoplastics," to describe his visual juxtapositions of mounted photographic fragments. Such a work "has a clearly discernible center of meaning and vision which permits a clear view of the whole," he wrote, "although it often consists of different optical and speculative superimpositions and intersections."[16] One of the earliest examples of Moholy-Nagy's photoplastics, *Der Abschied* (*The Farewell*) (fig. 5), presents a discordant picture of a cut-and-pasted couple and two dogs, amid a sweeping landscape of industrialization and new technology. The image shows the drama of a couple's farewell, evocative of popular postcards and movies from the period: the woman arches back in her draped dress, offering her languid arms forward to bid her suitor adieu. A grouchy bulldog stares forward, affixed beside the woman's heeled, pointed feet. Another flattened canine in profile faces

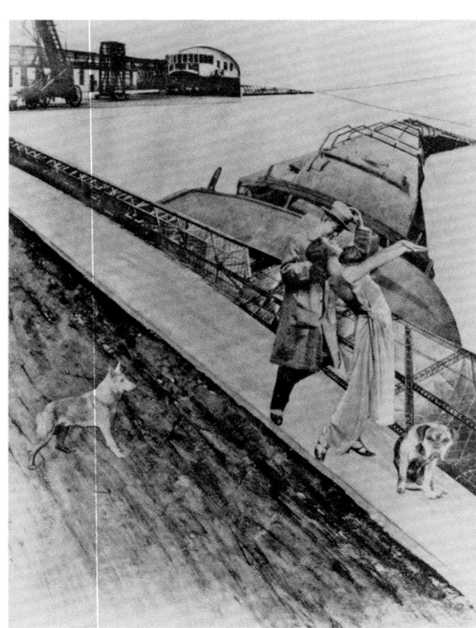

Fig. 5. László Moholy-Nagy (American, born Hungary. 1895–1946). *Der Abschied* (*The Farewell*). 1924. Gelatin silver print, 13 15/16 × 8 13/16 in. (35.4 × 22.4 cm)

toward the couple's ostentatious display, hovering atop the roughly painted bridge, under which a train runs. To make this work, Moholy-Nagy first arranged torn and cut imagery into a collage, and then took a photograph of the entire composition. From there, he continued to build upon the image, layering more found fragments and incorporating drawing and painting to enhance the surface, photographing what became the new arrangement after each alteration. For the white lines on the walkway of the bridge, for example, the artist used paint to build up or clean up the surface of the work. This additive process allows for disparate forms to gradually coalesce into a single image, much like the photogram itself.

Moholy-Nagy first began to explore the possibilities of fragmentation, collage, and photography in the early 1920s, shortly after he moved to Berlin. There, he became associated with Dadaist circles, and especially Raoul Hausmann and Schwitters, whom he often met at Romanisches Café, the famed artist hub, where they discussed and debated the new laws of pictorial construction in a technologically minded society. Hausmann imparted the young artist with the Constructivist principles of dematerialization and spatial dimensionality, and Schwitters's typographic work recalled Moholy-Nagy's earlier work as a letterer and sign painter across Eastern Germany before his move to Berlin. In her biography about her late husband, Moholy-Nagy's second wife, Sibyl Moholy-Nagy, demonstrates the decisive influence the group had on his political collage and photomontage work. Yet Moholy-Nagy chose to stray from the sensibilities of the preceding avant-garde; though he understood the "liberating outburst of the subconscious pandemonium in Dadaism," as Sibyl Moholy-Nagy put it, "he never became a part of it."[17]

Photomontage techniques popularized by these preceding avant-gardists presented the young artist with an apparatus to integrate the radical leftist politics, pedagogical ideals, and aesthetic questions he penned in his texts and raised in his classrooms at the Bauhaus. In his works from the period, when he was living and working across Germany, he adopted the formal approach of the glued Dadaist constructions, but set his own cutting, juxtaposing, and careful arranging of photographic prints apart from those of his predecessors. He saw the potential of his photoplastics to generate meaning, insisting upon the radical possibilities the medium could offer to the modern artist in a rapidly changing modern world. Dadaist photomontage could be likened, in Moholy-Nagy's own words, to "the Futurist, brutalist music composed of scraps of noise which sought to transmit an acoustic experience composed of various individual elements."[18] By contrast, his photoplastics resemble what he described as "the structure of a fugue or the order of an orchestra."[19]

In classical music, a fugue can be defined as a polyphonic or contrapuntal composition, written for several imitative parts that enter at staggered stages, later uniting to produce a harmonic whole. Moholy-Nagy wrote that both the fugue and his photoplastics, "consisting of more or less numerous superimposed layers, express unequivocal meaning."[20] The title of *Der Abschied* itself recalls classical music: "Der Abschied" was part of Gustav Mahler's 1908 symphony *Das Lied von der Erde* (*The Song of the Earth*). The hybrid musical structure of "Der Abschied" integrates successive, disparate strophes that contribute to the balance and import of the whole and epitomizes a central poetic idea.[21] The composition of Moholy-Nagy's *Der Abschied* is similarly organized around intersecting diagonal planes: the monumental train emerges from the top right, increasing in scale as it moves closer to the foreground of the image, and under the white bridge, which shrinks in width as one looks from the foreground of the image, where the couple and dogs are affixed, to the top left of the work. These curvilinear lines repeat, further unifying the picture into a coherent whole. Situated atop the blank paper ground, these lines direct the viewer's attention to, as Moholy-Nagy described, the "different optical and speculative superimpositions and intersections."

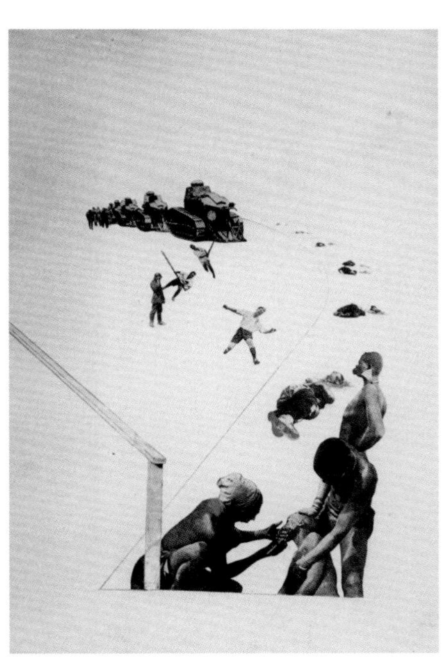

Fig. 6. László Moholy-Nagy (American, born Hungary. 1895–1946). *Militarismus* (*Militarism*). 1924. Gelatin silver print, 6⁹⁄₁₆ × 4½ in. (16.7 × 11.5 cm). The Museum of Modern Art, New York. Anonymous gift, 1939

Made at the beginning of his experimentation with photomontage, *Der Abschied* displays some of the spatial and perspectival strategies Moholy-Nagy would engage in his later writings, though it constitutes a more logical narrative (a couple's farewell) than later, more abstract examples of his photoplastic work. Like *Der Abschied*, *Militarismus* (*Militarism*) (fig. 6) uses the curved line to organize the composition, a structural device Moholy-Nagy applied to much of his photoplastic work. The spatial arrangement of *Militarismus*, however, is less linear: the cut-and-pasted tanks and soldiers float amid a white background, severed from an organized narrative schema. In this work and others that followed, Moholy-Nagy began to utilize his photomontage for social commentary, and seemed to take greater liberties with space and form. While the artist certainly distanced himself from earlier photomontage practices, as Sibyl Moholy-Nagy described, his photoplastics—with their satirical, often absurdist subject matter, unconscious sensibility, or dream-like arrangements—contain hints of Dadaist vernacular.

Moholy-Nagy continued to use overlapping layers of shadows and light in photographs he made in the second half of the decade, as in *Marseille, Rue Canebière* (fig. 7), which depicts the historic high street in the old quarter of the city of Marseille. He snapped the image through the decorative wrought iron railing of a balcony above the street. The ornate pattern work of the railing is blurred, layered atop the urban landscape of automobiles and pedestrians in top hats who traverse the sidewalks below. The two visual fields—the

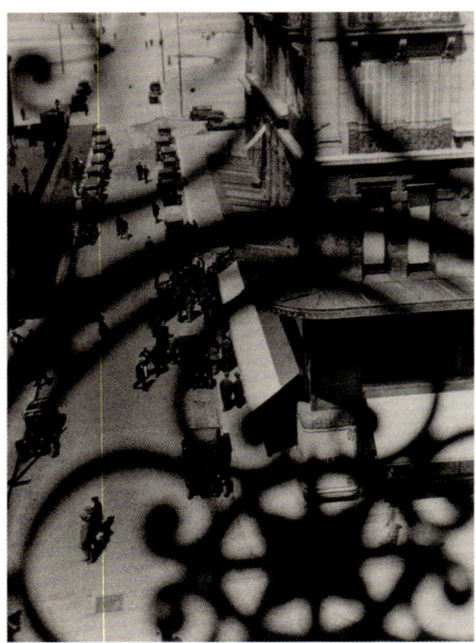

Fig. 7. László Moholy-Nagy (American, born Hungary. 1895–1946). *Marseille, Rue Canebière*. 1929. Gelatin silver print, 14¾ × 11 1/16 in. (37.5 × 28.1 cm)

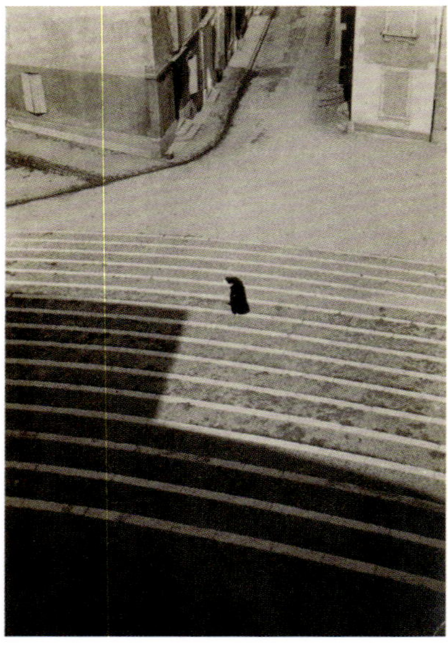

Fig. 8. László Moholy-Nagy (American, born Hungary. 1895–1946). *Nonne in Arles* (*Nun in Arles*). c. 1929. Gelatin silver print, 11 11/16 × 8⅛ in. (29.7 × 20.6 cm)

unfocused railing and the view of the street—are flattened together, producing an interplay of optical forms.

Other street photographs from this period also use an aerial perspective to juxtapose forms and figures below. In *Nonne in Arles* (*Nun in Arles*) (fig. 8), for example, a nun moves across a set of steps that leads toward an alley of stone slab buildings and doorways, cast in sunlight. Shadows cloak the foreground of the composition, creating rectilinear shapes that sever the picture into two. Shot from above, the shadows become layered atop the sunlit scene, creating an extreme perspective that lends a visual dynamism to the work. The spatial composition recalls Moholy-Nagy's earlier Constructivist sensibilities, and echoes the black-and-white geometric forms of the artist's earlier photograms. Even if each was made differently—one by means of the camera, the other camera-less—the two works similarly delineate the artist's incessant manipulation of light and shadow, each a new possibility of what he called "light-composition."

And so for the young artist, just twenty-five years of age at the start of this decade of experimental zeal, it was light—and its endless compositional possibilities and permutations—that became his primary subject. It became his medium, too—even more so than the camera itself. Light was his apparatus for poetic experimentation, whether through the street shot, the negative print, or the photogram. Indeed, in 1928 he described the photogram technique as "writing with light," and saw the photosensitive layer as "a tabula rasa, where we can sketch with light in the same way that the painter works in a sovereign manner on the canvas with his own instruments of paint-brush and pigment."[22] This act of writing, of mark-making, with light is evident throughout his work from the 1920s. Light became a way to show texture, surface, or shadow effects, to segment, distort, or fragment—or, in the words of the artist, to create a "new hidden world."

(1) Bertha Günther is now widely recognized as the unnamed "Loheländerin" (from the Loheland region) who introduced Moholy-Nagy to the technique, and whom he wrote of in 1927. See László Moholy-Nagy, "Die Photographie in der Reklame," *Photographische Korrespondenz* 9 (September 1, 1927): 259–60. Though previously not widely recognized, Günther and the school have been the subject of more recent scholarship. See Sandra Neugärtner, "Utopias of a New Society: Lucia Moholy, László Moholy-Nagy, and the Loheland and Schwarzerden Women's Communes," in *Bauhaus Bodies*, ed. Elizabeth Otto and Patrick Rössler (New York: Bloomsbury, 2019), 73–100.

(2) In her account of the couple's many walks in the Rhön region, Lucia Moholy describes how the two "talked about the 'production/reproduction' problem, which, quite independently, of the ideas of Christian Schad, Man Ray, El Lissitzky, became the starting point of our photogram activities." See Herbert Molderings, "The Light Years of a Life: The Photogram in the Aesthetic of László Moholy-Nagy," in *Moholy-Nagy: The Photograms. Catalogue Raisonné*, ed. Renate Heyne and Herbert Molderings (Ostfildern: Hatje-Cantz, 2009), 17–18.

(3) László Moholy-Nagy, "Production-Reproduction" (1922), trans. Mátyás Esterházy, in *Moholy-Nagy*, ed. Krisztina Passuth (London: Thames & Hudson, 1985), 289–90.

(4) Molderings, "The Light Years of a Life," 19. Though the early photograms were often attributed to Moholy-Nagy alone in publications and exhibitions of the 1920s, they resulted from the efforts of both Lucia Moholy and Moholy-Nagy. See Eleanor M. Hight, *Picturing Modernism: Moholy-Nagy and Photography in Weimar Germany* (Cambridge, MA: MIT Press, 1995), 60.

(5) László Moholy-Nagy, *Painting, Photography, Film*, trans. Jillian DeMair and Katrin Schamun (Zurich: Lars Müller Publishers, 2019), 25. Originally published in German as *Malerei, Photographie, Film* (Munich: Albert Langen Verlag, 1925).

(6) László Moholy-Nagy, *Vision in Motion* (Chicago: Paul Theobald, 1947), 197. As Hight notes, Moholy-Nagy described the effects possible in a photogram as "sublime, radiant, almost dematerialized," but the artist wanted to underscore that he did not seek to record imagery of the unconscious. See Hight, *Picturing Modernism*, 70.

(7) For an extensive analysis of the early 1922 photogram and the works that were produced thereafter, see "An Early Photogram and Its 'Revaluation,'" in *Moholy-Nagy: The Photograms*, 52–55.

(8) The triptych in the Greenhill Collection was the subject of a recent material analysis study, which demonstrated that the material constituents for two of the prints are nearly identical, whereas the third is markedly different. The materials and surface qualities of the prints were compared to other Moholy-Nagy photograms in MoMA's collection, and the paper used for the three prints is consistent with the range of papers the artist used in other works. See Lee Ann Daffner, "Material Characterization of Three Photographs by László Moholy-Nagy," internal report, The David Booth Conservation Department, The Museum of Modern Art, February 12, 2025.

(9) The inscriptions on the backs of the photograms in the Greenhill Collection appear to be made by different hands at different times (one in graphite, one in ink) and both sets of numbers seem to differ from the penmanship of the signature.

(10) Julien Levy, *Memoir of an Art Gallery* (New York: G. P. Putnam's Sons, 1977), 66.

(11) Moholy-Nagy acknowledged this history: "In 1835, Fox Talbot made the first crude photogram." See Moholy-Nagy, *Vision in Motion*, 187.

(12) Moholy-Nagy, *Painting, Photography, Film*, 25.

(13) Moholy-Nagy, quoted in Molderings, "The Light Years of a Life," 16.

(14) Moholy-Nagy, *Painting, Photography, Film*, 24.

(15) Moholy-Nagy, "Space-Time and the Photographer," in *Moholy-Nagy*, 348–52.

(16) Moholy-Nagy, "Photography Is Creation with Light," in *Moholy-Nagy*, 304. Lucia later explained the word "plastic" was chosen in part due to her and Moholy-Nagy's association with the artists of De Stijl and the currents of the movement that were dominant in that period, as well as a desire to distance themselves from earlier, Dadaist photomontage. See Lucia Moholy, *Marginalien zu Moholy-Nagy/ Moholy-Nagy, Marginal Notes* (Krefeld: Scherpe, 1972), 70. As Hight explains, "*plastik*" denotes "the organizing of different parts into a synthetic image with an independent meaning," as in neoplasticism. See Hight, *Picturing Modernism*, 150.

(17) Sibyl Moholy-Nagy, *Moholy-Nagy: Experiment in Totality* (New York: Harper & Brothers, 1950), 25.

(18) Moholy-Nagy, "Photography Is Creation with Light," 304.

(19) Ibid.

(20) Ibid.

(21) See Stephen E. Hefling, "Das Lied von Der Erde: Mahler's Symphony for Voices and Orchestra—or Piano," *Journal of Musicology* 10, no. 3 (July 1992): 293–341, https://doi.org/10.2307/763653.

(22) Moholy-Nagy, "Photography Is Creation with Light," 302.

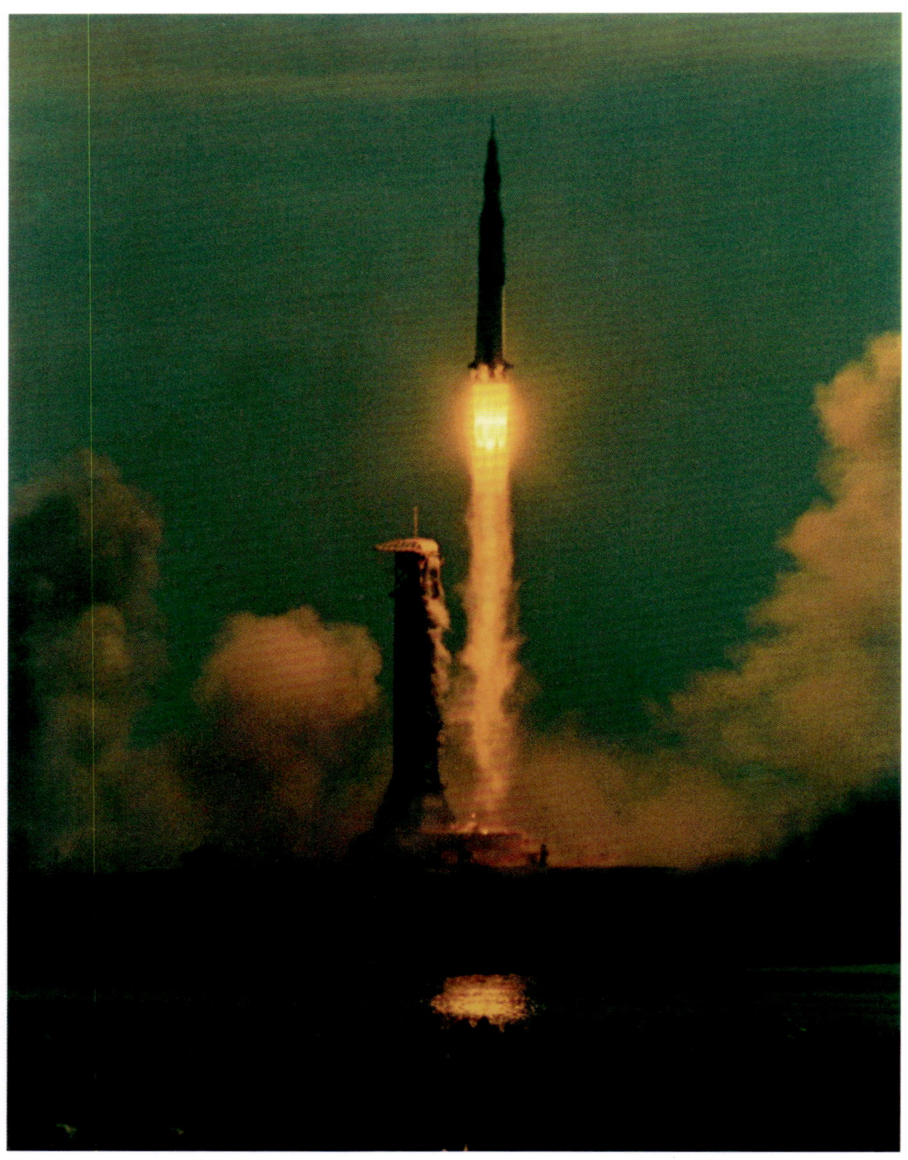

Hiro (Japanese, 1930–2021). *Apollo-11, 9:32 A.M. 7-16-69, Maiden Voyage To The Moon.* July 16, 1969. Dye transfer print, 38 × 29⅝ in. (96.5 × 75.2 cm)

Apollo 11 was set to launch on July 16, 1969, at 9:32 a.m. Eastern Standard Time from Cape Canaveral, Florida. Hiro, an in-house photographer for *Harper's Bazaar*, made it to the press site on a personal mission to photograph the event. NASA actively marketed the spaceflight to the American press, supplying reporters with a two-hundred-fifty-four-page press kit, audiovisual materials, photographs, and printed updates. The dissemination of images was critical to the space agency for securing its future budget and to the government for boosting the national morale as anti–Vietnam War and civil rights protests were gaining momentum.[1] The astronauts themselves were tasked with taking photographs. The most-reproduced image from the Apollo 11 mission is of Edward (Buzz) Aldrin Jr. walking on the moon, captured by Neil Armstrong, who is visible in the reflection of Aldrin's visor holding a 70mm camera. Michael Collins, who remained on the spacecraft, took panoramic views of the satellite planet.

Having worked in media for more than a decade, Hiro keenly understood that the launch would be a spectacle. He later recalled, "I came to the realization that there would be an enormous amount of worldwide publicity connected with this event and that I would have to approach this in a unique way in order to come up with original results. . . . To me, man's voyage to the moon represented the culmination of human energy."[2] Hiro loaded his camera with infrared film—a popular medium of the 1960s whose performance is highly dependent on the strength of the infrared radiation outdoors—recognizing how appropriate this unpredictable medium was for the occasion. Five seconds after liftoff, he clicked the shutter, catching the combustion flaming at the nozzle and the billowing clouds of exhaust flanking the engines. A group of spectators look on from the edge of the water, together with an estimated six hundred fifty million people tuning in on television. The artist applied color filters to achieve the orange-and-green palette and printed the work on wide-format photo paper in an attempt to capture the monumentality of the event. *Harper's Bazaar*, initially reluctant to cover this event without a clear fashion angle, finally accepted Hiro's pitch. The photograph appeared as an editorial page in the September 1969 issue. CL

(1) James Jeffrey, "Apollo 11: 'The greatest single broadcast in television history,'" BBC News, July 10, 2019, https://www.bbc.com/news/world-us-canada-48857752.

(2) Hiro, letter to unknown recipient, July 28, 1992, courtesy Sotheby's.

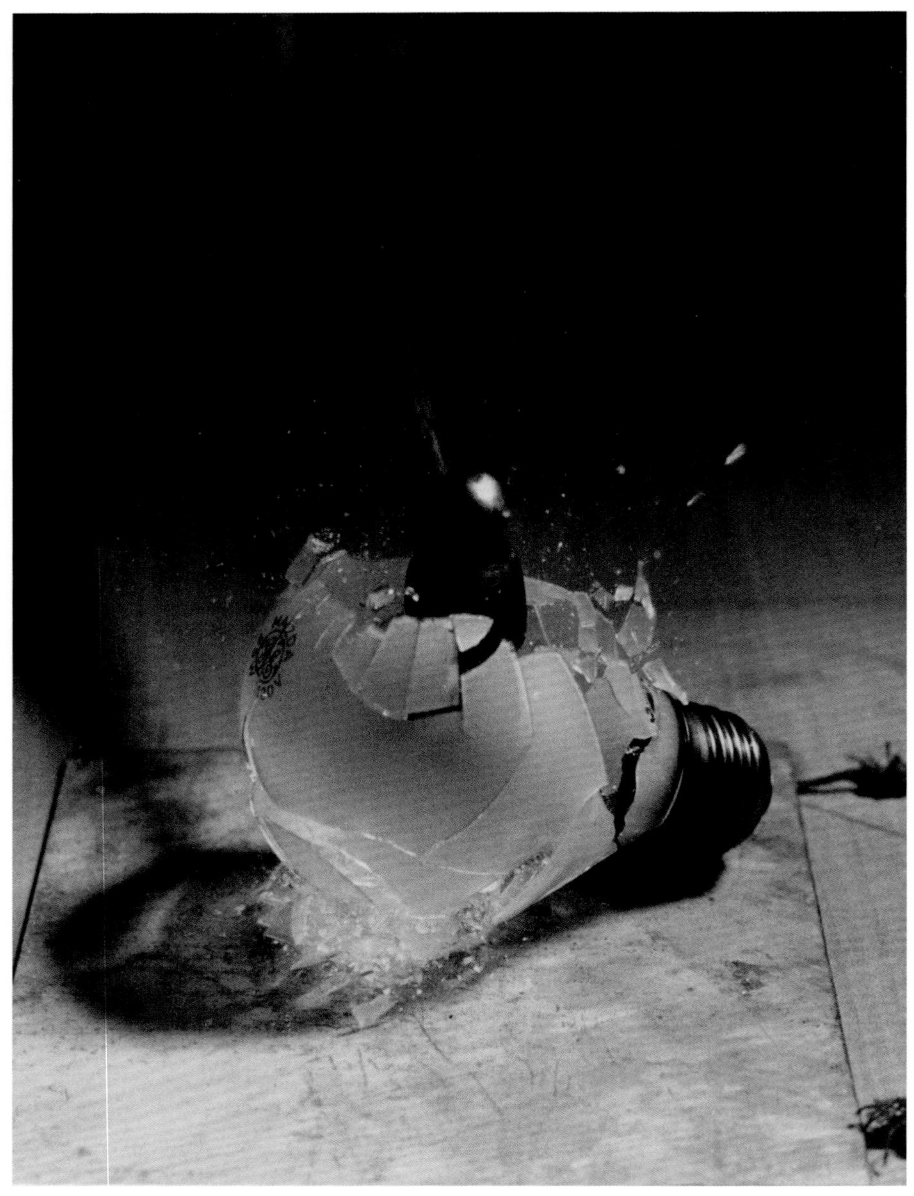

Harold Eugene Edgerton (American, 1903–1990). *Smash!* 1933. Gelatin silver print, 8 7/16 × 6 1/2 in. (21.5 × 16.5 cm)

Harold Eugene Edgerton's 1939 publication, *Flash! Seeing the Unseen by Ultra High-Speed Photography*, wowed the public with split-second photographs of objects and bodies in motion. The images were made possible by Edgerton's invention of the stroboscopic flash, which, due to its speed, power, and reusability, eventually rendered the flashbulb obsolete.

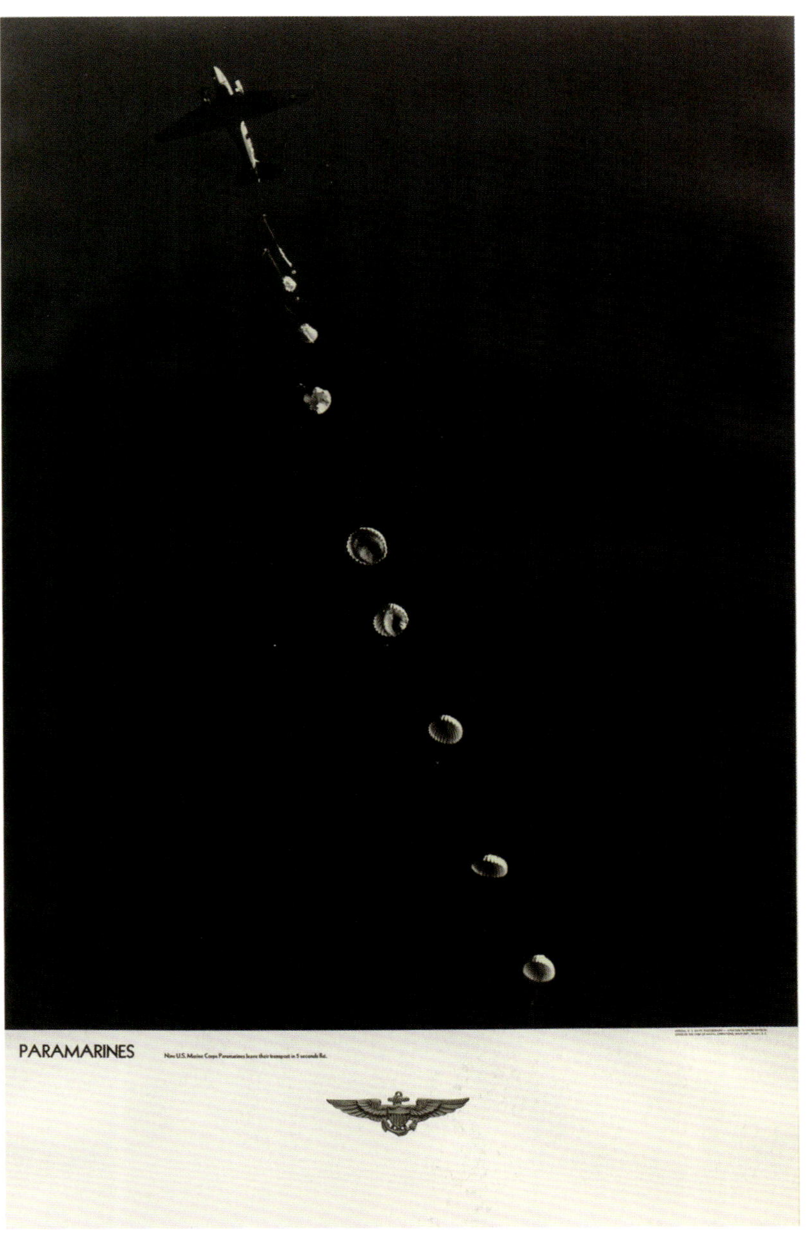

United States Marine Corps. *Paramarines (Nine U.S. Marine Corps Paramarines leave their transport in 5 seconds flat).* c. 1945. Collotype, 70 × 48 in. (177.8 × 121.9 cm)

Under the direction of photographer Edward Steichen (see also pp. 100–107), the Aviation Training Division of the US Navy produced posters such as this one to promote the many different roles of military personnel, including pilots and paratroopers. This stop-action photograph of marines training to parachute into combat zones marshals the medium's capacity to transcend normal vision.

CHANCE MEETING

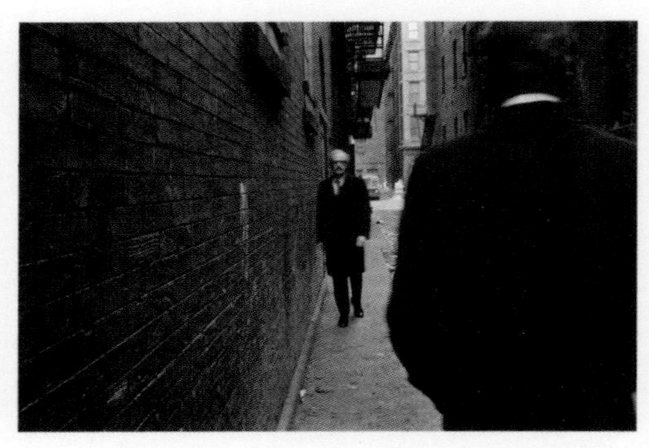

4

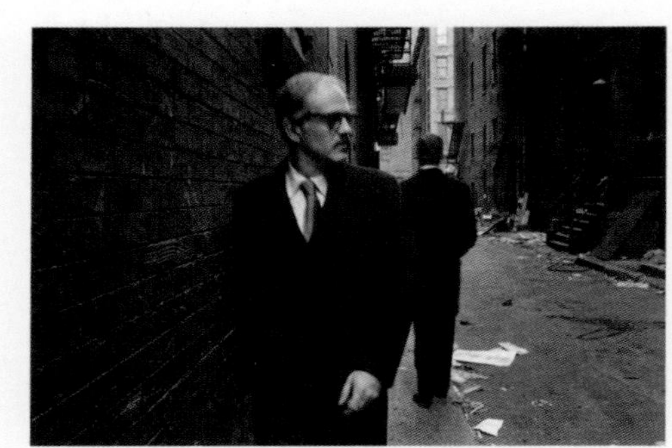

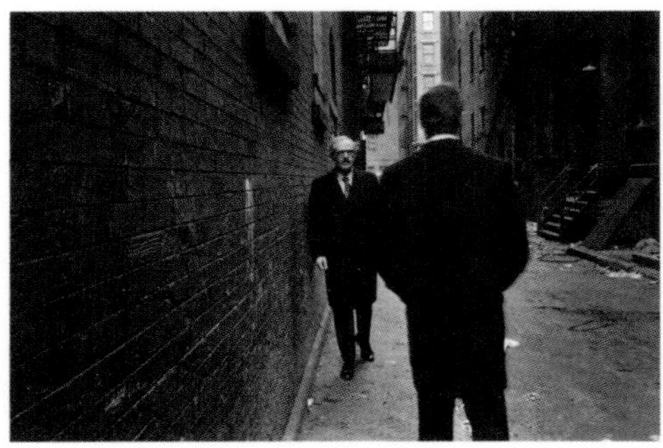

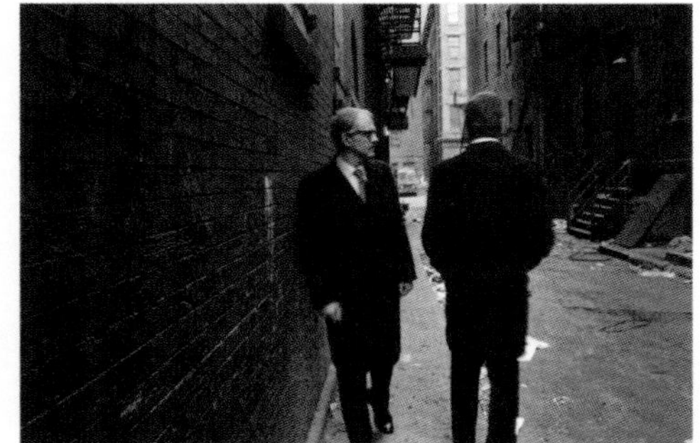

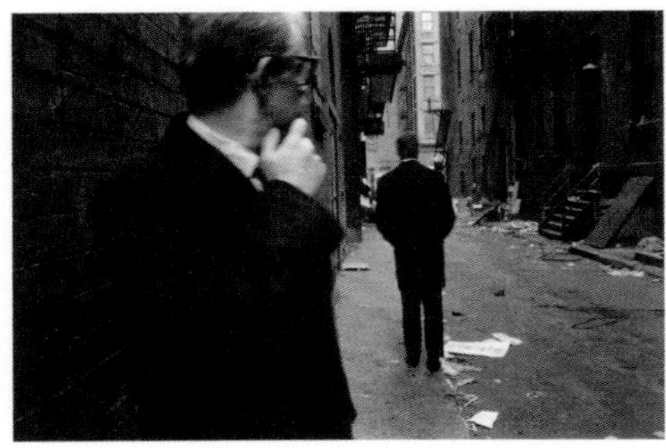

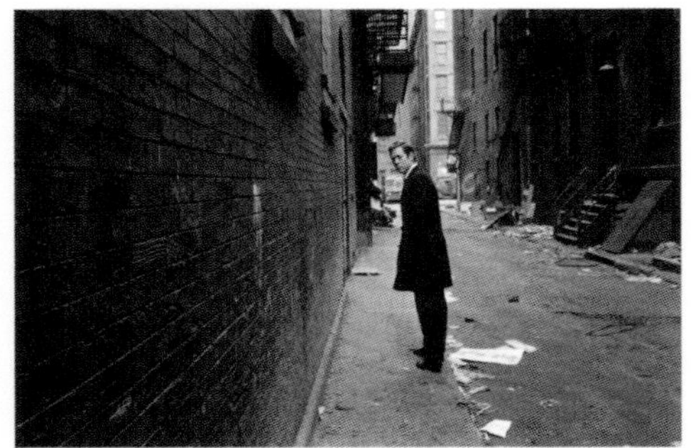

Duane Michals (American, born 1932). *Chance Meeting*. 1970.
Six gelatin silver prints, each approx. 3⅜ × 5 in. (8.6 × 12.7 cm)

"So what I did was, in a sense, to turn photography like a glove inside out," Duane Michals has said of his imaginative approach to images, often presented in series and accompanied by text, which broke dramatically with the conventions of postwar photography. "We were always wearing a glove like this, but then if you turn it inside out, I was doing the interior of the mind. So to me, photography's in the mind, it's not about the eyes."

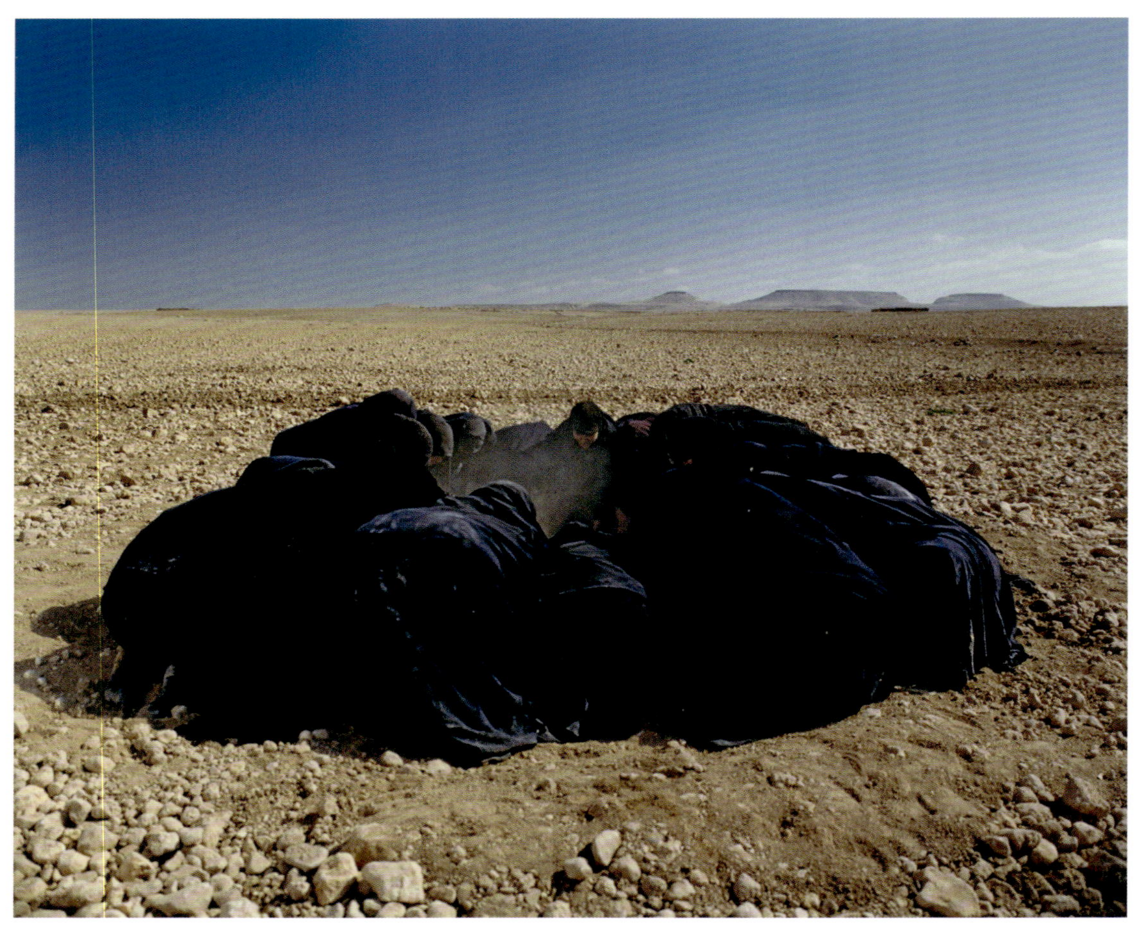

Shirin Neshat (Iranian-American, born 1957). Untitled from the series Passage. 2001. Silver dye bleach print, 19⅝ × 24¼ in. (49.8 × 61.6 cm)

A group of women digs at the earth in a circle. Dust rises off the ground, blowing into the air and onto the women's faces and chadors. Iranian-American artist Shirin Neshat created this image while making the film *Passage*, also in MoMA's collection. Neshat began working in video installation and film after deciding to take a break from photography in 1991. "Part of me was excited by how with the moving picture I could build more mystery, enigma, and sense of timelessness, while referencing sociopolitical realities," she explains.[1] Moving images have also allowed her to step out of the studio and work with other artists. Neshat learned to direct and execute complex narratives by putting together teams to develop audio and visual strategies. Storyboarding with multiple screens, she and her crew carefully orchestrate the relationship of the visual elements. The result is that every frame functions as a photograph. This practice gives the artist the choice to exhibit either the moving or still image of a work.

With cinematography by Ghasem Ebrahimian and still photography by Larry Barns and Grumij Fouad, *Passage* follows the actions of a burial. At the time Neshat conceived of the film, images of funeral processions for deaths caused by political violence in Southwest Asia and North Africa were constantly being televised. Working through melancholy, a lived experience and a guiding principle of Persian mysticism, the artist directs the audience's attention to public grief and mourning as a social act. In this frame the camera is low to the ground with the women, but distanced enough to also take in the landscape. Neshat draws the viewer into the picture with rich shades of blue and ochre without fully revealing the intent of this carefully choreographed funeral. Central to her work is what is not spoken: "In *our* culture, metaphoric/poetic language is the only means of expression for most of us, who are not permitted to speak freely. Poetry becomes a political statement, and the public becomes accustomed to reading between the lines."[2] CL

(1) Shirin Neshat, "Collecting Dreams: Shirin Neshat in Conversation with Glenn Lowry," in *I Will Greet the Sun Again* (New York: DelMonico, 2019), 76.

(2) Scott MacDonald, "Between Two Worlds: An Interview with Shirin Neshat," *Feminist Studies* 30, no. 3 (Fall 2004): 646.

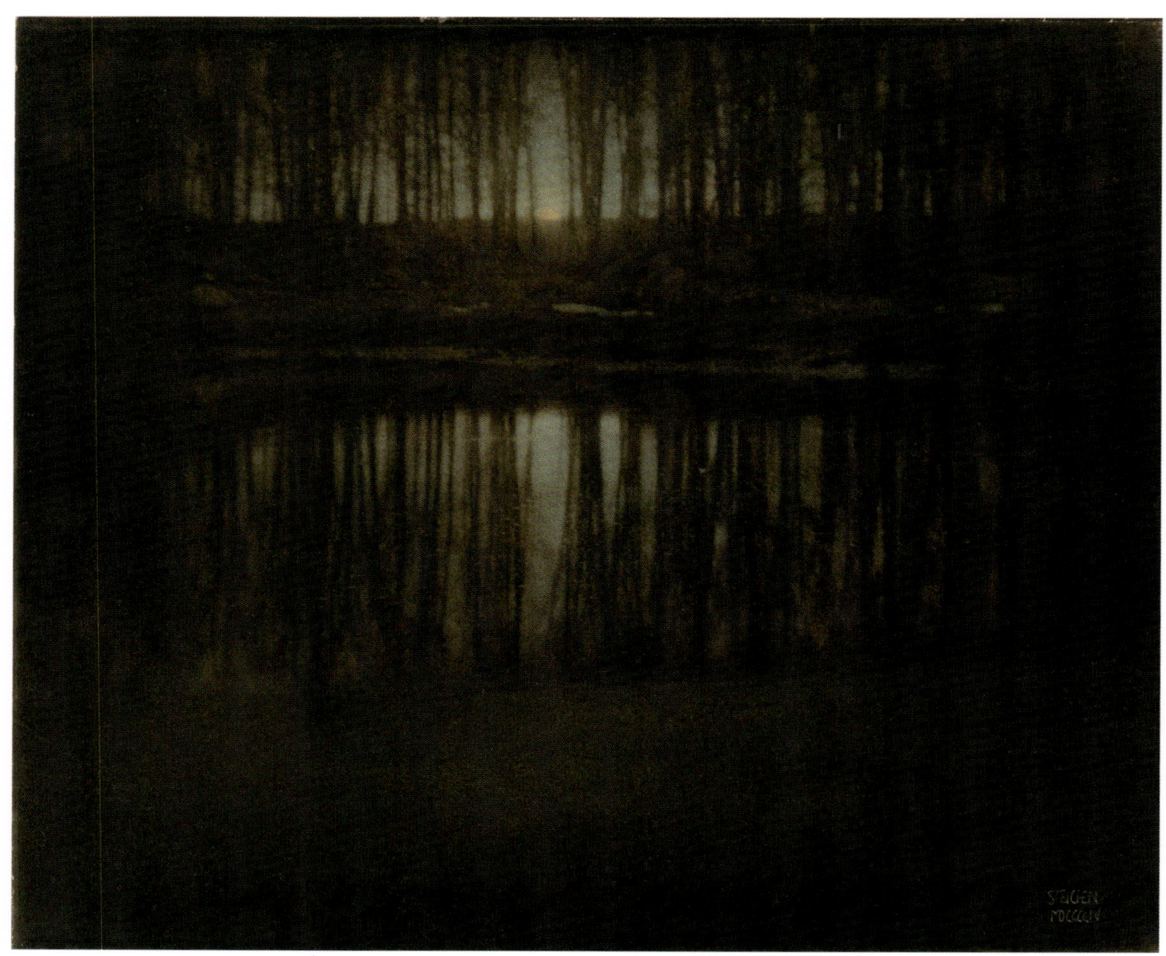

Edward Steichen (American, born Luxembourg. 1879–1973). *Moonrise—Mamaroneck, New York*. 1904. Gum bichromate over platinum print, 16 × 19⅝ in. (40.7 × 49.9 cm)

"It's a Whopper": Edward Steichen's Large-Scale Photographs

Lee Ann Daffner

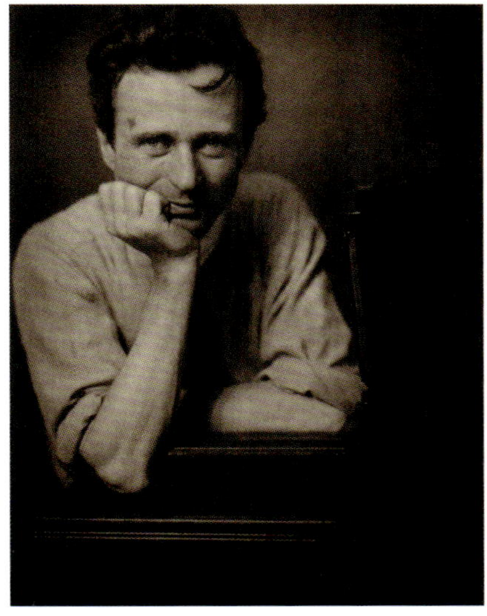

Fig. 1. Edward Steichen (American, born Luxembourg. 1879–1973). *Self-Portrait with Studio Camera*. c. 1917. Gelatin silver print, 13½ × 10⅝ in. (34.3 × 27 cm). The Museum of Modern Art, New York. Thomas Walther Collection. Gift of Sandro Mayer, by exchange, 2001

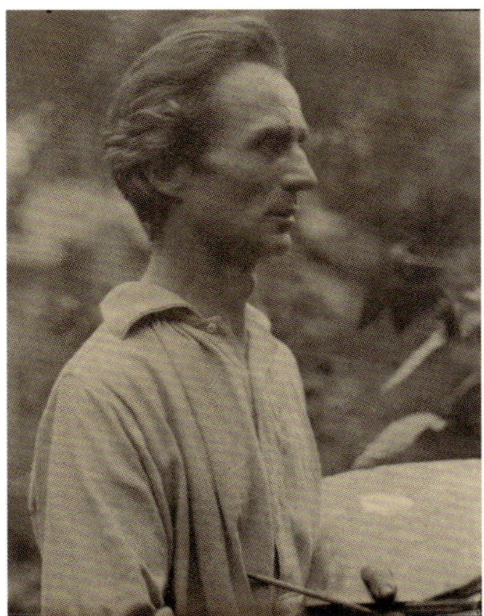

Fig. 2. Edward Steichen (American, born Luxembourg. 1879–1973). *Self-Portrait*. c. 1920. Gelatin silver print, 9½ × 7½ in. (24.1 × 19.1 cm). The Museum of Modern Art, New York. Thomas Walther Collection. Gift of Henri Cartier-Bresson, by exchange, 2017

Self-made, ambitious, and restless: this was Edward Steichen from the moment he stepped onto the photographic stage. Though until the early 1920s Steichen identified as both a photographer (fig. 1) and painter (fig. 2), seeing himself as an artist very much in both worlds, it was his mastery of intricate photographic processes that brought him acclaim and recognition. Two physical parameters—size and color—characterize his exhibition prints, often executed in multiple gum layers over platinum, yielding unique works of exceptional luminosity and bearing which seemingly fused his painterly craft with photography. Referring to this distinctive photographic hybrid, Steichen bragged to Alfred Stieglitz: "It's a whopper—and will compel attention."[1] The large scale of these photographs inspired the viewer to appraise photography in the vernacular of painting.

Moonrise—Mamaroneck, New York (1904; p. 100), in which an ascendant moon illuminates a woodland pond, is just one of at least twenty-five images Steichen rendered in layered photographic processes at a considerable scale.[2] While making these photographs, between 1901 and 1914, Steichen was also instrumental in the introduction of modern art to the United States, facilitated through his frequent transatlantic travel. In 1906, afraid he was being pigeonholed as a commercial portraitist, he packed up his successful New York City portrait studio and moved his family to Paris, where he could focus anew on his art.[3] In mapping the creation of *Moonrise*, we uncover key details of Steichen's multifarious creative process and the diverse locations in which his photographs could be made, even during a maelstrom of travel and artistic self-discovery.

Making *Moonrise*

> He never relies on accidents . . . that is the secret to his success. —Sidney Allen, 1903[4]

There are three extant sixteen-by-twenty-inch prints of *Moonrise*: in addition to the work in the Gayle Greenhill Collection, Steichen gave a print to The Museum of Modern Art in 1964 (fig. 3), while the third print resides in the collection of the Metropolitan Museum of Art (fig. 4). All three prints share the same foundation of gum bichromate over platinum; yet, belying photography's reputation as a medium of multiples, each is aesthetically and materially distinctive, differing in tonal interpretation, surface gloss, image detail, and even mounting. When viewing *Moonrise* today, with its translucent layers and turbid shadows, one might not immediately grasp the underlying steps necessary to create such a work. The prints were time-consuming, costly, and physically demanding, and despite Steichen's technical prowess, success was not certain. "Broke negative making the

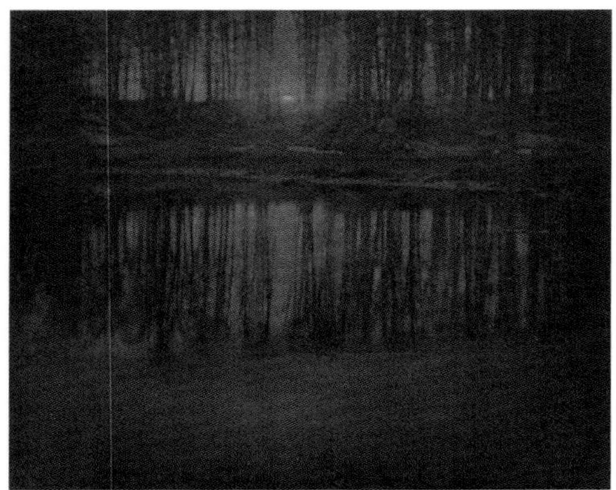

Fig. 3. Edward Steichen (American, born Luxembourg. 1879–1973). *Moonrise–Mamaroneck, New York*. 1904. Platinum and ferroprussiate print, 15¼ × 19 in. (38.7 × 48.2 cm). The Museum of Modern Art, New York. Gift of the artist, 1964

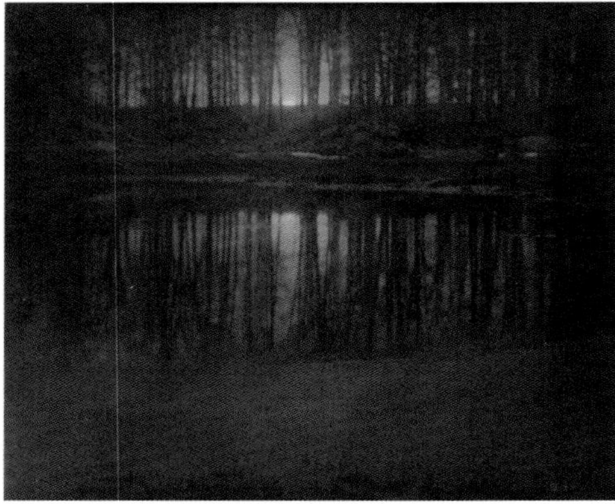

Fig. 4. Edward Steichen (American, born Luxembourg. 1879–1973). *The Pond–Moonrise*. 1904. Platinum print with applied color, 15⅝ × 19 in. (39.7 × 48.2 cm). The Metropolitan Museum of Art, New York. Alfred Stieglitz Collection, 1933. This print has a different title from the other two iterations

enlargement," the artist recorded in a letter to Stieglitz. "I cut my hand so bad I could not work for a week."[5]

For all their differences, each version of *Moonrise* began with the same negative, possibly four by five inches, captured in 1904 when Steichen and his family were vacationing in Mamaroneck, New York.[6] Once back in Manhattan and in the darkroom, printing could not begin until he had made an enlarged negative.[7] To do this, he first generated an interpositive, which was then enlarged via projection onto a sixteen-by-twenty-inch glass plate negative. These steps, and those that followed, required time to complete, as Steichen lamented to Stieglitz: "Two months hard work to say nothing of the expense which my bills at Obrig testify to. Big plates mean more failures and cost like h—l."[8]

With his enlarged negative readied, Steichen could turn to making prints. Rather than purchasing photographic paper, he prepared his paper himself by hand. The choice of "a good, pure paper" was critical, as it would shape the character of the print.[9] With one *Moonrise* print, he used handmade J Whatman paper, evidenced by the 1904 watermark visible at the top edge of the print (fig. 5).[10] To this paper he applied the sensitizing solution of iron oxalate and platinum salt. Once dry, the paper was pressed in a printing frame with the negative and exposed to very bright light. The print was developed in potassium oxalate and then cleared and washed to remove residual chemicals. The resulting platinum print, prized for its rich tonal scale, provided the monochromatic foundation for the ensuing steps.

From here Steichen built up the artwork in layers, printing multiple additional times from his negative. He brushed the platinum image with a pigmented gum bichromate solution that combines light-sensitive bichromate compounds in an organic colloid (such as gum arabic) with pigments in any color. Timing is critical with multiple-layered prints like *Moonrise*: a coated paper needs to be exposed to the negative relatively quickly, for maximum sensitivity; subsequently, each coat must dry between exposure and recoating, as a damp surface is more vulnerable to physical abrasion and chemical contamination. Upon exposure, the transparent bichromate-pigment coating hardens and becomes

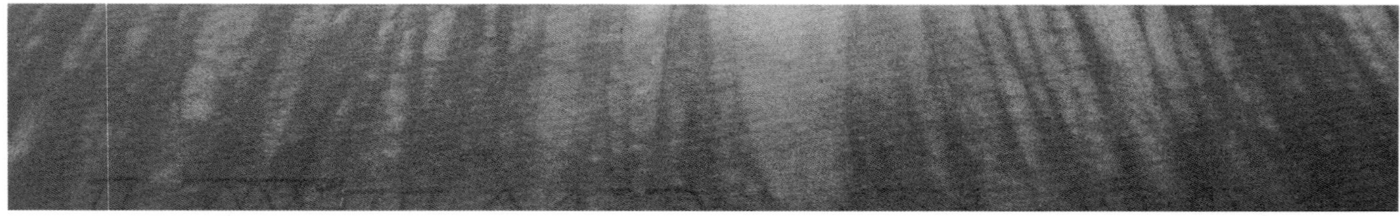

Fig. 5. Steichen's use of J Whatman paper is evidenced by the 1904 watermark visible at the top edge of the print (rotated detail of fig. 3)

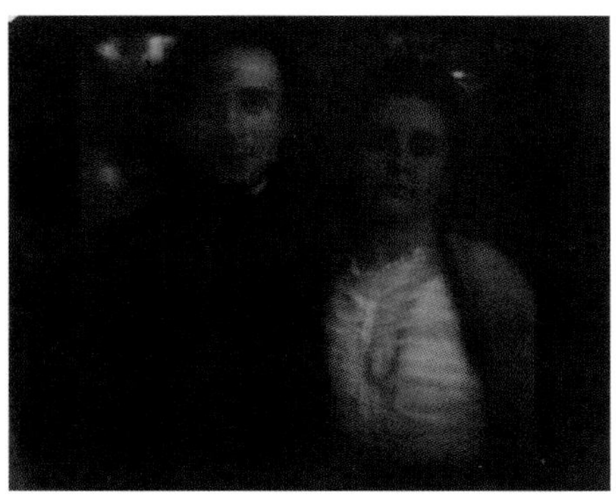

Fig. 6. Edward Steichen (American, born Luxembourg. 1879–1973). *Portraits—Evening*. 1903. Gum bichromate over platinum print, 11¾ × 15¾ in. (29.8 × 40 cm). The Museum of Modern Art, New York. Gift of Mary Steichen Calderone, M.D., 1973. Untrimmed print

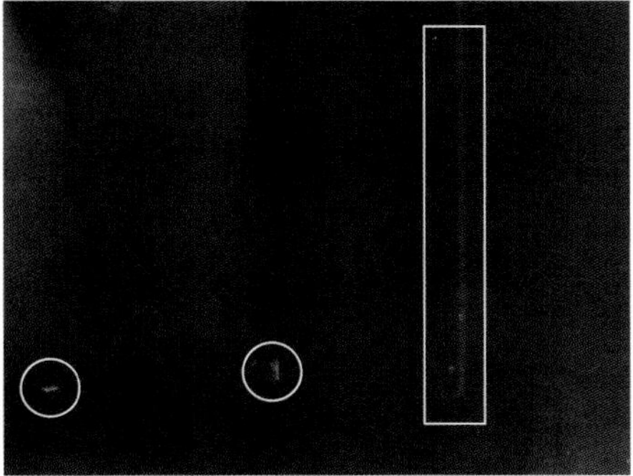

Fig. 7. The margins of *Portraits—Evening* show evidence of Steichen's printing process, including brushstrokes from the application of sensitizing solutions, registration marks (outlined with circles), and the line from the edge of the glass plate negative (outlined with a rectangle) (detail of fig. 6)

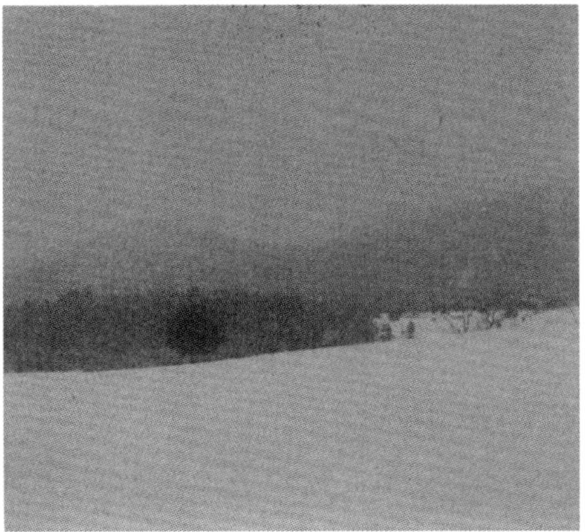

Fig. 8. Edward Steichen (American, born Luxembourg. 1879–1973). *Winter Landscape Lake George*. 1904–05. Gum bichromate print, 2¹³⁄₁₆ × 3⅛ in. (7.1 × 7.9 cm). The Museum of Modern Art, New York. Gift of the artist, 1961

insoluble in the areas where it is exposed to light. There are no chemical developers, as with the platinum process, but rather the unexposed portions are washed away in water. As Steichen built up the image in layers, he aligned each exposure with registration marks painted on the negative, which are visible in the margins of untrimmed prints.[11] The razor-straight edge of the glass plate negative of prints such as *Moonrise* or *Portraits—Evening* (figs. 6 and 7) can just be identified through the many glazes of pigmented gum.

In Steichen's skilled hands, these multiple layers of the gum bichromate process could obscure and soften an image or enhance a composition, depending on which pigments were used. Certain of his approaches yielded prints of exceptional delicacy, such as *Winter Landscape Lake George* (fig. 8). For darker, more mysterious works like *Moonrise*, he added depth and dimension by using pigments with stronger covering power. In letters and occasionally on test prints, Steichen left only a few tantalizing clues about the pigments used in his coatings and the sequence in which they were applied. His notes on the verso of an untitled 1904 print include: "Experiment in Gum / 1st printing solid lamp black (contrasty) / 2nd printing terre verte (flat) / 3rd sepia and black (very pale)."[12] The initial layer of lamp black pigmented gum on top of the platinum image reinforced the framework of the composition; next, the versatile, warm green terre verte pigment, well-known to painters for its transparent quality, blended and added complexity; finally, the topmost layer combined sepia and black pigments, adding depth and saturation like a toned varnish.[13]

The *Moonrise* photographs are remarkable for the luminosity that emanates from the rising moon reflecting on the pond. Steichen selectively etched or rubbed away image material to expose the bright paper in the moon and between the trees. This removal also allowed him to add Prussian blue to the sky, which he might have accomplished in any of three ways. Technical research carried out on a number of similar, large-format Steichen photographs suggests that Prussian blue pigment entered the work via either pigmented bichromate, watercolor, or ferroprussiate photographic process, commonly known as cyanotype. Archival sources do not reveal which process Steichen preferred; in fact, a letter to Stieglitz discussing the multiprocess print *Moonrise—Road to the Valley* (1904) is intentionally vague, merely confiding that Steichen had applied a layer of "plain blue print (secret)."[14] However, the blue passages of the *Moonrise* from the Greenhill Collection exhibit all the hallmarks of pigmented gum bichromate, while the *Moonrise* given to MoMA by Steichen appears to have been made through cyanotype.[15] Because the chemical signatures of Prussian blue pigment and cyanotype are nearly identical, these findings are subject to interpretation.[16]

The Studios

Bring over a few negatives you may want to work up.
I have a good darkroom enlarging camera Etc.
—Edward Steichen, 1909[17]

The three *Moonrise* prints were made for exhibition and sale: first in 1904, then in 1905, and finally in 1909.[18] The first and second printings were almost certainly made in New York, but the third was likely created elsewhere. Steichen was in constant motion; yet, even when traveling, he resourcefully transitioned between makeshift and professional darkrooms. Because his platinum and gum bichromate processes were safely handled under subdued light, not requiring the total darkness of a darkroom, he could work nearly anywhere.[19] At one juncture, he even remarked to Stieglitz, "I'm fixing an old barn for a studio and that will keep me busy."[20] During the years in which he made the *Moonrise* prints, Steichen primarily worked from three studios. In 1902, he became a member of the Camera Club of New York, gaining access to "wonderful darkroom faculties . . . the like of which I had never seen before."[21] Later in the decade, after relocating to France, he operated out of personal studios in his Paris apartment and at his country home in Voulangis.

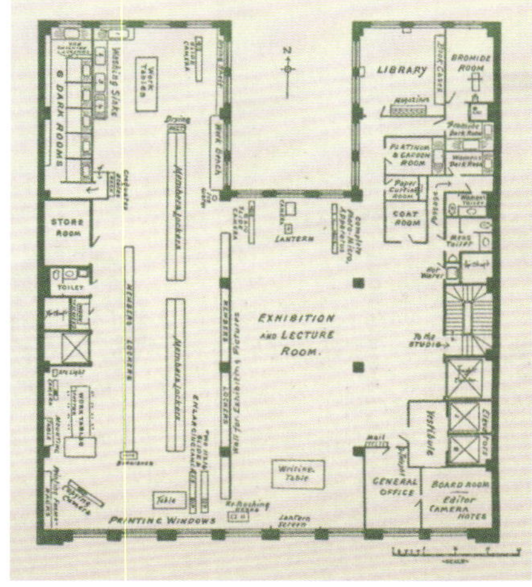

Fig. 9. Camera Club of New York floor plan. 1903. Manuscripts and Archives Division, The New York Public Library

The Camera Club provided five thousand square feet of state-of-the-art equipment, workrooms, and darkrooms stocked with processing chemistry, storage lockers, and exhibition spaces. A 1903 floor plan (fig. 9) indicates the path Steichen would have taken as he entered this venue from the elevator that opened onto the members' exhibition and lecture hall.[22] Striding past the corner office where Stieglitz sat—he was editor of *Camera Notes*, the club's photographic journal—Steichen headed straight to his locker to retrieve his negatives, papers, and supplies. He likely coated his papers with sensitizing solutions in the morning and, when dry, made the exposures the same afternoon. Loading the unexposed paper and glass plate negative into a printing frame (perhaps in the room for platinum or carbon printing), he carried the heavy printing frame to the south-facing window to expose it to direct sunlight. Here, the club also had an enlarging camera, useful for making the aforementioned interpositives and enlarged glass plate negatives. After each exposure, Steichen developed and fixed the print in the darkrooms at the opposite corner. For each successive layer for each print, these steps were repeated; it could take a week or more to build up a single print.

The deluxe accommodations at the Camera Club may have advanced certain aspects of Steichen's photographic process. In 1906, however, fed up with the pressures of commercial portraiture, he moved his family to an apartment in Paris, where he kept one studio. Additionally, from the

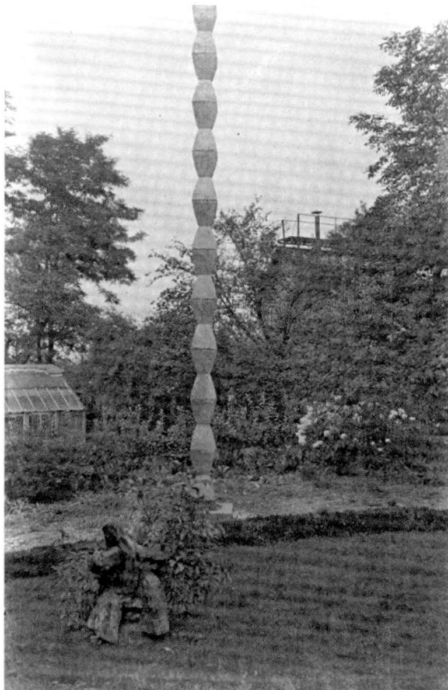

Fig. 10. Constantin Brâncuși (Romanian and French, born Romania. 1876–1957). *La Colonne sans fin de Voulangis (Endless Column at Voulangis)*. 1926. Gelatin silver negative, 5½ × 3½ in. (14 × 9 cm). Centre national d'art et de culture Georges Pompidou. Legs de Constantin Brancusi, 1957

spring of 1908 until 1924 Steichen leased a farmhouse property in Voulangis, affectionately dubbed Villa d'Oiseau Bleu. There, he had ample space for photographic activities, and in 1911 he installed a prefabricated building to serve as an additional studio. This north-facing structure had light, privacy, and, curiously, a catwalk where one could paint the surrounding countryside or expose photographs in bright sunlight.[23] A flexible space, adaptable to Steichen's full expressive arsenal, the studio also served as a setting for hosting artist friends. Painter Arthur B. Carles and sculptor Constantin Brâncuși were regular visitors; the studio's prefabricated walls and catwalk are visible in one of Brâncuși's photographs of his 1920 sculpture *La Colonne sans fin* (*Endless Column*) installed in Steichen's garden (fig. 10).

Changing Focus

> In those early days, a photographer came to Paris and knew us all. He was Steichen. He had been one of Stieglitz's men and came over excited about photography. Pretty soon he decided that ordinary painting did not interest him; one could do all that with photography. —Gertrude Stein, 1934[24]

During World War I, Steichen worked as chief of the Photographic Section of the Air Service, American Expeditionary Forces. In 1919 he returned to Voulangis to find his stored negatives in ruin from moisture and neglect. Though the war had left him in low spirits, his involvement with the Photographic Section had given him "a new kind of technical interest in photography" due to "making sharp, clear pictures from a vibrating, speeding airplane ten to twenty thousand feet in the air."[25] It can't have been lost on Steichen, whose life had been in constant movement, that things had accelerated to the point where he was perfecting his craft while literally in motion. In 1920 he dubbed one of his abstract still lifes *Space-Time Continuum*, one of many meditations on both the physics and metaphysics of Albert Einstein's theory of relativity. These musings on the entanglement of time and place may have contributed to Steichen's ultimate abandonment of painting, when, sometime between 1920 and 1923, he consigned his canvases to the bonfire.

Despite the loss of his negatives, Steichen doubled down on photography, immersing himself in its technology and relearning his craft through relentless experimentation. For a period of time he returned to making multilayered prints like those done before the war, albeit through a greatly simplified process. He now started with palladium print papers using commercially available "Japine" papers, which were celebrated for a parchment-like surface that resembled

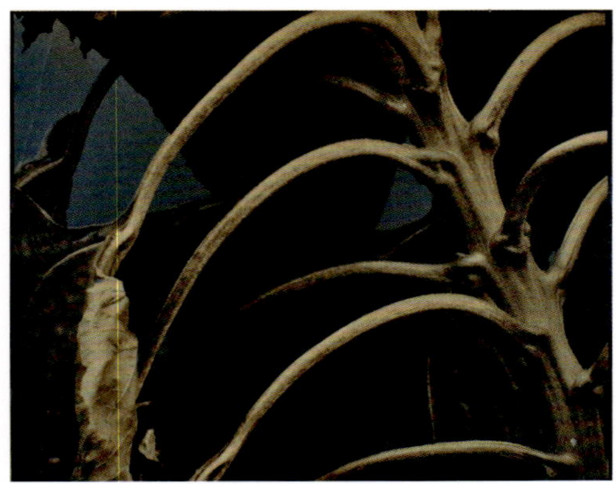

Fig. 11. Edward Steichen (American, born Luxembourg. 1879–1973). *Backbone and Ribs of a Sunflower.* c. 1920. Cyanotype and palladium print, 7⅞ × 9⅝ in. (19.5 × 24.6 cm). George Eastman Museum, Rochester, New York. Bequest of Edward Steichen, 1979

a gum print; on top of this initial print, he added a second, cyanotype layer by hand and printed from the negative again (fig. 11).[26] But this was short-lived; after a world war, the diaphanous sentiment of *Moonrise* may have seemed a quaint remnant of a more decorous age. In 1923, newly remarried and burdened by debt, Steichen surrendered Voulangis and returned to New York, diving into work for Condé Nast to become the world's highest paid and perhaps most recognizable photographer. In this way he was able to conquer his time-space problem: publishing and advertising put his work on display automatically and immediately. The sanctity of the image, however, never lost its centrality. Steichen merely found it increasingly in-camera, a perfect hybrid of artist and technician. During a period following one world war and helplessly on the road to another, Steichen opted for a louder, clearer voice to express himself, "with dreams of the Family of Man, flung wide on a shrinking globe."[27]

(1) Edward Steichen to Alfred Stieglitz, July 1904. Edward Steichen Archive, I.F.ii.2*. The Museum of Modern Art Archives, New York. These folders consist of photocopies, the originals of which are in the Alfred Stieglitz/Georgia O'Keeffe Archive, Yale Collection of American Literature, Beinecke Rare Book and Manuscript Library, Yale University.

(2) There are seven layered process photographs in MoMA's collection that closely measure sixteen by ten inches: *Moonrise—Mamaroneck* (1904), *George Bernard Shaw* (1907), *Portraits—Evening* (1903), *In Memoriam* (1904), *The Big Cloud* (1903), and *Chestnut Blossoms* (1904).

(3) See Edward Steichen, *A Life in Photography* (London: W. H. Allen, 1963); and Richard Whelan, *Alfred Stieglitz: A Biography* (New York: Little, Brown, 1995), 217.

(4) Sidney Allen, "A Visit to Steichen's Studio," *Camera Work*, no. 2 (April 1903), 27.

(5) Steichen to Stieglitz, February 1909. ESA, I.F.ii.2*. MoMA Archives, NY.

(6) A survey of one hundred contact prints made by Steichen between 1904 and 1914 suggests he employed a number of camera formats, with negatives ranging in size from two-by-two inches to four-by-five inches. See Steichen Family Papers, Yale Collection of American Literature, Beinecke Rare Book and Manuscript Library; and ESA, I.F.ii.2*. MoMA Archives, NY.

(7) The internegative was made by placing the original negative in contact with an unexposed negative plate and exposing it to light, resulting in a reverse-tone interpositive image on glass. The method for then making an enlarged negative was to project the interpositive image directly onto a sixteen-by-twenty-inch glass plate negative. Photographic literature of the time suggests "enlargements of greater dimensions are best made by daylight"; Rev. W. H. Burback, *Photographic Printing Methods: A Practical Guide to the Professional and Amateur Worker* (New York: Scovil & Adams, 1891), 109; see also John A. Tennant, "Enlargements from Small Negatives," *The Photo-Miniature* 9, no. 100 (April–September 1909).

(8) Steichen to Stieglitz, July 1904. ESA, I.F.ii.2*. MoMA Archives, NY. The Obrig Camera Co. was located at 165 and 167 Broadway in New York City.

(9) John A. Tennant, "Platinotype Processes," *The Photo-Miniature* 1, no. 7 (October 1899): 326; for more about high-quality printing paper, see John A. Tennant, "Gum-Bichromate Printing," *The Photo-Miniature* 2, no. 22 (January 1901): 407.

(10) Whatman papers were made by hand until 1937. See E. J. Labarre, *Dictionary and Encyclopedia of Paper and Papermaking*, 2nd ed. (Amsterdam: Swets & Zeitlinger, 1952), 363–64.

(11) Steichen may also have used tacks to hold the negative in place, as tack circles can be seen in the untrimmed margins of other MoMA enlargements: *Portraits—Evening* and *In Memoriam*.

(12) On the verso of Untitled, held at The Metropolitan Museum of Art, New York; Alfred Stieglitz Collection, 33.43.13.

(13) For more on these materials, see Rutherford J. Gettens and George L. Stout, *Painting Materials: A Short Encyclopedia* (Mineola, NY: Dover Publications, 1966).

(14) Steichen to Stieglitz, July 1904. ESA, I.F.ii.2*. MoMA Archives, NY.

(15) This *Moonrise* and several other blue-pigmented gum over platinum prints were catalogued in the artist's lifetime as platinum and ferroprussiate.

(16) Cyanotypes are chemically equivalent to Prussian blue. See Kaslyne O'Connor et al., "Moonlight or Midnight? Researching the Phases of Edward Steichen's Moonrise Prints," *Journal of the American Institute of Conservation* 59, no. 2 (2020): 111–22; and Anna Vila and Silvia A. Centeno, "FTIR, Raman and XRF identification of the image materials in turn of the 20th century pigment-based photographs," *Microchemical Journal* 106 (2013): 255–62

(17) Steichen to Stieglitz, April 1909. ESA, I.F.ii.2*. MoMA Archives, NY.

(18) Steichen first printed these works in 1904 and 1905 and then reprinted many works for the International Photographic Exhibition (IPHAD), held in Dresden in 1909, and the International Exhibition of Pictorial Photography, Albright Art Gallery, Buffalo, New York, 1910.

(19) Mike Ware, "The Technical History and Chemistry of Platinum and Palladium Printing," in *Platinum and Palladium Photographs: Technical History, Connoisseurship, and Preservation* (Washington, DC: Photographic Materials Group, American Institute for Conservation of Historic and Artistic Works, 2017), 49.

(20) Steichen to Stieglitz, undated letter (before 1917), Menomonee Falls, WI. ESA, I.F.ii.5. MoMA Archives, NY. In the same letter, he added, "Send (mail) me the Moonlights, and the sheep and i will stain them out here. I can do it easily and then send them back—We have a fine big garrot here that i can string them up."

(21) Edward Steichen and Kathleen Haven, *A Life in Photography* (Garden City, NY: Doubleday & Company, 1963).

(22) Camera Club of New York Floor Plan No. 3, West 29th Street [1903]. Box #1, Folder #B17, Camera Club of New York Records, Manuscripts and Archives Division, The New York Public Library.

(23) Compagnie des Constructions Désmontables et Sanitaire to Steichen, September 6, 1911. Fonds Constantin Brâncuși, Bibliothèque Kandinsky, Centre Pompidou. See also Mary Steichen Calderone, "Eduard Steichen as Painter: A Remembrance," in *The Paintings of Eduard Steichen* (Huntington, NY: Heckscher Museum, 1985), 10. According to Agnes Meyer, Steichen had a darkroom in 1909 in Voulangis. See Penelope Niven, *Steichen: A Biography*, (New York: Clarkson Potter, 1997), 301.

(24) Gertrude Stein, "And now," *Vanity Fair* 43, no. 1 (September 1934): 65.

(25) Steichen, quoted in Lee Ann Daffner and Audrey Sands, "Aerial Incendiary Bombs," in Mitra Abbaspour, Lee Ann Daffner, and Maria Morris Hambourg, eds., *Object:Photo. Modern Photographs, 1909–1949: The Thomas Walther Collection* (New York: The Museum of Modern Art, 2014), https://www.moma.org/interactives/objectphoto/objects/83912.html.

(26) Japine papers were a new line of print products with a paper surface that resembled parchment and that was completely different from the surface of conventional plain-paper prints. See Constance McCabe, "Noble Metals for the Early Modern Era: Platinum, Silver-Platinum, and Palladium Prints," in ibid., http://www.moma.org/interactives/objectphoto/assets/essays/McCabe.pdf.

(27) Carl Sandburg, "The Long Shadow of Lincoln: A Litany," in *Complete Poems of Carl Sandburg* (New York: Harcourt, Brace and Co., 1950), 635. *The Family of Man* would later serve as the title of the acclaimed exhibition of five hundred and three photographs celebrating universal aspects of the human experience, organized by Steichen at The Museum of Modern Art, where he was Director of the Department of Photography. The exhibition ran for four months in 1955 at MoMA and then toured the world for eight years, attracting more than nine million visitors. Steichen encountered the phrase "the Family of Man" in the poetic oeuvre of his brother-in-law, Carl Sandberg. The phrase was originally penned by Abraham Lincoln in 1861.

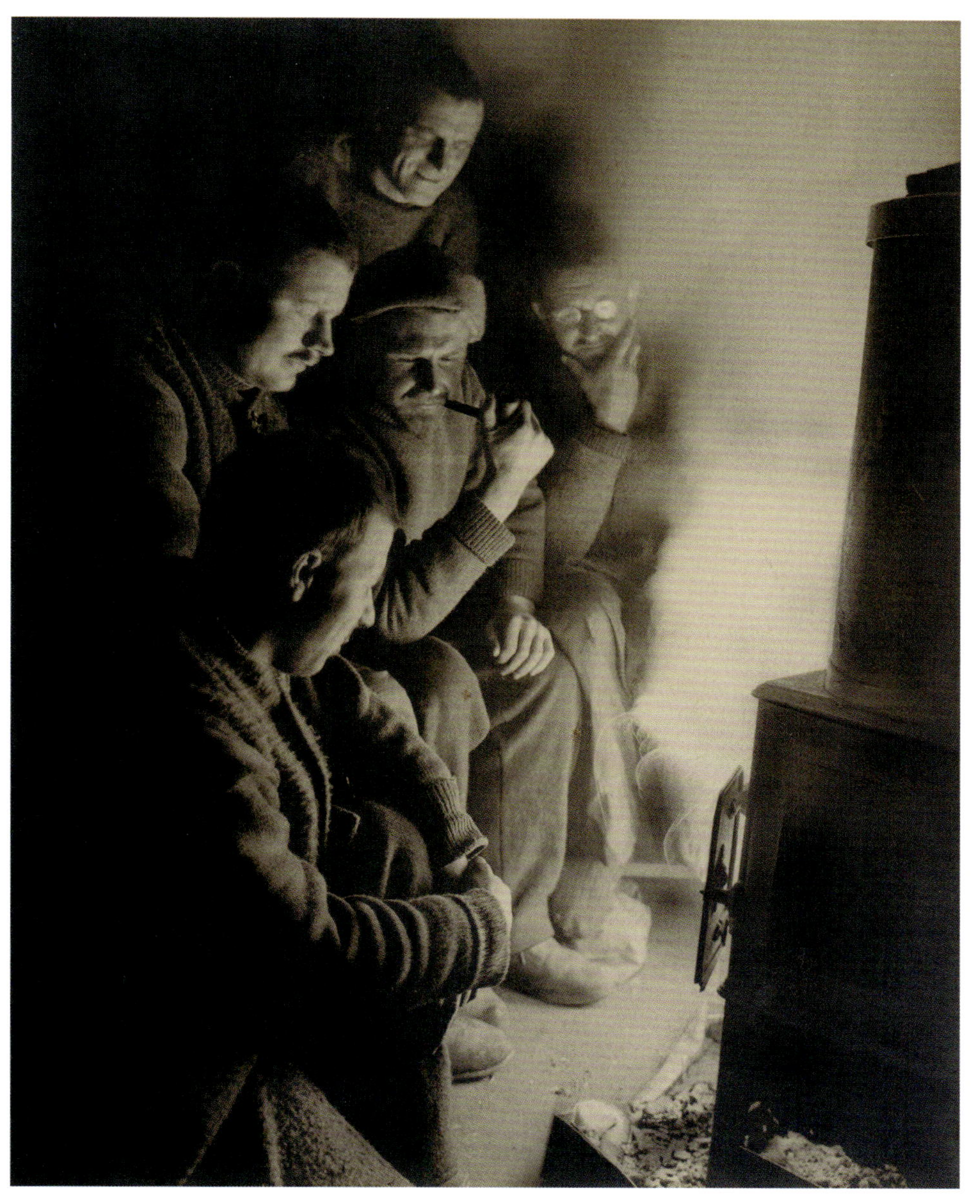

Frank Hurley (Australian, 1885–1962). *The night watchman spins a yarn.* 1915. Gelatin silver print, 23½ × 18¾ in. (59.7 × 47.6 cm)

During Ernest Shackleton's Antarctic expedition aboard the *Endurance*, crew members sometimes made the duties of the night watch—monitoring fires and changing weather conditions—a social activity, as they passed the winter with their ship frozen in the Weddell Sea.

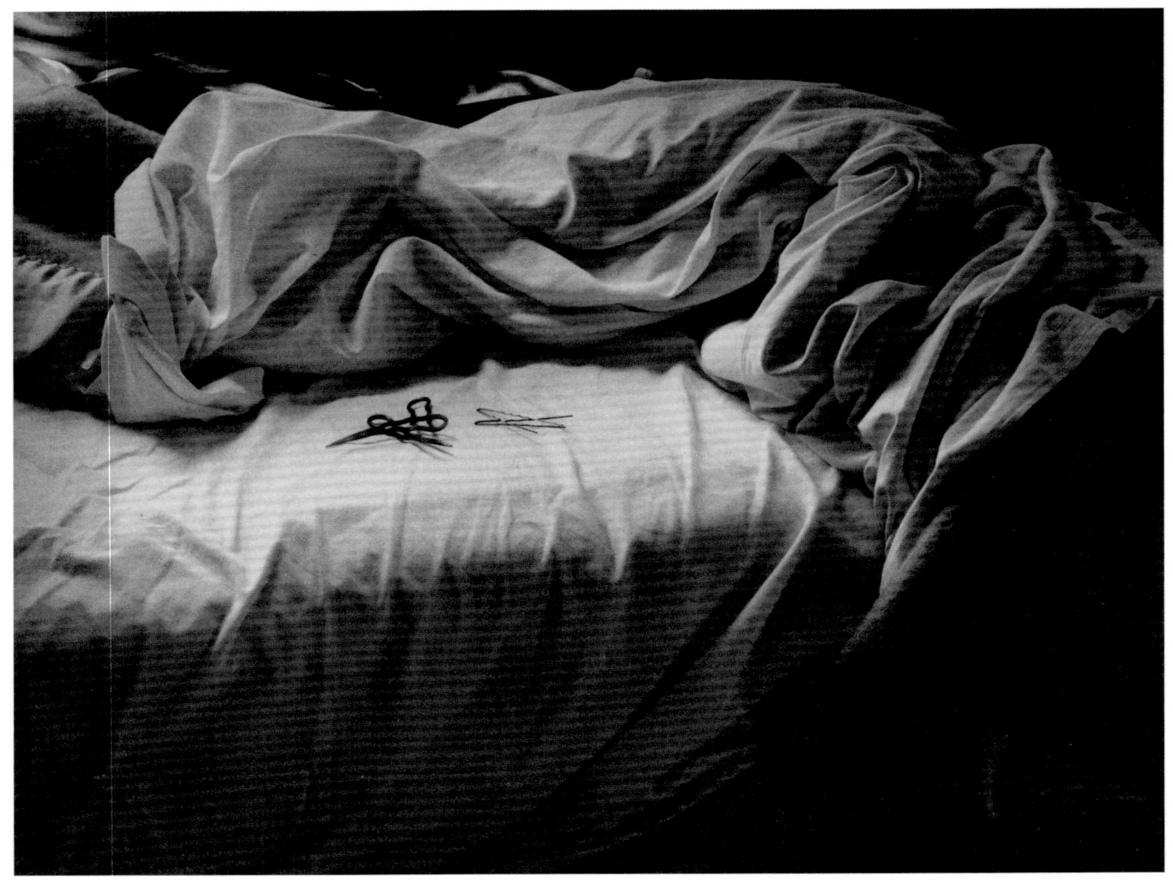

Imogen Cunningham (American, 1883–1976). *The Unmade Bed*. 1957. Gelatin silver print, $8\frac{11}{16}$ × $11\frac{1}{2}$ in. (22.1 × 29.2 cm)

Depicting the site of routine passages between sleep and wakefulness, *The Unmade Bed* meditates on the transitions that structure daily life. The photograph's broad tonal range, from the deep shadows of its background to the highlights of its foreground, suggests both dawn's light and dusk's gathering darkness. Tousled bedding, cascading through the image's upper half, expresses movement into the world while also anticipating its sleeper's return. Contrasting these unkempt bedsheets, two tidy stacks of hairpins and bobby pins rest in an illuminated patch at the picture's center, calling to mind rituals of putting up one's hair at the day's outset and letting it down at its end.

Through items that are regularly handled or hold traces of contact with the body, *The Unmade Bed* furnishes an intimate self-portrait of the artist, despite her physical absence from its frame. Cunningham created the artwork in response to an assignment Dorothea Lange, her fellow instructor at the California School of Fine Arts, had given to Lange's students, prompting them to photograph something they use every day. These objects of self-fashioning suggest a life that actively navigates the publicness of social and professional worlds while unfolding, as well, amid the privacy of one's own space.

By 1957 Cunningham was highly practiced in cultivating such nuance within the portrait. Early on, she had supported herself as a professional portraitist, opening a studio in her hometown of Seattle in 1910. The genre would remain a mainstay of the multifaceted career that ensued, unfolding mainly within the San Francisco Bay Area's vibrant photographic community. Ensconced there, she worked in dialogue with the modernist photographic vanguard as it emerged in the United States and abroad. Cunningham maintained a special interest in Germany's interwar photographers, including Karl Blossfeldt, whose photographs are also held in the Gayle Greenhill Collection (p. 77). Created contemporaneously with Blossfeldt's botanical still lifes, some of Cunningham's most recognizable images of the 1920s and '30s study the form of flowers and other subjects from nature. Like those earlier photographs, *The Unmade Bed* attends closely to light and how it defines structure and texture. SA

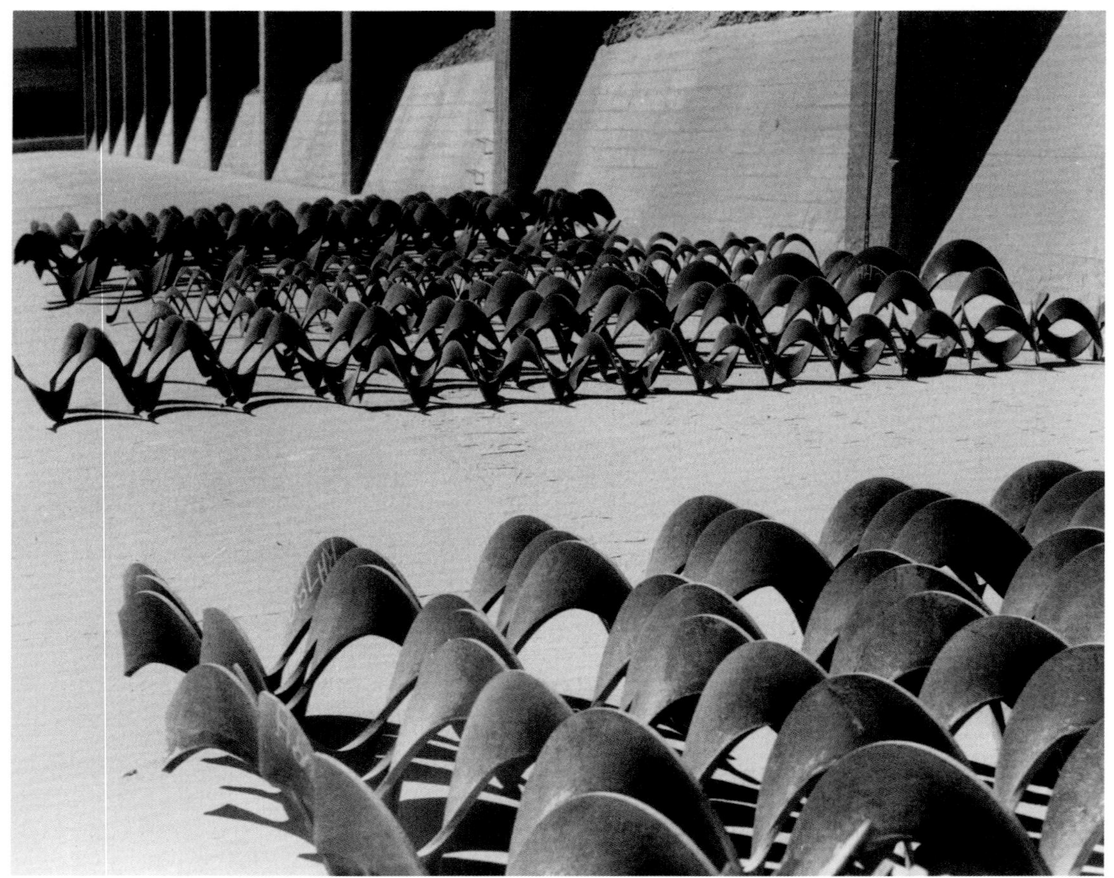

Manuel Álvarez Bravo (Mexican, 1902–2002). *Herramientas (Insectos)* (*Tools [Insects]*). 1931. Gelatin silver print, 7⅜ × 9⅜ in. (18.8 × 23.8 cm)

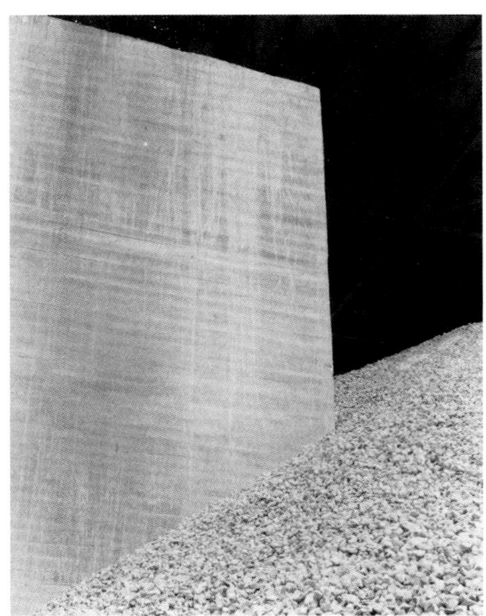

Fig. 1. Manuel Álvarez Bravo (Mexican, 1902–2002). *La Tolteca* (*The Toltec*). 1931. Gelatin silver print, 9½ × 7⁷⁄₁₆ in. (24.1 × 18.9 cm). Philadelphia Museum of Art. 125th Anniversary Acquisition. The Lynne and Harold Honickman Gift of the Julien Levy Collection, 2001-62-30

Manuel Álvarez Bravo's title for this photograph, *Herramientas (Insectos)* (*Tools [Insects]*), highlights the central ambiguity of his image: an industrial scene at Cemento Tolteca, a cement manufacturing plant north of Mexico City in the state of Hidalgo, that also, improbably, resembles an army of insects with arched backs, perched on tall legs, arranged in formation. The objects pictured are augers, the large screw-like steel tools used to move materials such as cement. The image is one of at least three that Álvarez Bravo printed following his time at the factory in 1931 as part of a Cemento Tolteca–sponsored photography contest. The contest submissions were displayed in an exhibition at the National Theatre in Mexico City in 1932. The contest judges, including artist Diego Rivera, awarded Álvarez Bravo first prize for an alternate view of the same factory, *La Tolteca* (*The Toltec*) (fig. 1).[1] In *La Tolteca*, one of the plant's concrete support columns is depicted like a gleaming monolith next to one of its raw materials, cement clinker, which will turn into concrete when ground and mixed with water and other materials.

Like *La Tolteca*, *Herramientas (Insectos)* has some of the trappings of modernist photographs made by artists around the world in the 1930s. Its high contrast plays up the rhythmic geometric forms, and its close cropping creates an enigmatic setting. However, as with most of his photographs, Álvarez Bravo avoided training his camera so closely on his subject that the image was devoid of other context. In this case, balancing form and context allows the photographer to show the scope of this important and enduring industry in Mexico. While cement had been used as a building material since pre-Columbian times, companies like Cemento Tolteca promoted it as the ideal material for modern government buildings and housing following the Mexican revolution. KB

(1) See "Algo sobre la exposición de la Tolteca," *Helios: Revista mensual fotográfica* (Mexico City) 3, no. 18 (January 1932), Documents of Latin American and Latino Art, International Center for the Arts of the Americas at the Museum of Fine Arts, Houston, https://icaa.mfah.org/s/es

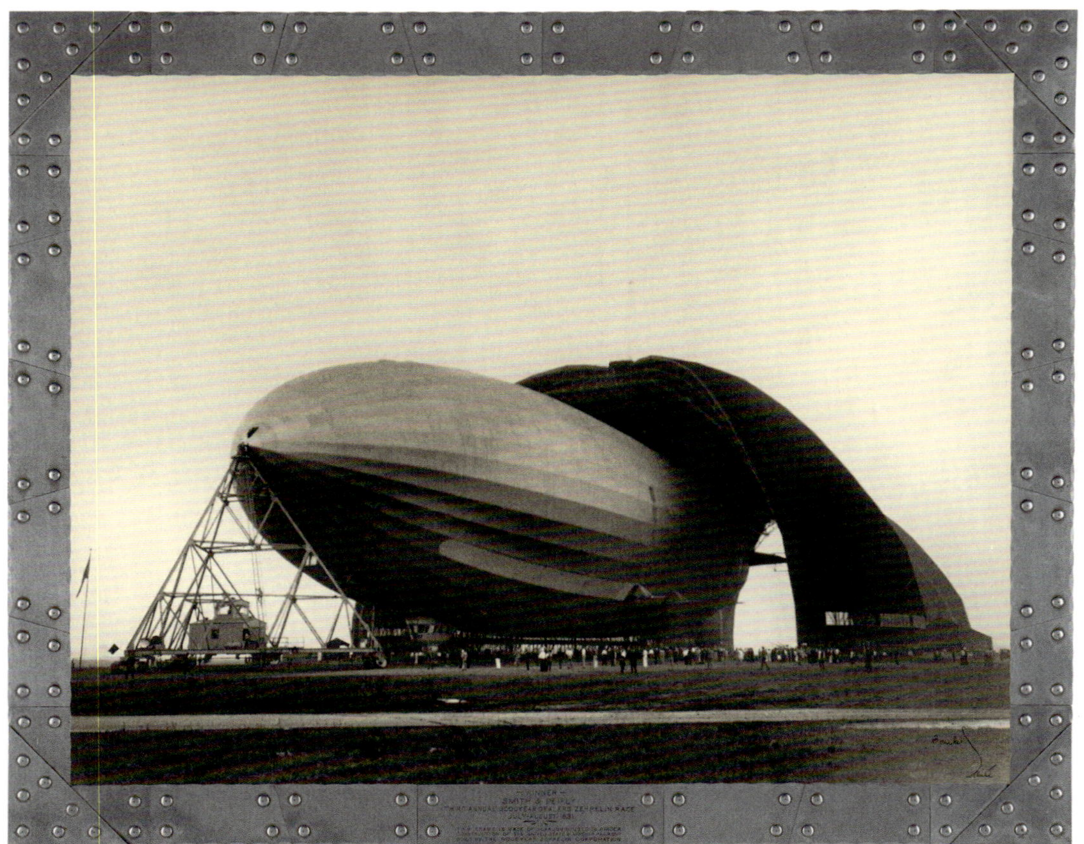

Margaret Bourke-White (American, 1904–1971). *United States Airship "Akron."* 1931. Gelatin silver print in aluminum frame, overall 20¼ × 25^{15}⁄$_{16}$ in. (51.4 × 65.9 cm)

Image Production / Aircraft Production

Lucy Gallun

In November 1929—just after the Wall Street crash of that year—production began on the largest helium-filled airship ever built, initially called the ZRS-4. Upon its completion a little under two years later, the giant rigid airship emerged from its hangar in Akron, Ohio, having been newly christened the USS *Akron* in honor of its hometown (p. 114). The spectacle of this appearance was captured by photographer Margaret Bourke-White, who was building a reputation for photographing the marvels of industry, from Ohio to New York City and beyond. The image, and its dispersal, served to bolster public enthusiasm for the immense scale, and economics, of industrial projects such as the airship. The possibilities of aircraft production were thus inextricably linked to image production, with photography helping to spark the new aviation age in the public imagination.[1]

Bourke-White had always been enthralled by feats of manufacturing. When she was a child, her father, Joseph White, an inventor and engineer—and an amateur photographer himself—would bring young Margaret along on visits to work sites, such as a plant in New Jersey that constructed rotary presses for offset lithography. "I remember climbing with him to a sooty balcony and looking down into the mysterious depths below. . . . I can hardly describe my joy," she later recalled. "To me at that age, a foundry represented the beginning and end of all beauty."[2] As an adult, after the end of her marriage, Bourke-White graduated from Cornell University and settled in Cleveland, where she opened her first photography studio. A 1943 article in *Popular Photography*, penned after her reputation had soared, described the humble beginnings: "Her studio was the living room of her apartment after the bed had been folded away. She mixed developers in the small kitchen sink and made her own enlarger."[3]

In Cleveland Bourke-White was introduced to Elroy Kulas, the president of the Otis Steel Company, and she pleaded her case for what photography could achieve for his business: "I remember standing there by his massive carved desk, trying to tell him of my belief that there is a power and vitality in industry that makes it a magnificent subject for photography," she wrote, "that it reflects the age in which we live . . . and that was why I wanted to capture the spirit of steelmaking in photographs."[4] She brought this same enthusiasm to her commissions to photograph the production of a Cleveland skyscraper, Terminal Tower, as well as to her photographs of emerging industries in Germany for editor Henry Luce of *Fortune* magazine. A few years later, Luce selected her photograph of Fort Peck Dam in Montana (fig. 1) to appear on the first cover of his new magazine, *Life*.

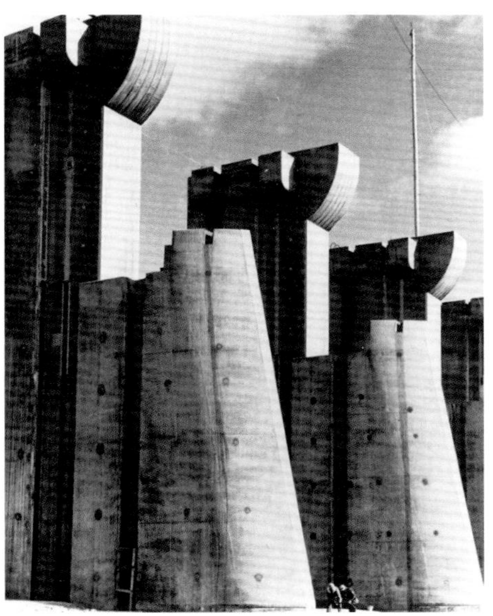

Fig. 1. Margaret Bourke-White (American, 1904–1971). *Fort Peck Dam, Montana*. 1936. Gelatin silver print, 13 × 10¼ in. (33 × 26 cm). The Museum of Modern Art, New York. Gift of *Life* magazine, 1964

Another of Bourke-White's major clients was Goodyear Tire and Rubber Company, whose headquarters was in nearby Akron. Here, too, she used photography as a tool to emphasize the magnificent fabrication achieved by

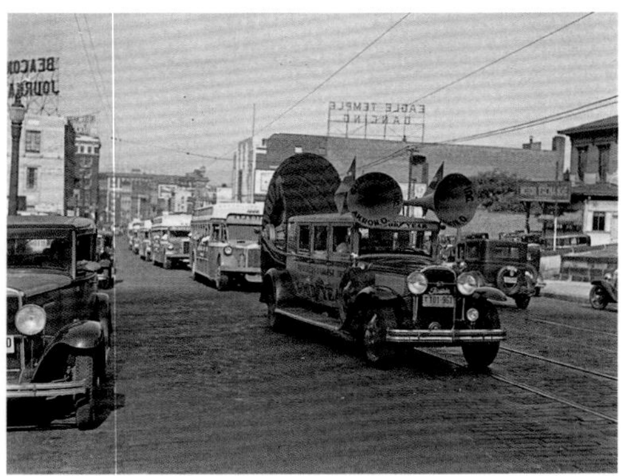

Fig. 2. Goodyear Tire and Rubber Company. Untitled (Procession of the Zeppelin Race). May 23, 1931. Nitrate negative, 4 × 5 in. (10.2 × 12.7 cm). Goodyear Tire and Rubber Company Records, Archives and Special Collections, University Libraries, The University of Akron

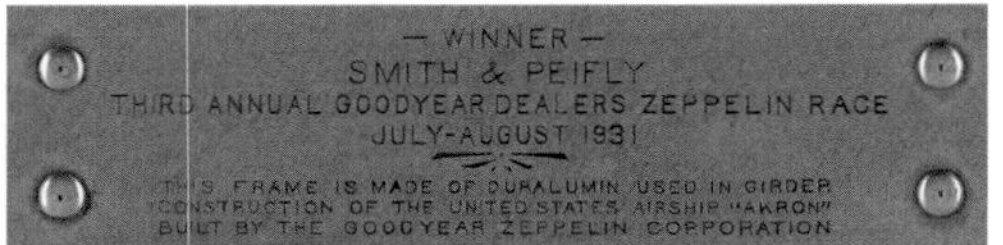

Fig. 3. Detail of frame of Margaret Bourke-White, *United States Airship "Akron"* (see p. 114)

her client. "If you photograph a rubber tire, it must look more like rubber than rubber itself. This became my specialty. In my glorification of the rubber tire, I concerned myself not only with the rubbery aspects of the tire itself but with the tire tracks and the tire's supernatural powers," she wrote.[5] This celebration of power and scale was clearly a priority for the company. In 1931, the year its record-breaking dirigible launched, the Goodyear company paraded the "winners of its Third Annual Zeppelin Race"—Goodyear dealers around the country who had achieved high sales in a two-month period—through the streets of Akron, led by a specially fitted Buick advertising "The World's Largest Tire" (fig. 2). To commemorate their participation, the high-achieving dealers also received individualized framed prints of Bourke-White's awe-inspiring photograph of the USS *Akron*'s launch. The frame of the print held in the Gayle Greenhill Collection identified one such recipient as Smith & Peifly, a Goodyear dealer and automotive supplier in Allentown, Pennsylvania (fig. 3). The frame's text also notes that the frame itself was made of "duralumin," a lightweight aluminum alloy used for the construction of the airship's girders. These girders—the rigid framework within the external envelope—can be seen in US Navy photographs that highlight the airship's use as a kind of flying aircraft carrier (fig. 4): Curtiss Aeroplane and Motor Company engineered a special model of biplane, the F9C-2 Sparrowhawk, that hooked onto the landing gear of the airship, and, from its resting place inside the hold, could be sent out on long-range reconnaissance missions.

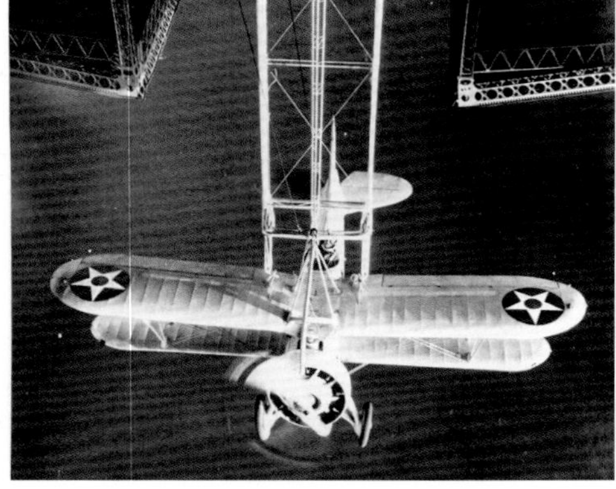

Fig. 4. Unidentified photographer. Untitled (Curtiss XF9C-1 "Sparrowhawk" fighter is lifted into the hangar of the USS "Akron" [ZRS-4], after hooking onto the airship's trapeze landing gear). May 3, 1932. Photographed during exercises over the Atlantic Ocean near Naval Air Station Lakehurst, New Jersey. Pilot is Lieutenant Howard L. Young. Official US Navy Photograph, now in the collections of the National Archives

"We're All 'Up in the Air' Out Here"

The sight of dirigibles and biplanes up in the air together recalls the crowded skies of Los Angeles during the first major airshow held in the United States, in January 1910 (fig. 5). The event was an international affair: a French pilot, Louis Paulhan, set the records for the longest and highest flights at the LA meet, while an American pilot, Glenn Curtiss (founder of the company that would go on to manufacture the Sparrowhawks that flew from the USS *Akron*), had set the speed record at the world's first airshow, held in Reims, France, one year earlier. "We're all 'up in the air' out here" announced a postcard depicting not the city of Los Angeles, but instead the open sky dotted with birds and various aircraft flying above the mountains (fig. 6). A poster for the earlier French event depicts a row of planes, followed by balloons, and finally, to the left of the towers of the Reims Cathedral, the oblong silhouette of a dirigible (fig. 7). Such airshows were an opportunity for eager viewers to see a wide range of aircraft all at one event, and the images portray the special experience.

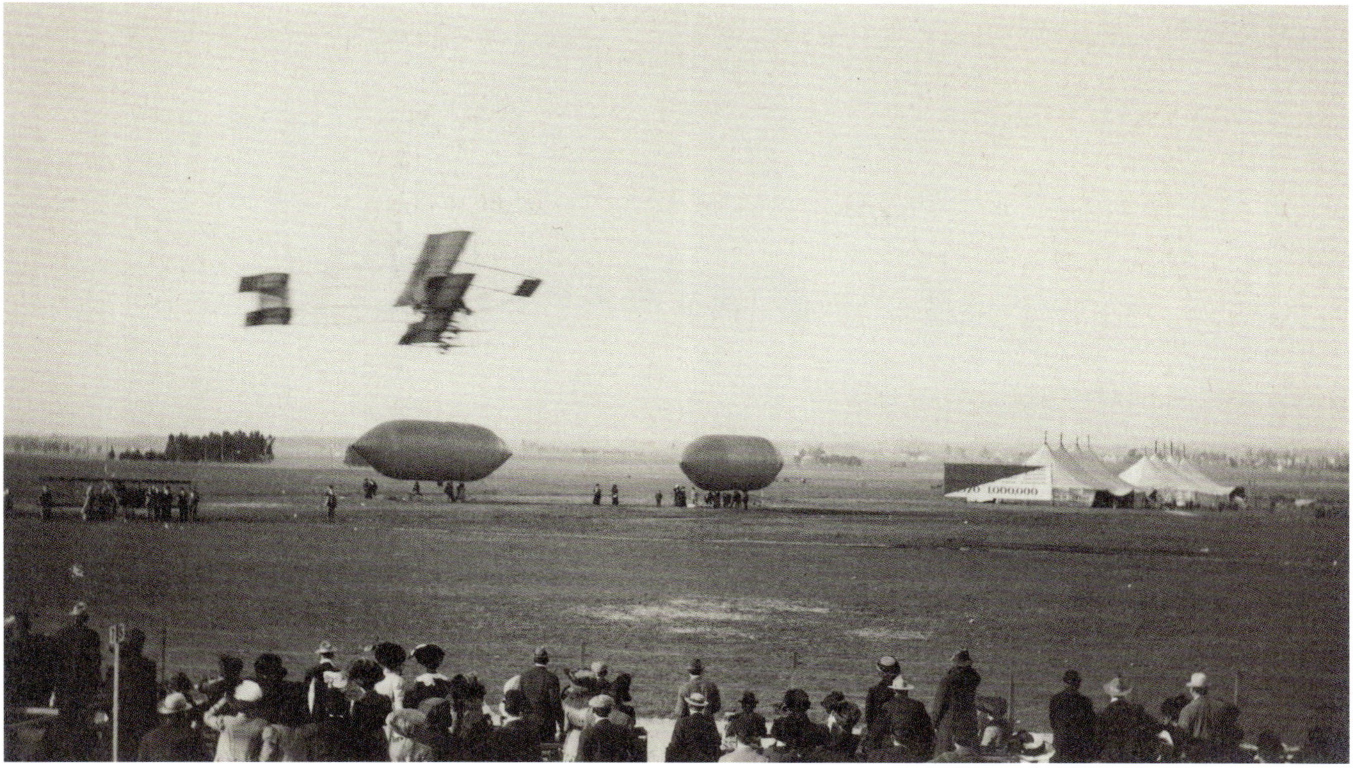

Fig. 5. Unidentified photographer. Untitled (First American Air Meet in Los Angeles). 1910. Gelatin silver print, 3 1/8 × 5 3/16 in. (7.9 × 13.2 cm)

The LA air meet drew at least a quarter million visitors, in a city with a population only twice that number. At the time, many Americans had never seen an airplane before. The event was financed by, among others, Henry Huntington, the railroad magnate and Los Angeles booster, and William Randolph Hearst, the newspaperman and politician. Felix J. Zeehandelaar, of the city's Merchants and Manufacturers Association, promoted the weeklong event in the *Los Angeles Times*: "I can truthfully say that nothing has ever taken place in this city that will attract so much attention or give Los Angeles so much widespread publicity as the flights that will take place next week."[6] Zeehandelaar went on to describe the means by which the excitement about the air meet reached its audiences: photography. "Aside from the columns of newspaper reports that have been published in all the papers throughout the United States," he wrote, "the events will be photographed and shown pictorially through the medium of nearly every illustrated magazine and publication. Several will have their own photographers in a balloon and on the ground to take pictures, and a film will be exposed for a moving-picture show that will be exhibited almost in every country in the world."[7] The excitement surrounding the air meet presaged the city's ascension as a center for amateur, commercial, and defense aviation.

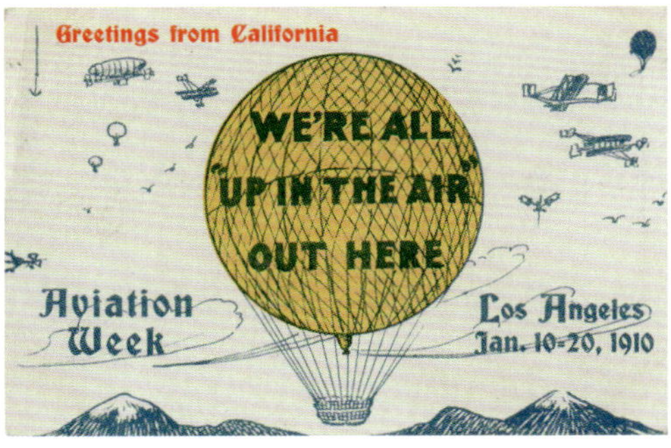

Fig. 6. Postcard from Los Angeles Aviation Week. 1910. 1910 Los Angeles International Aviation Meet Research Collection, California State University, Dominguez Hills

Also in attendance at the Los Angeles meet (though they did not make any public flights) were Orville and Wilbur Wright, the brothers who had made history with the first powered, controlled, and sustained flight in Kitty Hawk,

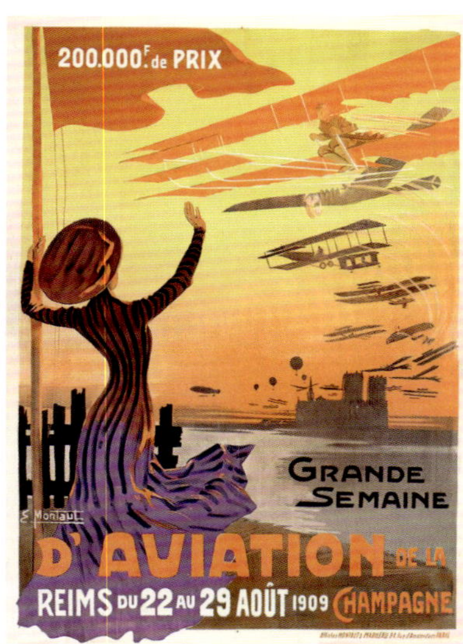

Fig. 7. Ernest Montaut (French 1879–1936). Advertising poster for the Grande semaine d'aviation de la Champagne, Reims. 1909. Color lithograph, 63 × 46½ in. (160 × 118 cm). Publisher: Affiches Montaut & Mabileau, Paris. Prints & Photographs Division, Library of Congress, Washington, DC

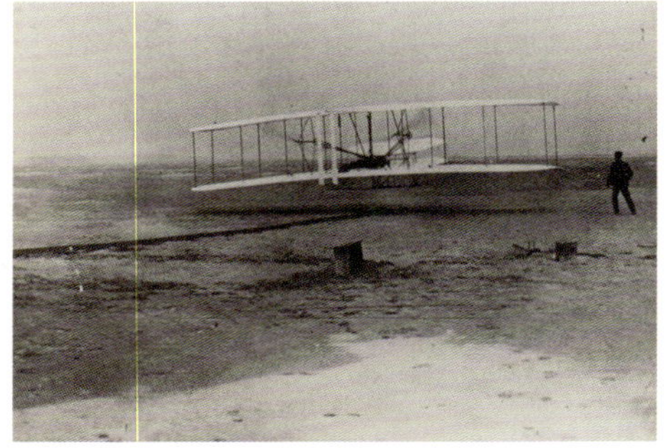

Fig. 8. John T. Daniels (American, 1873–1948). Untitled (Wright brothers taking off at Kitty Hawk). 1903. Gelatin silver print, printed later, 7⅛ × 9¼ in. (18.1 × 23.5 cm)

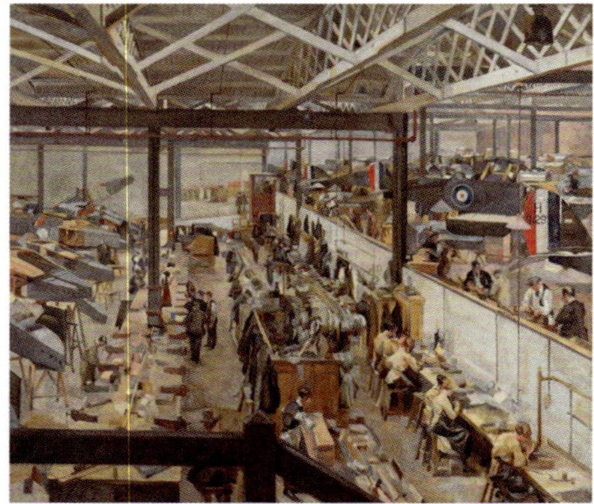

Fig. 9. Anna Airy (British, 1882–1964). *An Aircraft Assembly Shop, Hendon*. 1918. Oil on canvas, 6 ft. × 7 ft. (182.8 × 213.3 cm). Imperial War Museums, Art.IWM ART 1931

North Carolina, only seven years earlier. That flight had also been documented by a photograph, exposed within a camera that had been preset by Orville, and its shutter tripped mid-flight by John T. Daniels, a member of the US Life-Saving Station in nearby Kill Devil Hills, who besides never having witnessed a controlled flight also claimed never to have seen a camera (fig. 8). At the time of the image's exposure, Orville was himself at the controls of the Wright Flyer, as their biplane was named, lying flat atop the bottom wing, his shoes pointing toward the camera. Wilbur, on the right of the composition, had been running alongside to balance the plane, which had commenced its one-hundred-twenty-foot journey on the starting rail cutting diagonally across the picture. The image was preserved on a five-by-seven-inch glass negative, which the Wright brothers did not have developed until they returned to their home in Ohio. The Wright brothers were raised in Dayton—where they would eventually open an airplane factory—across the state from where Bourke-White would later capture an image of another record-breaking aircraft, the USS *Akron*. The print of the Wright brothers photograph held in the Greenhill Collection was, according to an inscription on its verso, sent to the *Cleveland Plain Dealer* and later given to the Cleveland Public Library—its own journey evidence of how the availability of photographic images is connected to a popular history of aviation.

While much of the Los Angeles event was geared toward record-breaking feats (including the fastest flight during the meet, the longest flight with a passenger, and so on), other activities signaled the significant potential of aviation, not only for personal thrills but also for commercial or military objectives. Toward the end of the week, on January 19, the program featured a demonstration of aerial bomb-dropping, with a lieutenant dropping sandbags from Paulhan's biplane onto white paper targets on the ground. The *Los Angeles Times* reported on the event the next morning under the headline "First Biplane Bomb Hits Aviation Field," with the accompanying article claiming, "Every war office in the world was watching. . . . It was the raising of the curtain on the war drama of tomorrow."[8]

During the decade to come, aviation production efforts ballooned as armed forces in various countries prepared for and undertook active warfare. Initially, aircraft were primarily used for reconnaissance, and then additionally for strikes.[9] In Britain, for example, at the beginning of World War I the Royal Flying Corps had just two hundred aircraft, a number that swelled to twenty-three thousand by April 1918, when it became known as the Royal Air Force. One major site of production was at the former Hendon airfield in North London (now the site of the Royal Air Force Museum). In 1910, just months after the Los Angeles air meet, Claude Grahame-White and Louis Paulhan both attempted to fly from

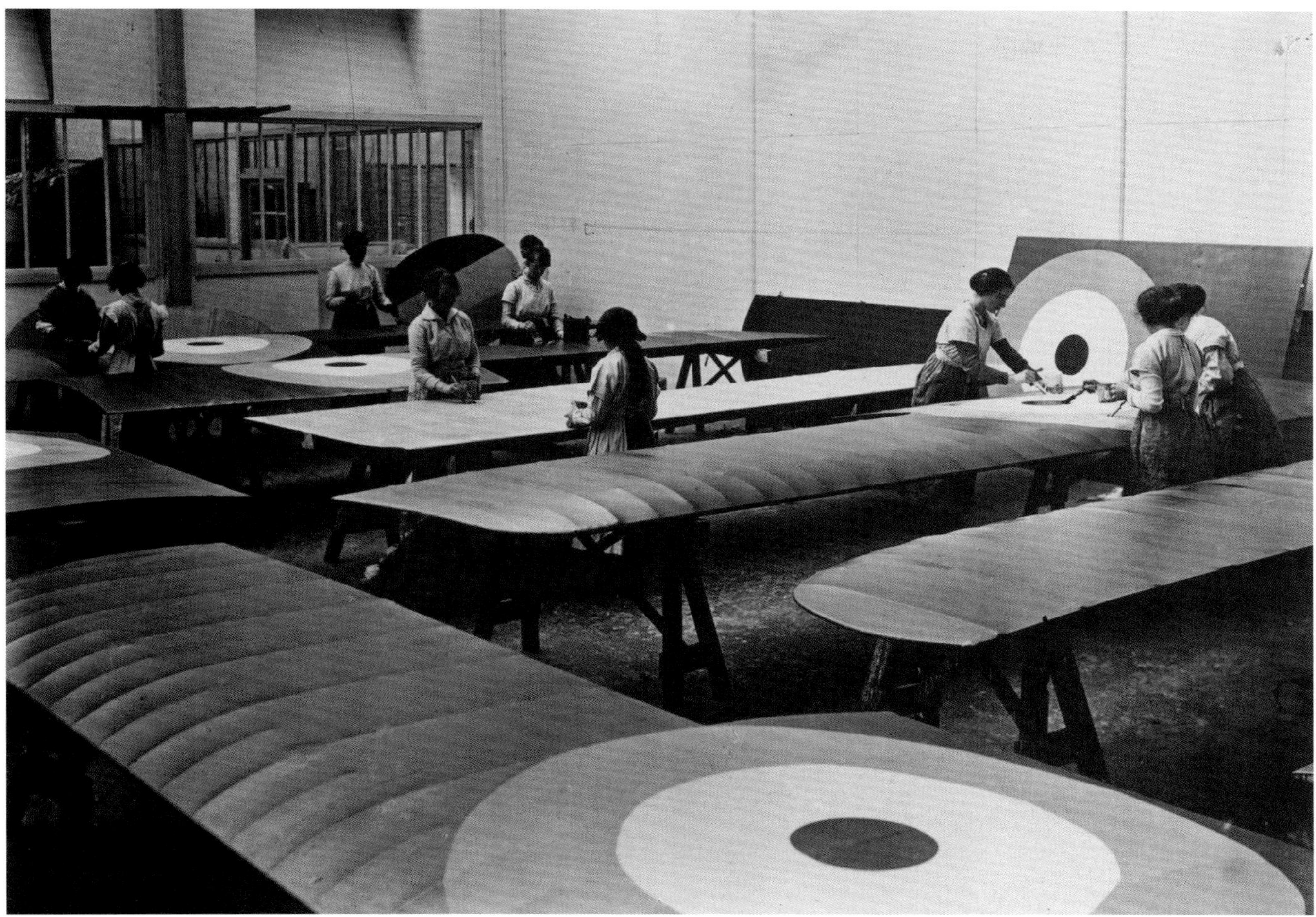

Fig. 10. Unidentified photographer. Untitled ("Women colouring planes"). c. 1917. Gelatin silver print, 6¼ × 8⅛ in. (15.9 × 20.6 cm)

London to Manchester, using Hendon as their base; Paulhan was ultimately successful. In 1912 the Hendon aerodrome was the site of the first air derby, which became an annual race and gathered huge crowds. The Grahame-White Aviation Company used the aerodrome as a commercial endeavor, and multiple flight training schools were located there, prior to it being commandeered by the military in 1916 for wartime aviation production efforts. In 1918 British painter Anna Airy, one of the first women to be commissioned by the Imperial War Museums as a war artist, depicted a detailed view of the full floor of an aircraft assembly factory at Hendon (fig. 9). In its wide hangar are rows of workbenches, and then the tails and wings of airplanes appearing one after another, with their distinguishing blue, white, and red roundels. As can be seen in numerous photographs, including many held in the collections of the Imperial War Museums, these roundels were also sometimes painted by women who had enlisted into the war effort. An inscription on the verso of a photograph held in the Greenhill Collection reads: "What the daughters of Britain are doing" (fig. 10). These daughters of Britain, like the painter Anna Airy, were involved not only in the expanding production of aircraft, but the expansion of imagery associated with it.

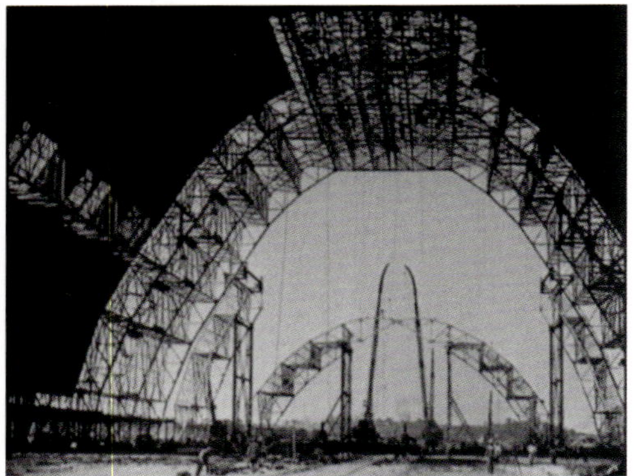

Fig. 11. Goodyear-Zeppelin Corporation. Still from 35mm film footage of the construction of the Goodyear Airdock and USS *Akron*. 1929–30. Goodyear Tire and Rubber Company Records, Archives and Special Collections, University Libraries, The University of Akron

"A Flying Age"

Bourke-White's widely circulated photograph of the USS *Akron* represented the completion of the dirigible's construction, and its emergence from within the Goodyear Airdock; but the Goodyear Company, through its subsidary Goodyear Zeppelin Corporation, also created film footage that documents the stages of its fabrication, beginning even before Rear Admiral William A. Moffett, the Chief of the Navy's Bureau of Aeronautics and a proponent of airships, drove the first "golden rivet" into the frame.[10] The footage begins with the erection of the purpose-built Airdock itself (fig. 11). To a certain extent, this immense hangar can be understood as just as much the subject of Bourke-White's photograph as the ship, and it was also record-breaking: for multiple decades it held the distinction of being the world's largest building without interior supports. The Airdock, which still exists today, has also had a significantly longer life than the ship it housed, which endured more than one accident before crashing on April 4, 1933, in the Atlantic Ocean. There were no lifejackets on the ship, and seventy-three of the seventy-six people on board died, along with two others who were aboard a Navy blimp that also crashed during an attempted rescue operation of the *Akron*.[11] It was one of aviation's first disasters, and the deadliest airship disaster in history.

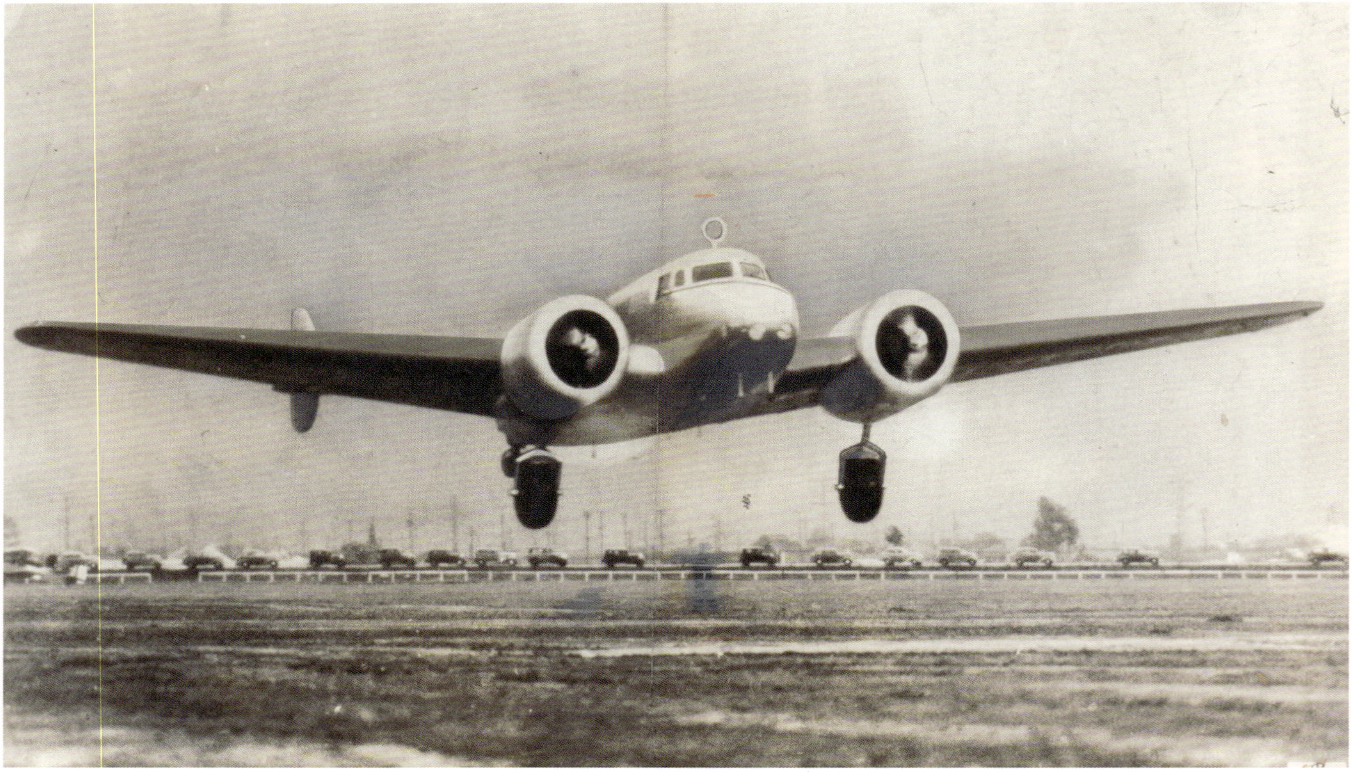

Fig. 12. Unidentified photographer. *Amelia Earhart's Plane on Takeoff; Start of Flight Around the World*. 1937. Gelatin silver print, 10¼ × 18 in. (26 × 45.7 cm)

Capturing that anticipatory moment of promise, Bourke-White's image offered an idea of what was possible with aviation production. With the wreckage of the USS *Akron* at the bottom of the ocean, the picture remained, with countless copies hung proudly on the walls of automotive shops around the country and then passed down through generations. Another picture that remained after the aircraft itself had disappeared is the image of Amelia Earhart's Lockheed Electra plane leaving Oakland Municipal Airport on March 17, 1937, headed for Honolulu (fig. 12). It was to be the first leg of the first flight around the world. The image of a plane, its nose tilted upward, would have been appreciated by the famous aviator. "I have often said that the lure of flying is the lure of beauty . . . that the reason flyers fly, whether they know it or not, is the esthetic appeal of flying."[12] Earhart had been the first woman and the second person to fly solo across the Atlantic Ocean, in 1932, and was at the height of her celebrity by the time of her 1937 attempt. After landing in Hawaii on March 18, she and the three crew members accompanying her were meant to begin the next leg of the around-the-world journey the following day, but her plane ground looped and was damaged upon takeoff, and was shipped back to California for repairs. The stages of her second attempt were not as thoroughly documented by photography, though Earhart understood the relevance of a record of her flights. "Aviation is woven ever closer into the warp of the world's news," she had written almost a decade earlier. "Ours is the commencement of a flying age, and I am happy to have popped into existence at a period so interesting."[13]

(1) One key figure in this relationship between aviation and image production was Edward Steichen, who served as Director of the Naval Aviation Photographic Unit during World War II, prior to his long tenure as Director of MoMA's Department of Photography. Alongside examples of Steichen's earlier work, such as the photographs achieved through multiprint processes chronicled in Lee Ann Daffner's essay in the present volume (pp. 101–7), the Gayle Greenhill Collection includes many photographs from his years with the US Navy.

(2) Margaret Bourke-White, *Portrait of Myself* (New York: Simon and Schuster, 1963), 18.

(3) William Hebert, "Margaret Bourke-White Goes to Hollywood," *Popular Photography*, December 1943, 25–28, 80.

(4) Bourke-White, *Portrait of Myself*, 49.

(5) Ibid., 81.

(6) F. J. Zeehandelaar, "Citizens of Los Angeles Asked to Do Their Duty," *Los Angeles Times*, January 7, 1910, 25.

(7) Ibid.

(8) "First Biplane Bomb Hits Aviation Field," *Los Angeles Times*, January 20, 1910, 17.

(9) The first sentence of the introduction to a widely cited 1914 publication on wartime aviation states: "The fighting aircraft has, beyond all question, arrived and come to stay." James Spaight, *Aircraft in War* (London: MacMillan and Co., 1914), 1.

(10) "Biggest Dirigible Started at Akron; Admiral Moffett Drives Golden Rivet in the First Ring of Navy Air Cruiser," *New York Times*, November 8, 1929, 1.

(11) Following the crash of the USS *Akron*, life jackets were issued to the crew of its sister ship, the USS *Macon*; when it, too, went down two years later, off the coast of California, only two crew members died.

(12) Russell Owen, "Amelia Earhart's Journal of Her Last and Fatal Flight," *New York Times Book Review*, November 28, 1937, 38.

(13) Amelia Earhart, *20 hrs. 40 min.* (New York: G. P. Putnam's Sons, 1928), 310.

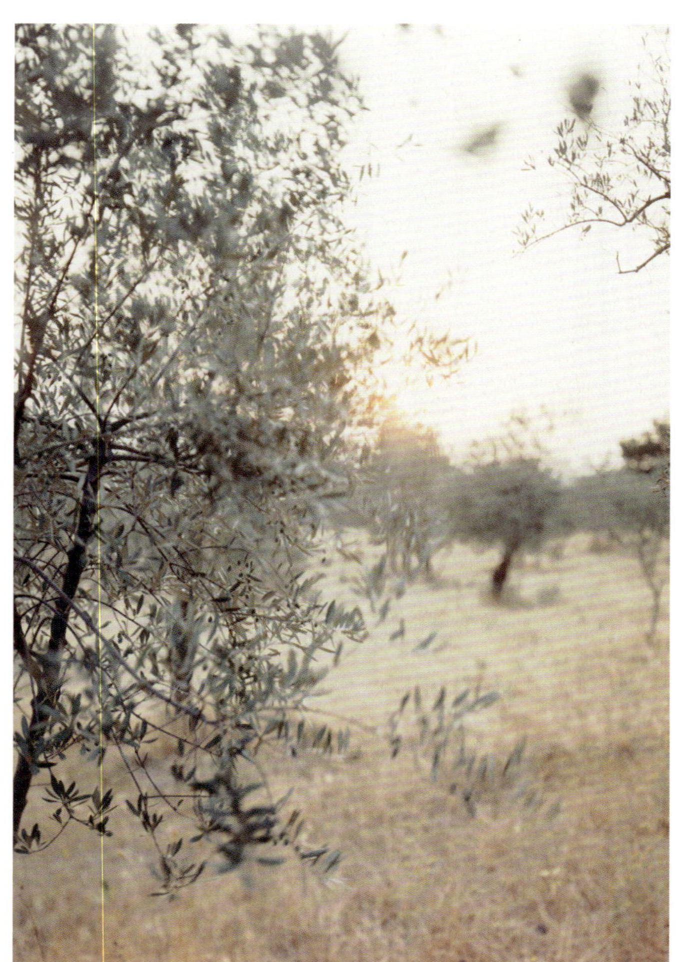

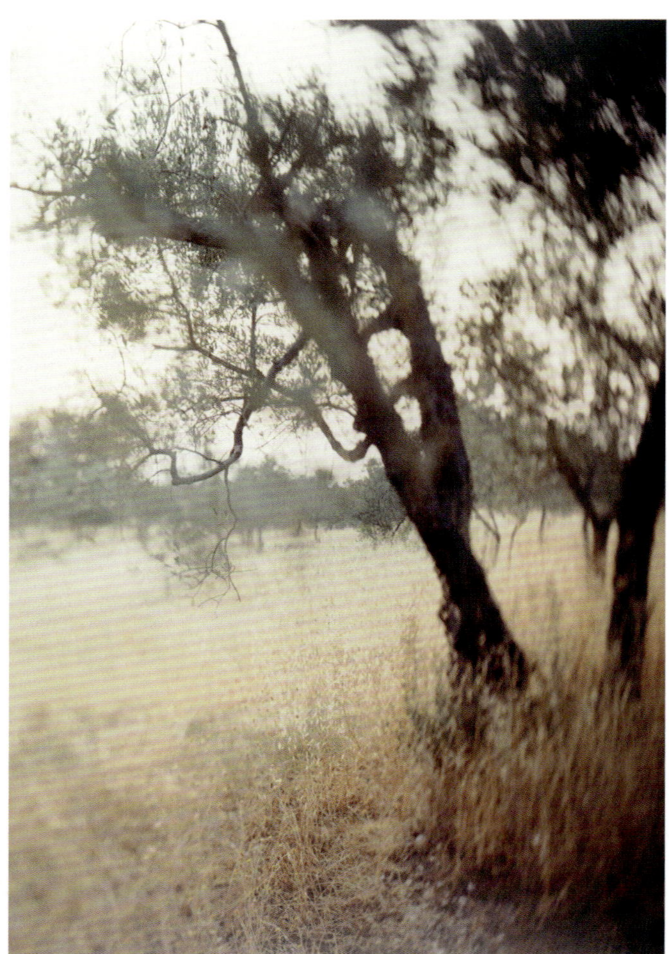

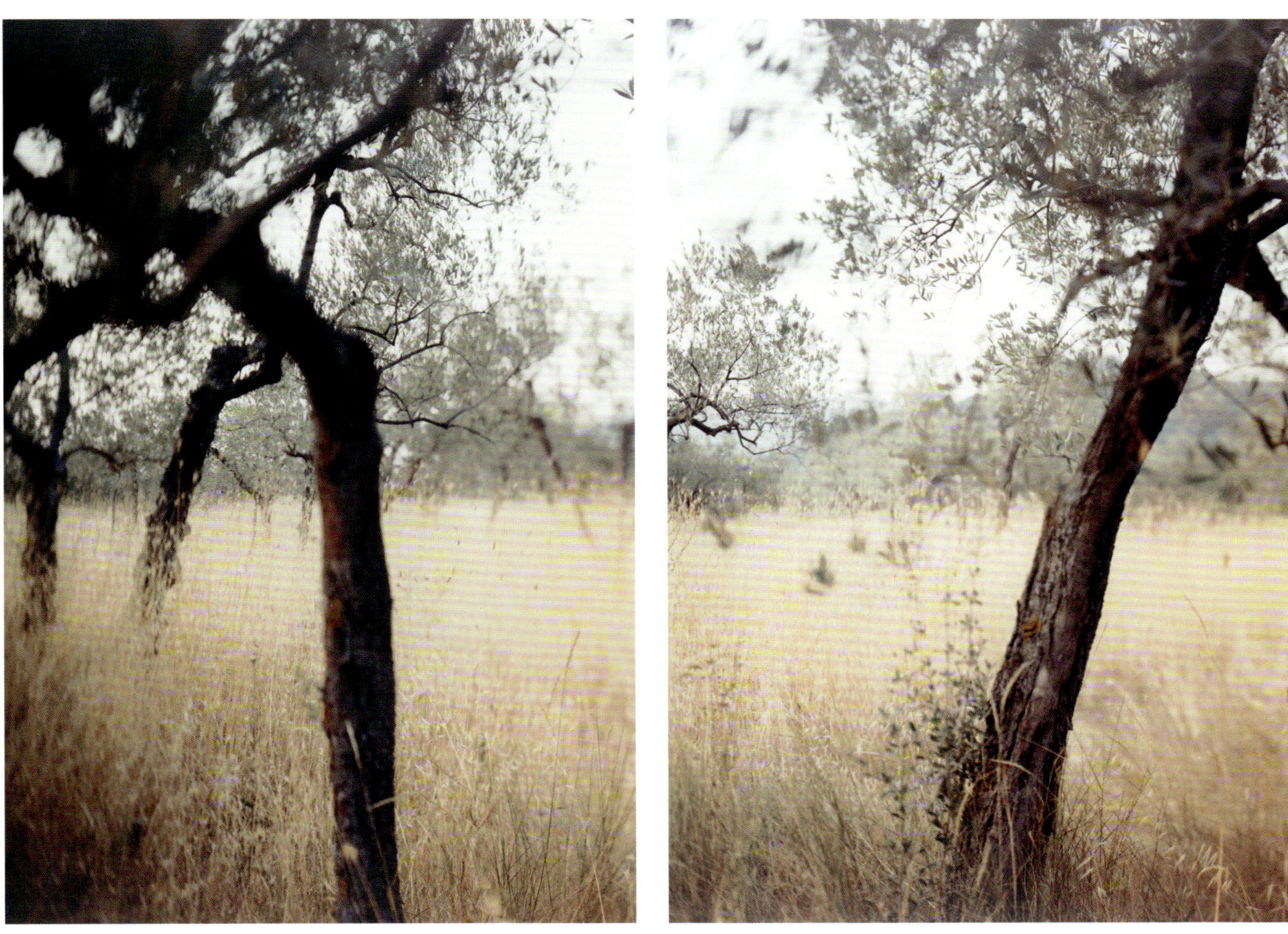

JoAnn Verburg (American, born 1950). *Olive Trees in the African Heat*. 2000. Four chromogenic prints, each 40 × 28 in. (101.6 × 71.1 cm)

For her explorations of olive groves, JoAnn Verburg sometimes uses tracing paper on the ground glass of her large-format camera, marking the horizon line of her first photograph, so that viewing her polyptychs is like "walking off the road and into the orchard."

Featured Photographers

The following photographers have work that is illustrated on the pages indicated and that was included in Robert F. Greenhill's 2019 gift to The Museum of Modern Art in memory of his wife, Gayle Greenhill, or in earlier gifts to the Museum by the Greenhills.

Acknowledgments

All journeys follow their own arc. Gayle Greenhill's journey at The Museum of Modern Art began almost four decades ago, in 1986, when John Szarkowski, then Director of the Department of Photography, invited her to join a newly formed Museum group called the Fellows of Photography. Gayle was often in conversation about pictures with her close friend Anne Ehrenkranz, and becoming part of MoMA's photography community, where Anne was (and is) involved, was a natural extension of that dialogue. In the ensuing years, Gayle and Robert F. Greenhill's keen interest and incredible generosity strengthened the Department's acquisition program. In 1992 Gayle joined the Museum's Committee on Photography, regularly meeting with Peter Galassi, who was by then leading the Department. The transformative significance of her and Bob's contributions have long been recognized by the Committee's dedicated stewards, including current Chairman Jon Lloyd Stryker.

Over those decades, Peter MacGill, at Pace/MacGill Gallery, was another of Gayle's frequent interlocutors on all things photography, together with gallery staff including Lauren Panzo and Kaelan Kleber. Peter fondly remembered Gayle's exacting eye during the inaugural Gayle Greenhill Photography Lecture at New York University's Institute of Fine Arts in 2018, an event where Quentin Bajac, then MoMA's Joel and Anne Ehrenkranz Chief Curator of Photography, also offered remarks.

The following year, in memory of Gayle, who passed away in 2017, Bob Greenhill offered MoMA a monumental gift of photographs, only a small fraction of which are presented in this book and exhibition. I'm indebted to former Curator Sarah Meister, who was closely involved with the gift and astutely observed that this remarkable body of photographs suggests "the spirit of adventure and exploration that were at the heart of Gayle's interests." Thanks are also due to Clément Chéroux, the Chief Curator following Quentin, who led early conversations about an exhibition project celebrating that spirit.

The Gayle Greenhill Collection is cared for by the incomparable staff of MoMA's Robert B. Menschel Department of Photography, all of whom I feel exceedingly fortunate to work alongside. I appreciate the encouragement of Roxana Marcoci, Acting Chief Curator and David Dechman Senior Curator of Photography, and the whole team: Dana Bell, Rosie Brock, Megan Feingold, Chiara M. Mannarino, Oluremi C. Onabanjo, Esmeralda Reyes, Caitlin Ryan, Marion Tandé, and especially Casey Li and Tasha Lutek, whose research has enhanced this book. Honorary Department members Saloni Mathur and Ananya Sikand brightened the office this year. My deepest gratitude goes to my close collaborators on this project: Kaitlin Booher, former Beaumont and Nancy Newhall Curatorial Fellow; and Samuel Allen, Curatorial Assistant, whose meticulous research, steady coordination, and wise suggestions have made a great impact.

I extend heartfelt thanks to the exhibition's many partners at the Museum. I am grateful for the guidance of Glenn D. Lowry, The David Rockefeller Director; Sarah Suzuki, Associate Director; Christy Thompson,

Senior Deputy Director of Exhibitions and Collections; Beverly Morgan-Welch, Senior Deputy Director of External Affairs; James Gara, Chief Operating Officer and Assistant Treasurer; and James Grooms, General Counsel and Secretary, together with their respective departments. The exhibition is realized thanks to the organization of Kristen Di Lonardo, Associate Exhibition Manager; and Ellen Conti, Associate Registrar, with Rob Jung, Tom Krueger, and the team in Art Handling and Preparation. The exhibition design was brilliantly executed by LJ McNerney and Montana Gray. Lana Hum, Director of Exhibition Design and Production, was an early champion and generator of ideas. Thanks to our colleagues in Marketing and in Graphic Design, headed by Stina Sawdust, including Claire Adkisson, Itamar Benitez, Claire Corey, and Christie Zhong; and to Sara Bodinson, George Benson, and Arlette Hernandez, who worked closely with us on the exhibition's interpretation and audio. Interpretive texts were edited by Jackie Neudorf and Virginia Gresham. Photography conservators Lee Ann Daffner, Nancy Reinhold, and Ashley Stanford examined and readied works for display. Peter Perez and his colleagues in MoMA's Frame Shop ensured each work would be presented in its best possible light.

Yoonjai Choi and Ken Meier of Common Name have designed this elegant publication that might itself be understood as a kind of "time machine" that transports us via photographs and their stories. Those stories come to life through the thoughtful texts authored by Allen and Booher as well as Daffner, Li, and Rachel Rosin. Like every MoMA publication, this one entailed contributions from an expert team led by Michelle Kuo, Chief Curator at Large and Publisher, including Sophie Golub, Hannah Kim, Anne Levine, and Curtis R. Scott. Special thanks are due to Libby Hruska, who ably edited the book with guidance from Rebecca Roberts and Anna Barnet; and to Joseph Mohan and Matthew Pimm, who beautifully produced it. The publication's gorgeous illustrations would not be possible without our terrific colleagues in MoMA's Department of Imaging and Visual Resources, directed by Robert Kastler. Thanks to Emile Askey, Robert Gerhardt, Tillie Lighte, Jonathan Muzikar, Martin Parsekian, John Wronn, and to the rights holders of the many illustrated works (listed on p. 129).

*Time Traveler*s provides an occasion to express our profound gratitude to two intrepid travelers: Gayle and Robert F. Greenhill. But this exhibition is just one of countless ways that this extraordinary gift will reach audiences in the years to come. Some works will form the Gayle Greenhill Collection of photographs at MoMA; others may be sold to establish the Gayle Greenhill Endowment Fund, which will support future exhibitions and acquisitions. I offer enduring thanks to the Greenhill family—Robert F. Greenhill and his children, Sarah Greenhill Wildasin, Robert F. Greenhill Jr., and Mary Greenhill Cagliero—for this visionary gift, in memory of a remarkable lover of photography.

Lucy Gallun
Curator
The Robert B. Menschel
Department of Photography

Contributors

Lucy Gallun is Curator in The Robert B. Menschel Department of Photography at The Museum of Modern Art, New York.

Samuel Allen is Curatorial Assistant in The Robert B. Menschel Department of Photography at The Museum of Modern Art, New York.

Kaitlin Booher is William and Sarah Ross Soter Associate Curator of Photography at the Columbus Museum of Art and former Beaumont and Nancy Newhall Curatorial Fellow in The Robert B. Menschel Department of Photography at The Museum of Modern Art, New York.

Lee Ann Daffner is The Andrew W. Mellon Foundation Conservator of Photographs at The Museum of Modern Art, New York.

Casey Li is Carl Jacobs Foundation Research Fellow in The Robert B. Menschel Department of Photography at The Museum of Modern Art, New York.

Rachel Rosin is Curatorial Assistant in Curatorial Affairs and the Department of Drawings and Prints at The Museum of Modern Art, New York.

Additional Citations

Page 3: Emmet Gowin, master's thesis statement (1967), repr. in *Emmet Gowin* (New York: Aperture, 2013), 11.

Page 6: William Bradford, *The Arctic Regions: Illustrated with Photographs Taken on an Art Expedition to Greenland* (London: Sampson Low, Marston, Low, and Searle, 1873), vii.

Page 10: May Ray to Ferdinand Howald, April 5, 1922, Ferdinand Howald Collection. Quoted in Merry Foresta, "Perpetual Motif: The Art of Man Ray," in *Perpetual Motif: The Art of Man Ray* (Washington, DC: National Museum of American Art, Smithsonian Institution, 1988), 28.

Page 11: William Eggleston, *Ancient and Modern* (London: Jonathan Cape, 1992), 28.

Page 13: Lee Friedlander, *Self Portrait* (New City, NY: Haywire Press, 1970), n.p.

Page 29: Tod Papageorge, *Passing Through Eden: Photographs of Central Park* (Göttingen: Steidl, 2007), ix.

Page 43: Philip-Lorca diCorcia, untitled artist statement, in *Philip-Lorca diCorcia: Hustlers* (Göttingen: Steidl, 2013), n.p.

Page 97: Duane Michals, interview by Jordan Weitzman, *Magic Hour,* podcast audio, June 15, 2016, https://magichour.press/episodes/2016/6/14/episode-1-duane-michaels.

Page 123: JoAnn Verburg, quoted in Susan Kismaric, "Present Tense," in Kismaric, *Present Tense: Photographs by JoAnn Verburg* (New York: The Museum of Modern Art, 2007), 29.

Photograph Credits

© 2025 Archivo Manuel Álvarez Bravo, S.C.: pp. 112–13, back endpaper top left. AP Images: p. 120 bottom. © The Estate of Diane Arbus: pp. 48–49. Archives and Special Collections, University Libraries, The University of Akron: pp. 116 top, 120 top. The Art Institute of Chicago / Art Resource, New York: p. 68 bottom. © 2025 Artists Rights Society (ARS), New York / VG Bild-Kunst, Bonn; © 2025 Estate of László Moholy-Nagy / Artists Rights Society (ARS), New York: p. 86. © Karl Blossfeldt Archiv / Ann and Jürgen Wilde / Cologne, Germany / Artists Rights Society (ARS), New York: p. 77. Margaret Bourke-White / The LIFE Picture Collection / Shutterstock: p. 115. © 2025 Estate of Margaret Bourke-White / Licensed by VAGA at Artists Rights Society (ARS), New York: p. 114. © Succession Brancusi - All rights reserved (ADAGP) 2025: p. 105. © 2025 The Estate of Harry Callahan: p. 79. © 2025 Center for Creative Photography, Arizona Board of Regents / Artists Rights Society (ARS), New York: p. 7, front endpaper top left. Digital Image © CNAC/MNAM, Dist. RMN-Grand Palais / Art Resource, New York: p. 105. © 2025 Estate of Imogen Cunningham: p. 110, back endpaper top right. Image courtesy of the Denver Art Museum: p. 72 top. © 2025 Philip-Lorca diCorcia, courtesy David Zwirner, New York: p. 43. © 2025 Estate of Harold Edgerton: p. 94. © 2025 William Eggleston: p. 11. © 2025 The June Leaf and Robert Frank Foundation: p. 45. © 2025 Lee Friedlander: p. 13. Courtesy the George Eastman Museum: p. 106. Courtesy the Gerth Archives and Special Collections, CSU Dominguez Hills: p. 117 bottom. Digital image courtesy of Getty's Open Content Program, 84.XM.349.11: p. 39; 84.XM.443.23: p. 40. © 2025 Emmet Gowin: p. 3, back cover. © 2025 Jan Groover: p. 82. Hearst Magazine Media, Inc. (photograph and text by Diane Arbus, *Harper's BAZAAR*, November 1961): p. 49. © IMW: p. 118 bottom. Courtesy Hiro Studio, Inc., © 2025 Estate of Y. Hiro Wakabayashi: p. 92. © 2025 Estate of André Kertész: p. 9. © 2025 The Lane Collection, Museum of Fine Arts, Boston: pp. 34, 35 top, front endpaper bottom right. Courtesy the Library of Congress, LC-DIG-ppmsca-15886: p. 57 bottom; LC-USZC4-13877 & LC-USZC4-13878: p. 118 top. Image © Loheland Stiftung Archiv: p. 85. © Man Ray 2015 Trust / Artists Rights Society (ARS), New York / ADAGP, Paris 2025: p. 10. © 2025 Robert Mapplethorpe Foundation: p. 78. Image copyright © The Metropolitan Museum of Art; image source: Art Resource, New York: pp. 57 top, 102 center. © 2025 Duane Michals: p. 96–97. © 2025 Estate of László Moholy-Nagy / Artists Rights Society (ARS), New York: pp. 84, 87–90. Photograph © The Museum of Fine Arts, Houston; photograph by Thomas R. DuBrock: p. 38. The Museum of Modern Art, New York, The David Booth Conservation Department, photograph by Adam Neese: p. 102 bottom. Digital Image © 2025 The Museum of Modern Art, New York, Imaging and Visual Resources Department: pp. 35 bottom, 89; photograph by Emile Askey: p. 95, front endpaper bottom left; photograph by Denis Doorly: p. 92; photograph by Robert Gerhardt: pp. 4, 22, 43, 47 (all), 69 bottom, 70 top and bottom, 71 bottom, 72 bottom, 78, 86, 100, 102 top, 103 (all), 114, 116 center, 117 top, 118 center, 119, 120 bottom; photograph by Jonathan Muzikar: pp. 60–65, 71 top, 81, 87 top, 98, 115; photograph by Martin Parsekian: pp. 48, 53, 122–23; photograph by John Wronn: front cover, pp. 1, 3, 5, 6, 7, 9, 10, 11, 13, 16, 29, 31, 32, 34, 35 top, 36–37, 45, 46, 55, 56, 69 top, 75, 77, 79, 82, 84, 87 bottom, 88, 90 (all), 94, 96–97, 101 (all), 109, 110, 112, front endpaper top right, back endpaper bottom left and right. © 2025 The Museum of Modern Art / Artists Rights Society (ARS), New York: p. 47 bottom. Courtesy National Archives, photo no. 80-G-416534: p. 116 bottom. © 2025 Shirin Neshat, courtesy the artist: p. 98. The New York Public Library: pp. 68–69 top; Manuscipts and Archives Division: p. 104. © 2025 Tod Papageorge: p. 29. © The Irving Penn Foundation: p. 81. Courtesy the Philadelphia Museum of Art: p. 113. © 2025 The Estate of Lucas Samaras, courtesy Pace Gallery: pp. 60–65, 68 bottom, 69 center and bottom, 70–72. © 2025 Cindy Sherman, courtesy the artist and Hauser & Wirth: p. 51. Courtesy Solander Collection: p. 33. © 2025 The Estate of Edward Steichen / Artists Rights Society (ARS), New York: pp. 100–103, 106. © 2025 Joel Sternfeld: p. 4. Josef Sudek © I & G Fárová: p. 75. © 2025 JoAnn Verburg: pp. 122–23. Photograph © Victoria and Albert Museum, London: p. 41. © 2025 William Wegman: p. 53. Digital image © Whitney Museum of American Art / Licensed by Scala / Art Resource, New York: p. 70 center

Leadership support for the publication is provided by the Kate W. Cassidy Foundation.

Additional funding is provided by the John Szarkowski Publications Fund.

Support for the exhibition is provided by the Annual Exhibition Fund. Leadership contributions to the Annual Exhibition Fund, in support of the Museum's collection and collection exhibitions, are generously provided by Jerry I. Speyer and Katherine G. Farley, Sue and Edgar Wachenheim III, the Sandra and Tony Tamer Exhibition Fund, the Kate W. Cassidy Foundation, Alice and Tom Tisch, the Marella and Giovanni Agnelli Fund for Exhibitions, The Contemporary Arts Council of The Museum of Modern Art, Eva and Glenn Dubin, Mimi Haas, The David Rockefeller Council, Anne and Joel Ehrenkranz, Kenneth C. Griffin, The International Council of The Museum of Modern Art, Marie-Josée and Henry R. Kravis, and Jo Carole and Ronald S. Lauder. Major funding is provided by The Sundheim Family Foundation.